Small Boat Through Holland

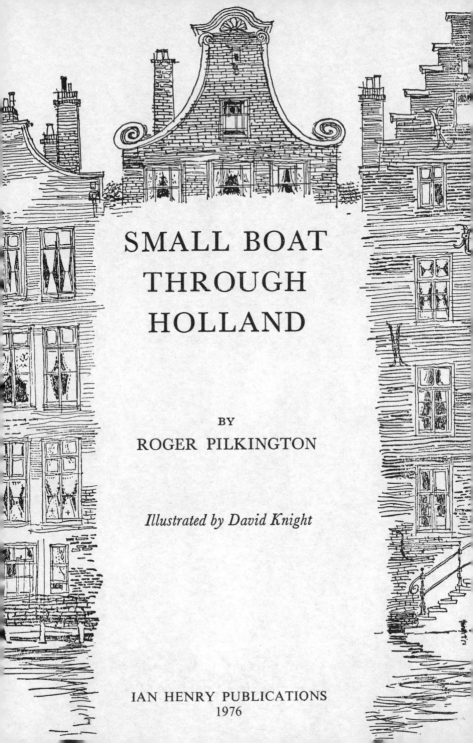

SMALL BOAT
THROUGH
HOLLAND

BY

ROGER PILKINGTON

Illustrated by David Knight

IAN HENRY PUBLICATIONS
1976

First published by
Macmillan & Co., Ltd.

This edition, 1976

ISBN 0 86025 807 6

Made and printed in Great Britain by
Galliard (Printers) Ltd, Great Yarmouth, Norfolk
for Ian Henry Publications, Ltd,
38 Parkstone Avenue, Hornchurch, Essex, RM11 3LW

FOREWORD

There is a strange belief current among boat-owners on our own waterways that a voyage overseas is beyond the achievement of any but a high-powered and elaborate boat staffed by a professional crew with the name of the ship woven in three-inch letters on their jerseys, a craft equipped with every conceivable navigational aid from echo-sounders to directional aerials. Yet the *Commodore* is certainly not a large boat. She has no automatic pilot, radar, ship-to-shore telephone, signal flags or other expensive toys from the exclusive yacht-chandler's window. The world may not be her oyster, but she has plodded through the waterways of eight countries without the least difficulty. She has no sail, and only one engine, but that is all that is needed to explore a network of waterways which in theory extends from Calais to the Sea of Okhotsk.

I would not for one moment wish to cast any doubts upon the great adventure of voyaging under sail, even though it has on several occasions been our lot to tow sailing craft out of difficulty or danger or flat breathless calm, but for river and canal voyaging a sailing boat is not so convenient as a motor craft, if only because there will often be no room to tack. Besides, the modest height of fixed bridges may bar the passage to any boat with a mast tall enough to mount a sail, and without a motor she will be obliged to keep to unobstructed fairways and cannot hope to penetrate right into the heart of such lovely water towns and cities as Ghent and Amsterdam.

As regards the single engine, it is often assumed that two motors are better than one. This I very much doubt; because the man with two motors may very easily rely too much on the belief that one of them is sure to function, and so pay too little attention to the condition of either of them. The *Commodore* on the other hand depends absolutely upon her one engine being in first class order, and so it receives every day a servicing and inspection more thorough than that which a car is likely to receive in the course of a year. There are of course certain parts of any motor which are more liable than others to cause trouble, but it does not take very long to discover which they are, and the *Commodore* carries her own supply of replacements for each one of those vital internal organs which may tire from prolonged exertion.

Carefully tended and allowed to follow her own head without too much interference from others, the *Commodore* has proved exceedingly reliable and even if she has no great speed we ourselves have been very content to let her carry us with her to one country after another. The voyage I shall here describe is no epic of drifting on a balsa raft in equatorial currents or living on the juice of fish squeezed in a lemon press, but a more comfortable journey with soft bunks and a warm fire on cold nights. For most of her route from England the *Commodore* was not crossing the open sea, but threading her way through inland waterways busy with commercial traffic. Of this I am in no way regretful, for awe-inspiring though the ocean may be it lacks the loveliness which can always be found in the waterside villages and the busy ports, the river valleys and lakes, the canals and locks and harbours where the ships come and go as they have done for centuries.

ROGER PILKINGTON

Highgate, 1958

I

Obstinacy of vessels — The Commodore's *character —*
Reticence over tonnage — Ghent and its shipping — Ter-
neuzen — Zeeland and the delta

A boat has a way of her own. Hidden beneath her plates or
planking there is a will every bit as strong as that of her owner,
and however carefully her skipper will formulate his plans for a
voyage his intentions may have to be modified to suit the tempera-
ment of the ship. This is obviously the case with the mammoths of
the ocean. Now and again a great liner will leave New York for
Southampton, but for some inexplicable reason will dock at Cher-
bourg instead — inexplicable, that is, to the landsman, who may
imagine that a liner is not much more than a floating railway carriage on a grand scale. The truth is, of course, that the vessel just
wants to visit France for a change of scene. A dock strike may be
the pretext, but it can hardly be the genuine underlying reason.

If such great men as Mr Onassis or the directors of Cunard
White Star find their plans subservient to the personal wishes of
their vessels it is hardly to be expected that humbler navigators will
always have the last word in arranging the summer voyages of the
Commodore, and surely this is only reasonable — for it is the
boat and not its human complement which is actually going to carry
out the work of probing into creeks or squeezing under the humped
bridges of canals. Many boats are very conservative and though
they may be ready enough to ride gaily along some particular and

favourite river they will obstinately refuse even to put their noses into another waterway on which their owners have set their hearts. Like a skilful child a boat can disobey orders in the most plausible ways. The water-pumps for cooling the engine may lock their teeth in solid defiance, just as though they were bound tight with silt. Fuel pipes may refuse even to drip, just as though choked with water or sediment. The engine itself may simply refuse to start for no mechanical reason at all but merely from disinclination — though pretended symptoms of magneto failure or faulty timing will be there to deceive. Nor is this behaviour confined merely to motor-boats. Sailing craft can be just as pig-headed and at times they will even turn upside down or shed their masts like so much waste timber rather than go where they have no desire.

The *Commodore* has a will of her own, and she has a surprising spirit too, coupled with an iron nerve which is more than human, and which appears to be situated in her rudder. Once in the Thames estuary she took it into her head to engage in a staring match with a liner home from the Cape. Proceeding straight towards the pinkish lavender hulk as it came frothing up the Sea Reach she paid no attention at all to the haughty and ostentatious blasts of its siren, but kept firmly on her course. I think that just for a moment we may have thought she was unwise to stand up to such a big bully but she knew better than we did that determination does not always go with bodily size, for in the end it was the liner and not she who changed course. With a lugubrious toot the big ship admitted her defeat and sheered off, and as she passed us one of the officers leaned out of the window of her Eiffel Tower of a bridge and spoke to us through a megaphone. I forget just what he said, but it was something about our being lucky to have a real boat under us and not just a floating heap of matchwood. Evidently he was envious.

The *Commodore* has more than just determination, however. She has a strong *wanderlust*, probably picked up in Germany when she served there for a while as the official barge of a British Admiral. Though never offensively domineering she seemed from the moment she became our own to long to go exploring and to visit waterways of which we ourselves had never even heard. When first we saw her handsome hull lying on the mud among the wrecks of the Admiralty Disposals list we had no thoughts other than to equip her with a single paraffin engine and a central heating system, and to explore the Thames and any such waterways connecting with it as were not either derelict from official carelessness or too narrow to pass her beam of ten and a half feet through their locks. Certainly we had several years of delightful voyaging in winter and summer alike on that lovely river, from the grimy and practical beauty of the docks up to the unspoiled Gloucestershire country-side where the cows stood knee deep and wide-eyed to watch us pass. We followed the Grand Union to Warwickshire too, and penetrated even into the sad dereliction of John Rennie's Kennet and Avon Navigation. The *Commodore* was so enthusiastic to take us on these voyages in our own country of England that she even miraculously contracted her seven foot eight inches of height over the water-line to such modest dimensions that she could pass beneath a bridge at Reading which offered headroom of less than five feet. Yet all the time she was secretly hankering after other waterways across the sea.

At first we were too absorbed in the excitement of these inland voyages to consider whether she herself had any other ambitions, but after a while we happened to notice from the log that when exploring the Thames she always ran downstream somewhat faster than she did upstream and we rightly surmised that this was simply because the one direction appealed to her more than the other. When we later discovered that at the end of her brief and peaceful naval career she had been towed home all the way from the Elbe with her naval engines derelict, and had passed right across Holland and Belgium on her journey, we guessed that her private desire might perhaps be to visit those same waterways again under happier circumstances. And if she wished to go abroad for her holidays, then we would be delighted to accompany her.

And so it came about that we began to desert the Thames for the waterways of other countries. At first it would only be for the summer holidays, and early in September of each year the *Commodore* could be seen running up on the tide past Margate or Southend towards the black and pungent water flowing down through the City of London. But after her first three trips abroad she developed such a thirst for exploration that bringing her back to England would have involved too much time, and at the end of the holidays we would leave her on some foreign slipway ready to be hauled up for hibernation in a dry and covered shed whilst we ourselves returned home by a larger but less homely packet boat to wait impatiently for the turn of winter to early spring.

All our voyages from England began by covering the same familiar course from London. Round the North Foreland, and inside the Goodwin Sands to the South Goodwin Lightship, the route led us to the small stretch of open water between our own shores and those of France or Belgium. Of the Channel and of the canals which lead into Belgium from the coast I shall say nothing in this book, because I have already described them in telling the tale of the *Commodore*'s voyage through Flanders and Brabant to the enchanting valley of the slow-flowing Meuse. Nor shall I have much to say about the *Commodore* herself as a vessel, because those who wish to know details of her design and engine and steering and dimensions will find them fully set out in *Thames Waters* or in *Small Boat Through Belgium*. It is enough to say that she is roomy and extremely comfortable, devoid of chromium-plating but endowed with the beauty of curves and figure which only naval parentage can succeed in providing. She is an excellent boat to manoeuvre, even if a sea on the quarter makes it necessary to work her wheel like a coffee mill, and she has the modest speed of six knots which she can stretch to seven and a half if need be, or even rarely to fourteen with tide and a strong wind behind her, and the dinghy lashed on the deck above her after cabin with its lugsail billowing in the breeze. She gallops so happily over oncoming waves that she will occasionally whirl her single propeller in the air from sheer elation, whilst in harbour a swell on her beam will rock her rounded hull like a cradle and gently send her crew to sleep.

But if I do not intend to say much of the *Commodore* as the vessel of which, according to her insurance policy, I am the Master under God, it is also because in all her voyages I think of her not as a vessel but as a ship. And there is an important difference between these terms. A vessel is a hull with its machinery, gear, tackle, and all those things such as 'removable bumkins, if any' which are men-

tioned in the Port of London's dock notices; but a ship is techni-
cally a vessel plus her complement of crew. Strictly speaking, there
is no such thing as the 'ship-building industry' of which we read in
the newspapers. One can build vessels and boats and steamers, but
not a ship. The material structure of the hull does not begin to be a
ship until life is aboard it in the form of the Master (under God)
and crew.

So if I write of the *Commodore* as a ship, it takes her human companions for granted. Usually they are four in number — my own
family, in fact — and occasionally there may be cousins or friends
too, but whoever they may be they are no more than that essential
element without which the *Commodore* would remain a mere vessel.

Most ships are 'registered', but the *Commodore* is not. She is to be
found neither in the Lloyd's Register of Yachts nor in the British
Register of Merchant Shipping, and she has always vigorously declined to be listed. Inclusion in the second of these catalogues would,
according to a letter received from the Ministry of Transport, en-
title her to the full protection afforded by Her Majesty's Government to such ships as are so registered, but the *Commodore* has
always felt that in a world in which three-halfpenny dictators with
broad grins and polished teeth can steal vast maritime and navigational enterprises with impunity the fullness of this protection is
open to question and is unlikely to be worth even the comparatively small sum which certification would involve. Besides, inclusion in either list would involve the *Commodore*'s tonnage being
stated for all to see, and this is something which neither she nor
ourselves would willingly contemplate.

Tonnage may be a very important matter, but it is really one of
private concern alone, and that is why the main beam upon which
the admiralty purists once carved a certain figure is now carefully
faced with a strip of mahogany to conceal it. After all, no gentleman would dare on casual acquaintance to ask a lady her weight,
and it seems to the *Commodore* immodest to disclose her own either
on her main beam or in any register which might reasonably be
expected to be found in the lockers of a harbour office. And not
only immodest, but imprudent.

Once when we were lying peacefully against the quay of a French harbour there was a knock on the hatch and a round red face with a black moustache peered down at us. It was the harbour-master.

'*Combien de tonnes?*' he asked through a cloud of garlic fumes, eyeing the main beam in vain.

His question caused us to think very hard, because in fact the *Commodore*'s tonnage varies from day to day according to the circumstances. On entering ports where dues are charged at so much a ton she has a tendency to diminish very rapidly in size until she is hardly heavier than a sailing dinghy. At the same time she has a knack of recognizing the kind of harbour where all craft below a certain figure are relegated to the corner where the sewer runs in and which — apart from a gentle flow of effluent — dries out at low tide. On approaching the quayside in such a port she sticks out her chest and inflates herself to dimensions which, if somewhat less than those of the *Queen Mary*, are impressive enough to ensure her a clean berth and deep water.

'*Tonnage!*' The harbour-master tapped his notebook impatiently, whilst we tried hard to read the purpose behind his question. It could hardly be a matter of dues, for the port was free below a very substantial figure. Nor could he be intending to turn us off the quayside, for he knew that within an hour we should be leaving on the tide, as we had already taken out our clearance at his office. The whole business was mysterious, and unable to guess why he wanted to know the tonnage at all we gave at random the figure of fifteen, and the harbour-master wrote it in his notebook.

'*Quinze tonnes*,' he said, 'You take a pilot.'

We said no thanks, the *Commodore* didn't want a pilot, but the harbour-master shook his head. Yes, we were to have a pilot. All ships over ten tons had to have a pilot. It was the regulation of the *Service Maritime*.

For a moment this puzzled us, because we knew very well that the Nautical Almanack gave a hundred and fifty tons as the lower limit of compulsory pilotage at this port. But glancing out towards the quay we soon understood. Two men in pilot's caps were looking anxiously towards where the harbour-master lay on our deck peering down at us. They struck us very much as Cassius impressed Caesar and it was clear that they were counting on the harbour-master's success in forcing us to take a pilot. Remembering that for nearly a week only one cargo vessel of more than a hundred and fifty tons had used the port we understood how they felt, and we were sorry for them — though not sufficiently sorry to agree to expend a couple of thousand francs just to have one of them run a straightforward line of buoys for us.

It was the *Commodore* herself who found a way of escape. The harbour-master was just scrambling to his feet when the end of our eel net, which was hanging from the mast, waved to and fro over our heads. There was no breeze to move it, and so we realized that the *Commodore* was trying to signal to us. Suddenly we understood her message.

'*Monsieur*,' we asked cautiously, 'you meant nett tonnage? Yes? *Bien!* The nett tonnage is only eight. It is the *brutto* that is fifteen.'

The harbour-master hesitated for a moment. Then he took out his notebook, crossed out the fifteen and inserted the lower figure.

'No pilot,' we said, trying to sound very sorry.

'No pilot,' he agreed dismally. And with a sigh he stepped ashore to break the sad news to the two hungry men.

Whatever her tonnage may be, the *Commodore* is happy to go anywhere on the right side of the Iron Curtain. The story of this voyage begins in London, with the *Commodore* sliding down through the busy Pool on the shoulders of an early morning tide. That same afternoon she was taking a rest in Ramsgate, but on the following evening she was lying at the foot of the deep wall outside the Demeysluis in Ostend, waiting for the dock gates to open to pass her into the Belgian canal system. Later in the week she could be seen moored under the trees in the centre of Ghent, having covered forty miles of pleasant but not very noteworthy canal and spent a leisurely day or two among the medieval glories of the great Flemish city of Bruges and lain at night beside the lawns flanking the canal to hear the sound of the incomparable bells of the Bruges carillon drifting down to her through the leaves, far beyond the roar of the trams and the clatter of traffic over the cobbles.

Up to this point her course was the same as when she had been bound for Antwerp and the Albert Canal, or for the Meuse and the forests of the Ardennes, but now instead of twisting in and out

of the medieval canals of Ghent towards the Scheldt she turned round outside the Law Courts and made her way back a mile or so out of the centre of the city to where a broad cut with high stone quays heaped with bales and boxes and sacks and piles of bricks joined the Canal de Bruges under the broad arch of a bridge. Along this waterway, the Verbindingskanaal, she passed under a series of girder swing-bridges towards the Muidesas lock at the upper end of a broad ship canal running from the inland port of Ghent to the Scheldt estuary at Terneuzen, in Holland.

The Terneuzen canal is an important waterway for two reasons. In the first place it is the highway from France and much of Belgium to the Dutch city ports of Rotterdam, Amsterdam and Groningen, as well as to the great rivers of western Germany — the Rhine, the Ems, the Weser and the Elbe. Day and night it carries the big black motor-barges by means of which the main bulk transport of goods in western Europe is undertaken. Nearly ten thousand of them dock at Ghent within a year, and though some come to the city by way of Zeebrugge and Bruges, or down the rivers Lys and Scheldt leading in from the industrial area of northern France, a great proportion of this traffic originates on the Rhine and reaches Ghent through the eighteen miles of the Terneuzen canal. Some of the barges are of a mere hundred tons — hardly bigger than a Thames lighter — but as no larger crew is required to handle a craft ten times the size the modern tendency is for a barge plying on the main waterways to be very much larger. All the main continental canals can pass craft of thirteen hundred tons burden, and the largest of the waterways are used by giants of three or four thousand tons, each carrying as much coal or cement or steel as half a dozen goods trains.

These massive craft usually belong to companies, and their master is salaried and probably has a comfortable home ashore in some canal-side town or port, but some — and particularly those up to five or six hundred tons — are privateers, boats which may be handed on from father to son. They are a family business and the family home too, and so they will be lavishly furnished. An air of cleanliness and comfort fills the roomy cabin behind the wheel, which serves as wheelhouse and family parlour combined. There are pots of flowers and lace curtains, wrought lamps and perhaps a picture or two, and in the case of the Belgian and French boats a crucifix. There are easy chairs, and a thick carpet covers the polished floor, and the rows of clogs and shoes outside the door is a reminder that not even the skipper may enter without first removing his working shoes. There is often the space and cleanliness for which a passenger would pay dearly on an ocean liner.

The Terneuzen Canal is not however a waterway only for inland transport. In its capacity as the ship canal for the Port of Ghent it has transformed that city into such a flourishing port that the burghers of Antwerp have necessarily come to regard it with something of the same misgivings as those with which a Liverpool man views the Manchester Ship Canal. Ghent has of course always been accessible from the sea by way of the Scheldt, but the upper reaches of the river were difficult and shoaled, and no ship of any great size could hope to reach it. A short cut to the Scheldt estuary was opened as early as the middle of the sixteenth century, and it not only avoided the difficulties of navigation over the tidal shallows but it reduced the distance by seventy miles. A century later the Sassevaart (as it was then called) was closed down by demand of the Dutch United Provinces at the Treaty of Münster, and it was not until 1795 that the canal was once more opened up by Napoleon. Just at that time Ghent was becoming a prosperous textile centre, and at the end of the Napoleonic wars the line of the canal was reconstructed and straightened, and provided with a new outlet at Terneuzen, eight miles beyond the Dutch frontier of today.

In 1900 the tonnage of sea-going ships entering the canal at Terneuzen was more than half a million. 141 were sailing ships, and the remaining 993 vessels were steamers. By 1930 the number had risen to 2,761, all but nine of them steamships, and in 1937 the last pure sailing ship carried its cargo up to the docks at Ghent. Not that sailing craft no longer arrive at the port — one or two still pass up the canal each month — but today they are all equipped with auxiliary motors. Some are Dutchmen, several are Scandinavian schooners carrying timber from the Swedish lakes or the Baltic ports, and the remainder are Germans.

The sea-going vessels which reach the Port of Ghent by way of the Terneuzen Canal come from every corner of the world. From Costa Rica and Venezuela, from Portugal and Russia, from Turkey and the Canary Islands, nearly two thousand ocean steamers and motor vessels pass up the canal in a year. To handle this considerable traffic the canal must of course be kept up to date, and during the last hundred years it has three times been widened and deepened. Today its depth is being increased to forty-one feet — ample for the largest ships which could dock in the city.

It is the variety of shipping which gives to the Terneuzen canal its own charm, for the country through which it passes is not spectacular. After leaving the dock area behind us we found ourselves in a clean waterway flanked with poplars on each bank, and beyond them the land stretched away on either side as flat as the Cambridgeshire fens and with just as few arresting features. Yet it was a busy land, a rich country of loaded wains and heavy horses. Farmers in broad straw hats looked up from the reapers as the tall funnels of some big ship glided slowly past the fields, and the children ran to the bank to wave to the *Commodore* as she passed their homes. The farms were prosperous but they were by no means always pretty. Sometimes they were thatched and whitewashed, but only too often they were gaunt and ugly, built of the particularly hideous glazed brick and tile which disfigures so much of the building of northern France and Belgium.

After a couple of hours we reached the frontier. Perhaps we had expected that to cross by canal from one country to another would be dramatic, but it was the easiest thing possible. When we drew over to the bank the Belgian officer removed his cigar from his mouth, asked us where we were next going — not that there was much choice, since the canal led only to Terneuzen — and waved us on again towards the Dutch post a few hundred yards further down and on the opposite bank. The three young Dutchmen were charming and courteous but they could not resist coming aboard out of sheer curiosity and they were happy to sit down for a cup of tea. They welcomed us cordially to Holland and each of them insisted that his own particular home town was the loveliest place in the world and that we must on no account miss it.

We must visit Haarlem.

No, no. Utrecht was even more beautiful.

Neither, said the third, could compare with Friesland. In Friesland we would love every moment of our visit.

But Haarlem had Frans Hals, too. And the bulbs — though not just now of course. . . .

Utrecht must be our first goal. The lovely River Lek flowed near it, and we could go on to Amsterdam by the Merwede canal.

But if we went by the more direct route we could pass through Haarlem. . . .

Whichever way we went we could reach the Zuyder Zee and across it lay Friesland, with water everywhere. Oh, it was a paradise for the boatman! Once we were there everything else would fade into insignificance.

Not Haarlem.

Certainly not Utrecht either. Utrecht had a higher tower than Haarlem, anyway.

But not such fine museums.

Well, what about the University?

In Friesland we would find the language more like English.

They could not speak Dutch properly, that was all.

The Frisian nobles were the oldest people to live in the Nether-lands. . . .

Nonsense! That was the Batavians.

Ah! They lived round Utrecht.

If they were not just a legend. . . .

Promising that we would try to visit Haarlem and Utrecht, and Friesland too, we moved on through the area of Zeeuwsch Vlaan-deren (the mainland part of the province of Zeeland) towards the Scheldt.

At Terneuzen, which is a little canal-end town and nothing more, we discovered that the tide would not be favourable for passing shipping out of the locks until midnight. Not that this mattered, because we would merely have to follow such shipping as turned to the right at the end of the mole, and so make our way up twelve miles of broad estuary of the Wester Schelde (the Scheldt channel towards Antwerp) in order to reach Hansweert, the southern end of the South Beveland canal. Most of the shipping would be turn-ing in at Hansweert too, bound for Rotterdam, Amsterdam or the Rhine, and there would in fact be a regular procession, the bridge-keeper assured us. This was most reassuring, for when the tide was down during the evening we could see that the Wester Schelde was very well supplied with sandbanks which at low water dried out for several feet.

At eleven o'clock the waiting barges, of which there were nearly thirty, started up their motors and the town basin resounded to the slow chug-chug-plop of their heavy oil engines. We let a dozen or so of them pass down to the gates and then we crept slowly in be-hind them. The lock was an almost circular one of stone, and at first we held ourselves comfortably against three craft tied abreast against the wall, but as more and more mast-lights came gliding slowly through the gates from the canal the lock-keeper determined to make the best possible use of the available space and he decided that the *Commodore* could just be squeezed into an otherwise wasted corner, right in the exit of the lock. This would obstruct one of the gates, but we could slip through the other one when it was opened and the second gate could then be swung back as soon as we were clear. The only real difference was that instead of trailing along behind the procession bound for Hansweert we now had no option but to lead out ahead with the rest of the boats behind us.

A possible solution was to ease off outside the lock and let ourselves be overtaken, but the one thing we knew about Terneuzen was that the tide was deflected by a small promontory of the flood dyke of the Wester Schelde in such a way that it ran into the lock cut, wheeled a quick circle against the basalt footings of the mole, and then made a hurried exit on the other side. We had seen this for ourselves before darkness fell, and a friendly bargemaster had in any case recommended us to look neither right nor left but to go full belt down the middle until we were well clear of the estuary shore and out in deep water. He had pointed to the little promontory in the gathering darkness and explained that he had seen two British yachts thrown on to it by the eddy, and wrecked.

On such occasions there is no need for alarm. One has only to remember that a yacht of any description is far more manoeuverable than a barge carrying a hundred tons of bricks, and that if dozens of such relatively heavy craft can use a route day and night all round the year it cannot be really dangerous. Admittedly the skippers may have local knowledge, but they certainly have no magical powers of keeping their boats off the rocks. Reputed dangers in frequented shipping fairways are common enough, but for a small boat they cannot be so formidable that they need to be viewed with alarm rather than with a mild degree of caution and alertness.

It took an hour to pack all the craft into the lock, but soon after midnight the inner gates were closed, the sluices were opened and we began to sink down between the cold wet walls at the back of the gates. The moment the men began to turn the windlass to wind back the first gate the bargemen cast off their ropes and started to crowd up right behind us, and as the *Commodore* preferred not to be pushed from the rear we shoved out from the wall and slid through the gap as soon as there was room to ease through. Then we pulled the accelerator well back and roared down the centre of the entrance channel just as we had been told.

On either side the big dykes rose up dark and high, hiding the town from view. An incoming barge appeared in the entrance, sliding half sideways on the eddy, but we had room enough to cut round behind it. Then we gave the *Commodore* the last inch of accelerator and shot across the mild stirring of the tidal swirl, straight out between the dyke-heads. And as we did so, the glint of the water ahead was suddenly shut off by a big mass towering up into the sky, and row upon row of circular patches of light. It was a liner bound for Antwerp, clipping close to the light on the point of the dyke to take the deep water on the bend.

Once the wash of the big ship had died away the surface was silky, heaving just slightly with the swell of the tide but otherwise devoid even of ripples. The night was hot and breathless, but up the Wester Schelde we could see the point lights beyond the receding shape of the liner. And soon we discovered that to keep in the deep water channel was in no way difficult, for the beacons were all of the sensible sector-type, with panels of coloured glass arranged in such a way that a light appeared variously coloured according to the angle from which it was seen. Where the light shone white there was deep water and safe navigation; where red or green it indicated a course across shoals or banks, or perhaps there was some intervening low promontory or other obstacle. We had merely to steer straight for the first white light until we crossed into the white sector of the next, for which we then aimed, and so in a little over an hour we came up to the jetties of Hansweert with the procession of barges left far astern of us. Soon we had passed through the great locks into the comparatively short but busy South Beveland Canal which cuts across the neck of the largest of the islands of Zeeland to connect the Wester Schelde with the Ooster Schelde and provide a through passage from Ghent or Antwerp to Rotterdam and the Rhine and Meuse.

On their western edges, where they meet the waves of the open sea, the islands of Zeeland are tipped with a deep line of high dunes, but elsewhere they are flat and green and extraordinarily fertile. They owe their existence to the curious fact that three of the greatest rivers of western Europe have chosen to converge so closely that their mouths form a single extended delta with a maze of banks and channels. For thousands of years the Rhine and Meuse and Scheldt have swept down towards this common ending, at times depositing masses of mud and silt in the area where first they meet the full flow of the tide, and in time of flood scouring channels through the flats of their own making. The sea too has played its part. Light winds have driven the waves to scoop up the sand and carry it inshore to raise banks above the surrounding water, and north-westerly gales have piled the North Sea up against the same islands to break them down by relentless pressure and to destroy in a single night the work of a century. Always the aspect of the Zeeland delta was changing until at last it became inhabited and the first dykes were built to keep out the water and to give stability to the islands among which the three great rivers merge.

To build defensive walls to keep the sea from swallowing the hundreds of miles of the island coastlines took hundreds of years, and it was not until the beginning of the sixteenth century that the islands of Walcheren and North Beveland, Schouwen and Tholen and South Beveland, Goeree and Overflakkee (these last two not belonging to the province of Zeeland itself) were all more or less stabilized. Some had arisen only to be inundated afresh, for at high tide the entire area was below sea-level, just as it is today. Six hundred years ago South Beveland itself was swamped in the violence of a storm. In the sixteenth century Schouwen was over-run by a flood and its villages wiped out. North Beveland too was so flooded that only the church steeples and the tree tops remained above water. In 1808 Walcheren was submerged, in 1825 Tholen. Always there was great loss of life and property, and yet with astonishing persistence those who escaped by boat or by clinging to the trees and rooftops began once more the weary task of digging and embanking, dyking, draining and pumping. On each occasion it required many years to rebuild the banks and to pump out the water; sometimes the land remained partially as marsh for more than a century.

Nor are the disasters confined to previous centuries. On the night of the 31st January 1953 a spring tide combined with a violent storm wind from the north-west. At times the gale reached a velocity of ninety miles per hour, and it drove the high water of the

North Sea once more against the dykes of Zeeland. In countless places the banks were broken down. Thousands of homes were washed away, roads and railway tracks were swept aside. Horses and cattle stood knee deep on the high banks until one false step sent them to drown in the swirling torrents. As the waters swept on their way to flood nearly a twelfth of the entire country of the Netherlands fourteen hundred people lost their lives, the heaviest toll falling upon the islands of Schouwen and Overflakkee. That the death roll was so much less than in 1570, when a hundred thousand lives were lost, was only due to the immediate efforts of the Dutch themselves, and the quick assistance rendered by Belgium and the United States, Italy and France and Norway, in fact by every country which could supply sandbags and rafts, motor-boats and helicopters. Without modern equipment it would have been impossible to rescue as many people as were in fact saved when the flood swiftly engulfed their homes, but aircraft were able to spot men and women waving flags on the roof ridges of houses which had not yet collapsed and to give their position by radio. Motor boats and amphibious army vehicles came to the rescue and helicopters picked survivors from gables and branches of trees.

'God created the whole world except Holland, which was created by the Hollanders,' runs an old French saying. And this is true enough, for without its dykes much of Holland would long ago have returned to the bottom of the sea. It may well be however that the flood of 1953 will prove to be the last in the history of Zeeland, for the Netherlands government has now embarked on an ambitious plan to build a vast sea-dyke bridging the gaps from island to island all the way from the neighbourhood of the Hook of Holland, passing by Goeree and Schouwen to the Scheldt entrance at Walcheren. Such an enterprise may need decades for its completion, but when once the huge sea-wall is in place the islands of Zeeland should not only be safe but they will almost cease to be islands at all. Little by little the shallows of the water between them will be pumped dry and the channels of the rivers confined to regulated courses.

It is not only storm that has flooded Zeeland and inundated the crops and pastures and farms. Sometimes the land has been drowned deliberately in order to expel an invader or to protect a city from attack. At the end of the Second World War the dykes of Walcheren were breached by bombing to cut off the German garrison, and centuries earlier the same land was flooded in the long and desperate struggle against the Spaniards in which the Zeelanders themselves were in the forefront of the revolt out of which the Dutch nation was born.

II

No page of history can be blacker than that of the Spanish rule
in the Netherlands. Under the imperial edicts of Philip II,
'King of all the Spanish dominions and the Sicilies, titular King of
England, France and Jerusalem, Absolute Dominator of Asia,
Africa and America, Duke of Milan and the Burgundies and Here-
ditary Sovereign of the Seventeen Netherlands,' Christian men
went daily to the stake and the gallows, and women courageously
sang psalms as the grave-diggers bound them and shovelled the
earth on their faces to bury them alive — for such was the punishment ordained for those who dared to exercise even the slightest
degree of freedom of religious thought. Parents who read the Sermon on the Mount to their own children were to go to the stake —
unless they desisted and repented, in which case Philip graciously
allowed the men to be beheaded and the women to be buried alive
instead of bound and burned. To ferret out the offenders more
effectually the Inquisition was brought to the Netherlands, and
Spanish troops were stationed there to support and assist the
authorities in the Christian task which they had laid upon themselves.

The most infamous servant of the system was one Peter Titelmann, who even went so far as to boast that he seized for preference
the innocent and the virtuous, because they made no resistance.
In one town after another his arrival was followed by summary con-
victions and the most callous and brutal executions. In one village
an entire family which admitted praying at home that their sins
might be forgiven was burned alive. Eight people in another house
in the same village were convicted of Bible-reading and prayer,

and were sent immediately to the stake. Thousands of Netherlanders, men, women and young children, were tortured and burned
before admiring audiences of Spaniards and Papal officials for the
crime of worship. Their tongues were torn out or sealed with rings
of heated iron that their exhortations to others might not be heard
as they made their way to the stake, or to have their living flesh torn
from their bones with red-hot pincers.

No refinement of cruelty was beyond Titelmann's invention.
Bertrand le Blas, a cloth-manufacturer of Tournay, broke through
the crowd at mass in the cathedral and snatched the consecrated
wafer from the priest, trampling it with his feet and crying 'Misguided men, do ye take this thing to be Jesus Christ, your Lord and
Saviour?' So paralysed were the onlookers that le Blas could have
escaped, but he was determined to take the consequences of his
action, and he remained where he was. Unresisting, he was taken
before the Inquisition, where he defiantly maintained that nothing
could make him repent of attempting to rescue the name of his
Redeemer from such profanation. He was tortured three times, and
then dragged on a hurdle to the market, where his right hand and
foot were twisted off with red-hot irons. His tongue was torn out, a
hook was fastened through his body, and he was swung slowly to
and fro over a gentle fire until roasted, but to the very end le Blas
remained staunchly faithful to his belief.

Such a death, which was suffered by others also whose names
have not been preserved, 'was carefully selected as among the most
poignant that man can suffer. They were usually burnt alive. They
were burnt alive, not infrequently by a slow fire. They were burnt
alive after their constancy had been tried by the most excruciating
agonies that minds fertile in torture could devise' — when Lecky
wrote these words on the victims of the Inquisition he may have
been grinding a rationalist axe but he was certainly telling the
truth.

The almost incredible bestialities exercised by the agents of
Spain and the papacy towards people of such astounding fortitude
make very terrible reading. One is tempted to pass quickly over the
blackest pages with just that same feeling of guilty escape with which
one turned swiftly from the glossy pictures of Belsen and Buchen-

wald to the less uncomfortable pieces of news, but it was out of the unflinching courage with which these terrors were borne that the Dutch nation struggled painfully to birth, and the bravery with which the men and women of the Netherlands faced an inhuman foe was to leave its mark for ever on the character of the people, endowing them with an abiding hatred of persecution, and a determination to help the oppressed. When in 1956 the Hungarian revolution was ruthlessly crushed by the Russian forces the whole free world passed resolutions of condemnation and many countries received those who had escaped to freedom, but in no other country were they so generously treated as in Holland. It was not the Dutch miners who devised pretexts for refusing to work with Hungarians; in Holland the refugees were received with open arms and genuine friendship, as were the Jews in the years of Hitler, and the English dissenters in the days of James I.

In Italy and Spain the rack and sword and stake achieved their effect of terrorizing the people, but in the Netherlands it was different. The native courage of a people who had had to fight against wind and wave for the very soil on which they lived gave them the strength to defy even the most brutal coercion of Titelmann and his accomplices. Instead of capitulation there arose the spirit of rebellion, and in 1567 King Philip decided to put down the seething revolt once and for all. For this task he selected the Duke of Alva.

The Duke of Alva's name still haunts the Netherlands countryside. His famous Blood-Council set out to exterminate not only protestants but papists too, and to seize their property over their smouldering bodies. No proper trial was necessary, and where formerly people had been burned in ones or twos the Blood-Council's executives now exterminated them by the score. Eighty-four on a single day in Valenciennes, forty-six in Mechlen, five hundred on a single night elsewhere — Alva's executioners were tireless in their master's service. All through the country the fruit-trees and fences and doorposts were laden with the exhibited bodies of men and women who had been strangled, burned or beheaded.

Quite apart from the countless Netherlanders slain in skirmishes, starved to death in sieges, torn limb from limb in the streets (as at Maastricht) or driven to death by being herded into the Scheldt (as

at Antwerp) the Duke of Alva was able to boast when he finally retired to Spain that he had been responsible for the slaughter of not
less than twenty thousand victims seized under the devices of the
Blood-Council. In recognition of his diligence he received not
only the continual approbation of his king, but the rare gift of a
jewelled sword and a flamboyant hat from the Pope. No wonder
that in our own century the Dutch saw in Himmler something of a
reincarnation of the earlier butcher of their people.

Perhaps the spirit of freedom might indeed have been drowned
in the torrent of blood if the Holy Office had not in its enthusiasm
issued a remarkable edict, in 1568. This extraordinary pronounce-
ment sentenced *every inhabitant of the Netherlands* to death as a
heretic, regardless of age, sex, or occupation. Only a handful of
named people were excepted, and ten days later Philip ordered the
decree to be put into force and the methodical extermination of the
Netherlanders to be begun.

Yet the effect of the new policy was different from that which he
expected. Terrified for their lives, and with their leading citizens
for the most part already murdered or in exile, the Netherlanders
at last had the one satisfaction of knowing just where they stood.
It no longer needed even a vestige of heresy or treason to send
them to the gallows. They were under sentence of death, and in
such a position they had nothing to lose by revolt. Resistance was
centred round the great figure of William the Silent — so-called
because whilst a hostage in France he had had the fortune to hear
from King Henry of France that that monarch and Philip were
planning a secret convention to rid France and the Netherlands of
all protestants by a general massacre. Prince William — then himself a Catholic — had not betrayed his horror at this piece of news,
but from that moment forward he had been secretly resolved to
free the Netherlands from their impending fate.

The first town in the whole of the seventeen provinces to throw
off the rule of the Spaniards was Brielle, on the southern side of
the northernmost mouth of the Meuse, and in an indirect way it
owed this distinction to the action of Queen Elizabeth I of England,
whose intentions at this time were to avoid offending the Duke of
Alva rather than to assist the persecuted Netherlanders. The only

safe refuge for the men of a nation condemned to wholesale extermination was on the water, and numbers of Dutchmen had acquired
ships and taken to the sea to live a precarious life as pirates preying
on other ships — and particularly on Spanish ones. William the
Silent afforded these men a certain status as an official fleet, and he
wisely restrained them so far as he was able from attacking ships
other than those of the Duke of Alva and his Spanish forces.

Many of these corsairs, the 'Sea Beggars' as they were called,
happened to be lying in Dover harbour ready to pounce upon
Spanish supply ships coming through the Straits, when in response
to threats from the Duke of Alva the Queen of England forbade
them to be supplied with victuals. Desperately short of provisions
and with their crews almost starving, twenty-four ships of the Sea
Beggars fleet had no option but to put out from Dover and to secure
provisions by a raid on the opposite coast.

The goal selected was the rich harbour of Enkhuizen in the
Zuyder Zee, but when the squadron had sailed as far as the top of
the coast of North Holland the wind changed and they were unable
to round the point and sands of Den Helder into the approaches to
the Zuyder Zee. They accordingly turned down the coast once
more and entered the Brielsche Gat, the most northerly channel of
the great delta, and ranged themselves off Brielle.

When they appeared, a ferry was crossing the river — just as
might be the case today — and after landing his passengers the
ferryman, Peter Kloppelstok, rowed out to the fleet. Kloppelstok
was a secret supporter of William and his rebels, and the Sea
Beggars sent him to row to the town of Brielle to demand of the
magistrates its immediate surrender. Brielle was well fortified and
it had in reality little to fear from the mere two hundred and fifty
ill-equipped men lying off the shore in their tattered vessels, but
the ferryman assured the authorities that the ships contained a total
complement of about five thousand armed men. This ingenious lie
had a most startling effect. Terrified at the prospect of an attack by
such a strong force of the Sea Beggars — men whose mere name
caused people to tremble for the safety of their possessions — the
authorities and all but a mere fifty of the poorer inhabitants of
Brielle quickly snatched up their valuables and fled from the town

in panic. The corsairs landed, carried one of the gates by assault and lit a fire against the other until it was sufficiently charred to be battered in with an old mast. By mid-afternoon the first city to be freed from the Spanish Inquisition had been liberated, never to be retaken.

On receiving news of the unexpected loss of Brielle the Duke of Alva was beside himself with rage, and he at once dispatched a force from Utrecht to recapture the town at all costs. Sailing across the Maas to the delta island of Voorne on which Brielle lay, the Spaniards ranged themselves outside the northern gate and demanded in their turn the surrender of the town. Certainly the Sea Beggars could not have held out, but a carpenter of the town dived into the water with an axe, swam to the sluice in the enclosing dyke, and hacked away the boards so that the water roared through the gap to flood the ground and cut off the troops from the approach to the city on that side.

The attackers then shifted to the southern gate, where they were met with an unexpected salvo of cannon. At the same moment a few of the Sea Beggars were found to have rowed out from the harbour and to have set fire to several of the deserted troop transports and cut the rest adrift. The combined result was to cause a general alarm among the investing forces, and with the sea streaming towards them, their ships gone, and only the rapidly diminishing strip of the top of the dyke left as a means of escape, they turned and fled whilst there was yet time. Many of them slipped and stumbled in the mud amidst the rising water and were drowned, but enough survived to sack Rotterdam in the rage of their frustration.

The surprising success at Brielle caused a wave of hope to run across Zeeland, and the people of Flushing on the island of Walcheren rose spontaneously, drove out the Spanish garrison, and held them at bay. News of this fresh success was carried to the Sea Beggars at Brielle, and a number of them set sail at once in three ships to strengthen the defenders. Ironically, if gorgeously clad in the brilliant vestments and friars' robes seized from the hated figureheads of the papacy and Inquisition in Brielle, they must have presented a strange sight as they sailed into the harbour vowing vengeance upon the Spaniards, but their arrival secured the city until it was further strengthened by the arrival of a considerable force of protestant volunteers from England.

Almost immediately Veere, on the north-eastern side of Walcheren, rose also and declared for William of Orange, but between these two towns a mere eight miles apart, a strong Spanish force held the city of Middelburg. Skirmishing and surprise attacks flared up throughout the island, and such was the hatred born of the cruelties of the Spanish occupation that no prisoner on either side escaped hanging or execution. On the whole the Zeelanders behaved with more restraint than might have been expected of men who had seen their own families hauled to the rack and stake and their women buried alive for refusing to forgo a prayer or a reading from the Bible, yet here and there revenge and cruelty were bound to break out. The Sea Beggars ferociously slaughtered a group of priests at Brielle. In Walcheren prisoners taken from the Spanish forces were tied back to back in pairs and flung into the swirling tide of the Wester Schelde or the Veere Gat, and at Veere a surgeon cut the heart from a Spaniard and nailed it to the bowsprit of a ship lying in the harbour so that the citizens could fasten their teeth in it in the fury of their hatred for men whose behaviour had long since deprived them of any semblance of humanity.

Once, when on her way back to England, the *Commodore* led us towards the island where these horrible events had taken place as a prelude to the great sweep of tolerance and freedom across the villages and cities and dykes of Holland. Her crew was temporarily swelled by two Swiss students who had hitch-hiked to Holland to join her, and though they were cousins they might each have come from a different planet. The one, Paul, was widely travelled and he had already been to England several times. He had in fact a somewhat professional interest in journeying, and particularly in 'Social Tourism', a subject of very serious study about which he was engaged in preparing a monumental *doktorarbeit* with the financial assistance of the Swiss Federal Railways. He gave us clearly to understand that the *Commodore* was not an example of Social Tourism, but I am not sure that we ever understood very clearly what this activity or phenomenon really embraced even though

Paul explained to us that his research led him to Butlin camps where he made a number of technical notes. It seemed however that our ignorance was shared by others. When Paul's investigations had taken him to London he had requested an audience with a high official of the T.U.C. in the expectation that this interview would yield valuable data, but he confessed to us that he had been somewhat disappointed. He had been received with the greatest geniality by a titled trades-unionist ranged behind a big desk at Transport House and for a while they had talked about the weather, but when Paul asked him point blank for his views on current developments in social tourism a shadow of something strangely like perplexity had passed over the broad brow of his host and after murmuring something to the effect that it was a very interesting problem he had looked at his watch, apologized for having to leave immediately on very urgent business, and had shown Paul out with a hearty handshake and best wishes for the success of his research.

Our other visitor, Rene, was much more Alp-bound. Never before had he been further from home than when going to college in the cantonal town at the foot of his native valley. He had indeed been in a boat before — there was a row-boat on some mountain lake near where he lived — but he had never in his life actually seen either a sailing-boat or a motor-ship of any kind, though he knew from pictures in books that they existed. As the *Commodore* chugged complacently down the river towards the delta Rene sat on her bows with his eyes stretched wide in astonishment at everything he saw, from barges to windmills and from old-fashioned tugs to bucket-dredgers. But the highlights of his voyaging were yet to come, for soon we passed through into the channels of Zeeland and in the fairway off Duiveland we met a long sleek vessel of some fifteen hundred tons, thrashing through the water to overhaul the slower barges ahead. As its stern came into view and Rene saw the broad white cross on the red background his emotion knew no limits.

"*'n Schwizes Schiff!*" he shouted. "*'n Schwizes!*" And he rushed below to bring up the little Swiss pennant off his rucksack, insisting that we should run it up to the yard-arm whilst he stood on deck waving and shouting through his hands to the astonished crew of the Swiss boat. Rene had never imagined that any Swiss craft existed other than the landlocked passenger steamers on the lakes, of which he had seen pictures.

Another shock was soon to come his way however, for off Schouwen we dropped a bucket over the side, hauled it up for him, and invited him to taste it.

'*Salzig!*' He licked his lips, took two or three large gulps from the bucket and then suddenly emptied the whole pail over his head. For a moment he was speechless, and then he broke out into wild laughter. The sea was salty! *Donnerwetter!*

With his widely travelled and worldly wisdom Paul said Yes, the sea was always salt — surely Rene must have known that. Rene replied that he had indeed heard so; they had told him so at school in the geography class, but it had seemed incredible that such a thing could really be true. Certainly he had not thought that the sea could be so salt that one could actually *taste* it. Never in his life had he imagined that the sea could really be briny. Surely it would kill the fish.

This was a reasonable point of view and it led us into a deep discussion of *Osmoregulation* and the *Widerstandsfähigkeit* of fishes, with a note or two on the structure and function of vertebrate kidneys and semi-permeable membranes, but Rene was more interested in the sheer phenomenon of the sea than in biology and so we eased off amid the silky calm of the Ooster Schelde and threw out a line astern with a buoy on the end. Soon Rene was trailing through the water behind us, taking mouthfuls of sea water and blowing it out again, waving an arm in the air and calling repeatedly to us that he was in the sea, and the sea was really salt. Even when we had hauled in the rope again and pulled him aboard he had every now and then to dip the bucket overboard and pour the water exultantly over himself, licking the trickles from his lips to make quite sure there was no deception.

Our course led us through the Zandkreek between North and South Beveland. The water was low, and on the exposed banks the golden seals lay contentedly in the sunshine, raising their heads to watch us pass and occasionally exchanging comments about the *Commodore*, but they certainly showed no fear — probably they knew that they were protected by law and that we were just as amiably interested in them as they were in us. Long ago their ancestors would have been more wary of the approach of a ship, for the Zeeland fishermen were armed with heavy harpoons of polished steel. A fat seal yielded plenty of meat and clothing and oil for the lamp at home, and only the breast of a Spanish mercenary was a more highly favoured target for the barbed head which carried behind it the weight of a heavy shaft and the power of a strong and practised arm.

Beyond the narrow channel the water opened out among the sandbanks, and punching against the inward flow of the tide the *Commodore* slid across the current into the same harbour of Veere where once the Spaniard's heart had dripped blood into the water beneath. Ahead lay the lock, and beyond it the course of the Walcheren Canal which leads by way of Middelburg across the island to Flushing.

There is probably no such thing as a Dutch water-town which is not charming, but Veere is certainly one of the loveliest. At the same time it is a sad place. Once it was a flourishing port of 15,000 people, for in 1444 Mary, the daughter of James I of Scotland, married the Lord of Veere, a circumstance which established the wool trade between the two countries and led to Veere becoming the port of the staple. But of this prosperity there is today no more than a nostalgic trace in the rich beauty of the houses of the Scottish merchants on the quayside of the fishing harbour, and even though the Schotse Huizen with their gaily painted shutters are as perfect as ever they were the population of Veere has shrunk to little more than a thousand. The lovely bells of the slender carillon tower on the town hall still ring out over the marshes and fields, and on the *Commodore* we could lie in the harbour and listen lazily to a concert by the municipal carilloneur or

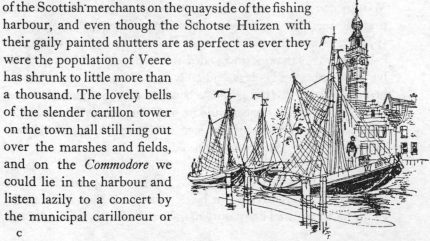

beiaardier, but even the most cheerful of country airs seemed counterpointed with melancholy as it filtered down through the leaves of the trees lining the wharf, where now only a few fishing-boats lay moored with their nets hoisted up their masts to dry. The huge Church of Our Lady too, protestant since the days of the rising, was a forlorn relic of what once it must have been. Burned in the seventeenth century, converted into a barracks in the early nineteenth by the English first and then by the French, it seemed no longer able to keep pace with the deterioration of its outside as well as with the decay of its interior, and propped in scaffolding it had an air of despairing to avoid becoming irrevocably a ruin.

Forgotten and sighing, Veere inevitably has its legends. There is the tale of the burgher who discovered that his wife had fallen in love with a young man of the town, and who lured him out into the Veere Gat on pretence of a fishing expedition. In this channel there still lies a big sandbank named the 'Schotsman' after a wool ship of Scotland which was wrecked upon it, and to this bank the husband took his companion at low tide. The two men landed together, but the husband quickly jumped back into the boat alone and pushed out. Then, lying off in deeper water, he expressed his feelings very clearly to his victim, and began to enlarge in detail upon the unpleasant experiences of any man marooned on a bank in a rising and roaring tide, and he described how for many days the corpse would be carried with each flow up the Zandkreek and the Mastgat and Volkerrak channels, and down again on the ebb to pass the scene of his misguided intrigue. Having delivered this appropriate sermon he turned away and rowed back into Veere.

The young man cried and yelled and wept as the tide crept inch by inch further up his legs and body, but his shouts could not be heard in the town. It is possible however that the husband knew that the local fishing boats would be returning on the flood, for just before dark one of them drew in sight of the sandbank, and the now thoroughly penitent lover was rescued.

Another tale recounts that an old beggar woman was walking beneath the trees to Middelburg when she was approached by a handsome stranger dressed in black, who made the familiar bargain which promised her plenty of gold and silver in return for her soul if she would only do his bidding. With the contract agreed, he sheared off her hair and compounded it into a paste which the woman was to take to the port and smear on the bows of the ships lying at the quays. This she did, and when soon afterwards the boats put out to sea the whole flotilla was caught in a violent gale and every ship was lost with all hands. Imprudently the woman boasted that it was her own doing, and she was at once taken before the magistrates at Middelburg. The same day she was burned alive — as a practical demonstration that the devil's clients would not be allowed to tamper with the shipping on which Zeeland depended for its life and trade.

It was on the ferry from Veere that Albrecht Dürer had a somewhat exciting experience, as recorded in the diary he kept of his journey to the Netherlands in 1520. Just as the boat reached the quayside of Arnemuiden and the passengers were disembarking, a *grosses schiff* rammed the ferryboat, and in the confusion Dürer let the other passengers out ahead of him. Before he could step ashore the boat was carried away from the quay by the ship which had struck it, and the sail was torn in pieces. The wind caught the ferry and drove it from the shore, out towards the open sea.

Aboard were Dürer, his companion, two old women, a baby, and the skipper. They yelled for help, but nobody came to their assistance, and all the captain could do was to shout that the ship was unladen and all the crew unfortunately on shore. He could do nothing, he explained. 'There was fear and alarm, the wind was strong,' Dürer wrote, but he went up to the boatman and told him to take heart and put his hope in God and think hard what ought to be done. Thus encouraged, the *schiffmann* pulled himself together and decided that if the jib could be set they might be able to make harbour again. Dürer and his companions together managed to hoist it half way up the mast, and the adventure ended happily.

Though nowadays Veere is no more than a faint shadow of the port at which Dürer saw ships 'from every nation', the town may have been fortunate to have fallen to comparative unimportance, for it thus escaped damage during the Second World War. But not so Middelburg, which was ravaged from end to end by the fighting. Whole streets were destroyed, and yet with their traditional energy and with a charming refusal to be tempted into the sterile uniformity of town planning or the blank curving façades of bleak architectural modernity the Zeelanders have rebuilt their famous city. The incomparable city hall with its rows of tiny gold-capped dormer windows in the deep sloping roof has been excellently restored, and it is today as lovely as ever it was.

On the Walcheren Canal we met very little traffic, for the waterway was only used by Dutch barges and *tjalks* carrying goods to and from Middelburg. Nor was the canal itself of any particular interest, for it consisted merely of a succession of straight cuts linking the three main towns of the island, and between Middelburg and Flushing one of its banks carried a road and the other a railway. It was not one of the ancient waterways of the Netherlands, and indeed it was only constructed to restore communication between the Scheldt channels on either side of the island when Walcheren became joined to its neighbour by the embankment of the railway from Rosendaal to Flushing — just as the South Beveland Canal was cut to overcome the similar obstruction further up the same railway line where an embankment joined South Beveland to the mainland of Brabant and closed the shipping route. But it was not unattractive in its own unassuming way, and always we had a bell tower in view — at first that of Veere, then Middelburg's city hall, and finally the belfry-tower of Flushing itself at the opposite side of the island.

Flushing, or Vlissingen, is a busy port, and just off its entrance the deep water channel of the Wester Schelde sweeps close in beside the Walcheren shore. The bulk of the town lies low, but it is protected by a dyke vast enough to carry a street and a row of hotels on its top. There too is the magnificent bronze of Admiral de Ruyter, gazing defiantly out over the sea which he roamed so successfully that he could attack English ships in the West Indies and even sail up the Thames to Gravesend or the Medway to Rochester in order to burn or capture the ships of the neglected English navy. The *Royal Charles* was actually seized at her moorings. Samuel Pepys recorded ruefully that 'the Dutch did take her with a boat of nine men, who found not a man on board her, and her laying so near them was a main temptation to them to come on; and presently a man went up and struck a flag and jack, and a trumpeter sounded upon her "Joan's placket is torn".' The Dutch sailors then took her down the estuary at a time 'both for tides and wind when the best pilot in Chatham would not have undertaken it, they heeling her on one side to make her draw little water, and so carried her away safe'. No wonder Pepys was alarmed. 'The truth is, I do fear so much that the whole kingdom is undone . . . I presently resolved of my father's and wife's going into the country; and, at two hour's warning, they did go by the coach with about 1300£ in gold in their night bag. Pray God give them good passage, and good care to hide it when they come home! But my heart is full of fear . . . for I think, in any nation but our's, people that appear so faulty as we, would have their throats cut.'

Sitting outside one of the hotels on a summer's night we could see the glow of the ferry harbour of Breskens across the wide estuary, and watch the lights of the ships turning the bends in the channel from Antwerp. Once long ago they might have been bound for London with a cargo of grain, with every now and then an innocent sack of wheat hiding within its depths a precious copy of William Tyndale's scriptures, safely printed by a Flemish printer in Antwerp and consigned to some merchant in the City of London who could be relied upon to ensure its secret distribution. Now however they were the tankers and liners and cargo carriers outward bound on the ebb to ports in every continent. Every few minutes in the stillness of the night air we could hear against the background of the sweet bells of the carillon a deep slow throbbing from the propeller as one after another the great ships cut inshore to glide past in a blaze of lighted portholes within a hundred yards of de Ruyter. The throb would become slower or perhaps cease for a moment as a ship eased off and a cutter raced out from a jetty at the foot of the dyke to pick up the pilot — for it is at Flushing that the pilotage for Antwerp begins or ends.

Down behind the sea-wall, in a broad street inundated in the flood of 1953, we found another fine bronze, this time of a young man with a coil of rope. His name was Frans Naerebout, and he was a pioneer of life-saving at sea. His most famous exploit was when the packet ship *Woestduyn* ran on a bank off the coast of Zeeuwsch

Vlaanderen opposite Flushing, in a violent storm. Naerebout put out at once in a small boat, single-handed, and by superb seamanship he came alongside and took off several of the passengers. There was room only for a few without capsizing his small craft, but Naerebout reached Flushing safely and immediately set off into the storm again and succeeded in bringing the whole complement to safety.

> *Nog kookt de zee, nog brult de wind,*
> *Nog is er volk in nood.*
> *Frans snelt opnieuw ter redding aan,*
> *Hij vreest gevaar noch dood.*
> *En neemt de rest*
> *Trots zee en wind*
> *Behouden in zijn boot.*

Even now there are children in Holland who have learned from their parents and grandparents the song in which the story of the rescue is told.

On another occasion some ships were trapped in pack ice in the mouth of the Scheldt, and as the floes surged to and fro in the tide and swell the sharp edges cut right through the planking and the ships began to sink. It was impossible to launch a boat, and to walk over the thin floes would have meant certain death, but once again Naerebout came to the rescue of the crews. He swiftly mounted a boat on sledge-runners, and setting out from Flushing he skated quickly over the thin ice, pushing it ahead of him. He could only carry a small load at each time, but passing to and fro between the ships and the shore he once more saved all hands.

Eventually Naerebout became chief pilot of the Dutch East India Company, and once more he had the chance to show his ability. A laden ship from the East Indies which was caught in a gale off the Scheldt lost her rudder and was partly dismasted. Naerebout went out to her and got aboard, and using only the wind and the tide he took the crippled vessel down through the Channel before the gale, and brought her safely into Plymouth.

It was at Flushing too that a young man who was to become famous in protestant history first made his acquaintance with

Holland when in 1585 Queen Elizabeth I at last determined to send a small English force to help the Netherlanders to rid themselves of the Spanish yoke. Her new-found zeal for their cause was certainly political rather than religious, for whilst her forces were preparing to sail to Flushing in order to aid the long-suffering protestants of the Netherlands the Queen's policy nearer home was somewhat different. The same 'Good' Queen Bess was hunting down dissenters with the greatest energy and either hounding them out of the country or having them dragged to the gibbet if they did not conform with the practice of the English Church.

The English force based on Flushing was to be commanded by the Earl of Leicester, but the Queen refused to render any assistance at all without some guarantee of security, and it was to arrange the necessary terms that she sent Sir William Davison to Holland as her envoy. To him the Dutch handed over the keys of Flushing as a guarantee of good faith, and he in turn passed them to his private secretary for safe keeping. This young man slept with them under his pillow. His name was William Brewster.

Throughout the time that Sir William Davison remained in Holland as the Queen's representative, Brewster stayed in his service; then, when the diplomatic mission was completed the two men returned to the court in London. Here Sir William was very soon to experience Elizabeth's ingenuity, for when Mary Queen of Scots was condemned to death the Queen instructed Davison to sign the death warrant. Popular feeling mounted at Mary's execution, but the Queen easily transferred the resentment from herself to Sir William Davison by hinting that he had signed the death warrant without her authority. To lend colour to this explanation Davison was brought to trial, disgraced, and imprisoned in the Tower of London.

Brewster might well have deserted his employer and saved himself from being involved in his disgrace, but he was a man of staunch character. He knew that Sir William was innocent, and he chose to remain close to him all through the time of imprisonment. Not until his employer was released did Brewster return to his home in Nottinghamshire and settle down once more in the little village where he had grown up. Two years later, when still prob-

ably no more than twenty-five years old, William Brewster succeeded his father as postmaster of the manor of Scrooby.

Whilst serving in the Netherlands Brewster must frequently
have come into contact with the Dutch form of Protestantism, and
no doubt he had heard and perhaps seen something of the heroism
of the men and women who had gone willingly to the stake rather
than deny their conscience. He had not been back in Scrooby again
for more than two or three years when news reached the village
that several young men whom he had known from his student days
at Cambridge had been hanged for their insistence that they and
not the Queen and her bishops were the best judges of their duty
towards God. At once Brewster's mind was made up; if freedom of
worship was forbidden, then the meetings would have to be in
secret. Soon he had gathered round himself a little band of fellow
non-conformists which began to meet in his house at Scrooby, and
it was from that circle that the Pilgrim Fathers were one day to
spring — even if Brewster himself was the only one of the original
Scrooby meeting to reach America.

Among Brewster's friends who went to the gallows for their
faith was Henry Barrow. Imprisoned in the Fleet for seven years
before his final execution, Barrow wrote books and tracts in which
he vigorously attacked religious dogma and the persecution carried
on by the Queen and her bishops, and campaigned for the right of
freedom of worship. Page by page his writings were secretly conveyed out of the prison, and despatched by friendly merchants to
Holland — just as once Tyndale's Bibles had been smuggled in
the opposite direction. At Dordrecht Barrow's tracts were secretly
printed, and the copies were smuggled into England again for cir-
culation.

The Queen was not particularly pleased to hear that heretical
literature was entering her dominion by the back door, and she
instructed her representative in Holland to do all that he could to
discover where the printing was done, and to have it stopped. He
in turn chose a spy to pursue the matter, and the man selected was
Francis Johnson, a minister living in Middelburg. Strangely
enough, Johnson himself had already been driven from England
for refusal to toe the proper ecclesiastical line, but that did not

mean that he approved of Barrow. His own quarrel was with the practices and forms of the Church of England and he wished to see it put right from the inside, whilst for men like Barrow, who proclaimed that the Church of England itself was an entire misconception of the relations between God and man, he had no sympathy at all. Barrow was a Congregationalist, but Johnson was a militant and critical Anglican, and for that reason he was delighted to undertake the task of preventing the printing of Barrow's works.

Thus commissioned, Johnson followed the trail of the tracts until at last it led him to a printer's shop in Dordrecht, and entering the shop in the pose of a customer he was lucky enough to find sheets of a tract by Barrow actually on the press. But he was too cunning to reveal his hand immediately, and he waited until the entire edition of three thousand copies had been run off. Only then did he pounce, and under his authority the tracts were seized and all but two of the copies were burned.

The two surviving examples Johnson deliberately kept from the fire as souvenirs. One he sent to a friend but the other he kept for himself, and on his return to Middelburg he began out of curiosity to read it. By the time he had read it through he was so thoroughly convinced by Barrow's arguments that he hurriedly made his departure from Middelburg and took a ship for London, where he hastened to the Fleet prison, sought out the author, and begged his forgiveness for the destruction of the edition at Dordrecht.

Henry Barrow received Johnson without a word of reproach, and before long the two men were firm friends. Johnson himself became a non-conformist, and learned what it meant to meet with others in continual fear of arrest. Soon he was acting as pastor to a clandestine congregation in London. Eventually his activities were discovered, and like many before him he was arrested and put on trial. His sentence was perhaps not so brutal as it would have been under Alva, but it was severe enough, for although he escaped hanging he was sentenced to be deported immediately to the safe distance of the wild continent of America. At Southampton however he contrived to escape from the prison ship in which he was confined for shipment and he fled back to Holland, where men were relatively free to follow their conscience. In ones and twos the people of his own congregation and Barrow's followed him, and together with others they formed the nucleus of the famous church in the Begijnhof at Amsterdam.

Walcheren is an island of memories of siege and struggle and flood and war, but today these things lie hidden below the surface. Seen from the canal bank the countryside is one of thriving farms where tractors haul the modern machinery of agricultural science to harvest the crops grown in the rich black silt left by the great rivers long ago. Yet although it is a prosperous island with modern ways Walcheren is one of the few remaining areas of Holland where traditional costume is regularly worn, more as a matter of pride than of custom. In Vollendam and certain other towns and villages near to Amsterdam the pretty costumes have become something of a fancy dress, donned to attract tourists by their quaintness and to lure them into souvenir shops and restaurants with American bars, but throughout Zeeland the most exquisite dresses appear unostentatiously, magnificently, and in an astonishing variety of detail which varies from village to village. Many different styles can be seen on market day in Middelburg when the women of the farmsteads come to do their shopping. A bodice may be stiff and starched, or it may rise high off the shoulders in fluted wings worked with embroidery. The long skirt may be striped or plain or brocaded, and there will be rows of coral beads from the East Indies, held at the neck with gold clasps which perhaps have been treasured in the family for generations. The spotless cap may be short and pointed, or there may be a spread of delicate butterfly wings of elegant lace, and often there will be corkscrew or pendant ornaments of solid gold protruding at either side of the forehead, with perhaps a blue silk bow at the back of the head.

These lovely dresses, with all their array of several coloured petticoats peeping impudently from beneath each other, are not by any means confined to the farming people. They are found in the towns too, and when on the dock-side at Flushing we stood to watch the berthing of a passenger vessel just arrived from overseas we noticed further along the quay the wife of the master, straight and tall and round-featured as a portrait in the Rijksmuseum, waiting to welcome him home. Quite unselfconscious, she was more imposing than the wife of an ambassador at a court function and as the wind fluttered her head-dress of lace she took it off for a moment to adjust it. Beneath it her head was encased in a heavy casque of solid burnished gold, which flashed brilliant in the sun for a brief moment before it vanished from view once more as she pulled her cap quickly over it again and secured the lace with the gold ornaments at her temples.

Yet this was no uncommon possession. Many a young girl or wife of a Zeelander will owe something of her upright carriage to the heavy heirloom lying under her cap, a helmet of beaten gold pierced along the central line and capable perhaps of turning the assayer's scales at a weight which today would represent a dowry of ten thousand guilders or a thousand pounds.

III

The South Beveland Canal — Shopping on the water —
Mondragon's expedition — The route through the islands —
Dintelsas and the great flood — Willemstad — The for-
tunes of a bargemaster

It was at Hansweert that we first encountered the delightful open-faced honesty of the Dutch. An armed guard appeared on the lock-side, saluted, and drew from his pocket a little printed catalogue which he handed to us.

'That is a list of criminals internationally sought by the police,' he explained as he shone his light on the booklet. 'Please be so good as to tell me whether your names are listed.'

We scanned the list and handed it back to him with the assurance that for some reason or other we were not included. He thanked us, saluted once more, and told us that we might proceed. We drew up on a dredger outside the lock to wait for daylight, and then we set off along the canal.

It is always an interesting experience to arrive at some new place in the dark, for when the dawn first begins to illuminate the countryside the view is invariably quite different from what one has imagined. Perhaps we had pictured a sweet story-book prospect of cows and milkmaids on lush meadows, and of cottages with gay gardens and here and there a windmill, but as the light stole across the sky we found that the view over the landscape was not beautiful. Nor was it ugly, however. It just did not exist, for the land area of the Zeeland islands lies far below the normal tide line and even further below the height which the sea may reach in times of sudden flood, so that to the boatman the fields and hamlets are hidden from view behind the massive dykes which fringe river and creek and canal alike. The South Beveland Canal passes in a straight line from one side of the island to the other, but the most that one can hope to see is the orange-tiled ridge of the roof of a farm just behind the bank, or the tip of some distant spire of a church, or the moving sail of a mill.

Yet the canal is interesting enough, for it is one of the busiest in Europe. An endless stream of inland shipping converges upon the southern entrance at Hansweert from Flushing to the west, Terneuzen to the south and Antwerp to the east. Ahead through the northern locks at Wemeldinge the channels of Zeeland lead through to Dordrecht and Rotterdam, to Amsterdam and the whole of Holland, to the lower reaches of the Meuse, and to the Rhine. Day and night the unceasing procession of inland transport throbs through the short waterway with the produce and raw materials of France, Belgium, Holland, Germany and Switzerland, and it is in its shipping rather than its landscape that the charm of Zeeland is to be found.

The craft which had followed us out of the small lock at Terneuzen were for the most part Dutch privateer boats of up to two hundred tons. The majority were motor-barges, but one or two were sailing craft aided by an outboard propeller on a long shaft which could be lowered over the side by a pulley block. This screw

was driven by the donkey engine near the bows which at other times could serve to work a derrick or haul up the anchor. Some of these one-time sailing barges had huge elephant-ears or leeboards and their stems curved bulkily under the broad bows in a style peculiar to the country. They were steered sometimes with a wheel, but often by a massive wooden tiller on which carved lions or signs of the zodiac were gaily painted in reds and greens and browns. Other craft were Belgians, mainly of the sharp-bowed *spitz* type capable not only of forging through the currents of the estuary channels but of penetrating into the smaller rivers and canals of their homeland.

The largest barges had used the main ship-locks at Terneuzen, but now in the South Beveland Canal all classes of boats were once more united. The more massive craft ranged from powerful tankers of several hundred tons to towed butty-boats of as much as three and four thousand tons apiece. Laden, these motorless mammoths of the canals and rivers would push so powerfully with their bulky bows that the water-level would surge upwards on the banks, even as far ahead as the diminutive tugs which pulled them. Then, as they passed us, the water would slide quickly back behind their sterns to fill the gaps they had left. Unladen, the same giants towered up to the top of the canal banks and drifted half sideways behind their tugs as the wind caught their huge bulk and swung them over the surface — for such craft wasted none of the available and considerable depth of the waterways upon such refinements as a keel.

Besides these there were the smart, clean-lined express boats from Switzerland, shapely and strong and capable of the ten knots which would give them speed enough to pass the Binger Loch and the narrows of the Rhine gorge without delay. Not that delay was the only means of loss of profit on a voyage, but for craft passing far up the Rhine the days saved by greater speed against the current would be worth more than the cost of extra fuel to achieve that speed, or a reduction in tonnage carried per horse-power. Among these craft the *Commodore* passed almost unnoticed as she pressed her little hull of questionable tonnage into the curving corner of the Wemeldinge lock, close inside the gates.

Hansweert and Wemeldinge are almost invisible from within the canal banks, but their shopkeepers appear on the locksides in spotless aprons of white and blue to hold up smoked eels and loaves of bread, beefsteaks and sausages and baskets of eggs or cans of milk. The skipper of a canal boat has no time to seek out the shops for himself and the tradesmen must deal with him as he moves past. From the point of view of the *Commodore* no country in Europe proved so convenient for household shopping as Holland, where domestic supplies were brought right to her hatch. We could be asleep at anchor in a country lake when a tapping on the side of the hull would wake us to discover a rowboat alongside us in which the local greengrocer had brought out his range of stock. Sometimes when we were waiting for a swing bridge to open, a message boy with a cycle would hail us from the bank. Eggs? Cheese? Bread? Some pork chops? Very good, they would be delivered. No, no, we were not to wait. He would find us somewhere further on, and lower our purchases aboard from a bridge.

Often we would see a deep-laden shop-boat swing alongside a passing barge, throw a hook round a stanchion or through the scuppers, and supply all the odds and ends needed by the bargemaster's wife whilst the customer to which it was hanging proceeded doggedly on its way. Marked with a border of green and white squares on the gunwale, these mobile shops are to be found in any inland harbour of importance throughout Holland, and sometimes in rivers or busy canals too, far from a village. The shopkeeper does not appear to mind how far he may be carried while supplying a boat, for sooner or later another ship from the opposite direction is sure to bear his craft back again. Once in Zeeland we had a ship-shop hooked on to our side for more than five miles whilst we bought what we needed from a stock which started with fuel oil and wire hawsers and ended with daily papers and fruit. There were strawberries and cream to be had too, and these were not just stocked for the rare yachtsman who might pass that way but for the families on the commercial craft. The master of a barge half the size of a Channel packet and capable of carrying as much cargo as six or eight goods trains is not likely to be so poor that he cannot afford luxuries. Nor is he socially on the level of the genial steersman of a narrow-boat on a winding canal in England. His son may be at the university — and paying full fees too, for not many of the places at a Dutch university are aided by a scholarship or local authority award of any kind.

Between Hansweert and Wemeldinge there was only the converging perspective of the canal banks and the double line of traffic, yet the canal itself cut across the path along which the forces of Alva passed in their memorable relief of the town of Goes, a few miles further west. The island of South Beveland was then almost connected with Walcheren opposite Middelburg (today the fusion is completed by the broad railway embankment) and with Flushing on the one side of it and Veere on the other in the hands of the patriot rebels, the position of the garrison of Middelburg was precarious. The creeks and rivers around Walcheren and the Beveland islands were swarming with the craft of the Sea Beggars and Zeelanders, and it was thus clear to the Duke of Alva that Middelburg could not hold out indefinitely unless the forces in the town of Goes on South Beveland were reinforced so that they could hold open the only other approach to the island of Walcheren.

Today South Beveland is no true island but just as on the west it is connected to Walcheren so too on the east it is continuous with Brabant. At the opening of the sixteenth century it was similarly joined to the mainland, but one of the rare recurrent tempests broke down the dykes and cut a broad way through from the Ooster Schelde to the Wester Schelde. The roaring sea engulfed a hundred villages and hamlets as it swept on its way, and the area inundated became known as the 'drowned' or *Verdronken* land. Here and there throughout Zeeland there are patches of *Verdronken* land, once inhabited and above the sea — just as throughout Holland there are today large tracts of land which in the days of the Spaniards were below the waters — but the flooded area which separated South Beveland from the Duke of Alva's forces stationed in Brabant was several miles from side to side. Yet it was across this stretch of shallow water that the veteran Spanish commander Mondragon decided to take a relieving force to Goes. Not that the water was merely ankle-deep. On the contrary even at low tide it lay several feet in depth over the whole of the area, and the flats were intersected by three deeper channels, through which streamed out some of the water of the Schelde.

Mondragon's undertaking was a very bold one. Ten miles of underwater banks and eroded dykes had to be followed, and in three places the troops would be obliged to swim. If the crossing should take longer than the time between half ebb and half flow, the entire force would be drowned. Yet Mondragon decided that the plan was possible, and at the head of three thousand picked men, each bearing his own supply of provisions and gunpowder on his head, the Spanish commander waded into the chill water on the Brabant shore in the darkness of an October night in 1572. Ahead of him were three men with local knowledge of the sands and channels, and behind him a body of soldiery who had no experience of such an undertaking. Yet on occasions which demanded courage and endurance the discipline of the Spanish forces was superb, and though up to their chests in the waves and sometimes forced to swim across some deeper gulley between the banks they plodded doggedly in perfect order across the lost land towards the island. By next morning the force was ashore at Yerseke, close to the eastern bank of the modern canal, and only nine out of the three thousand had been drowned in the adventure. South Beveland was easily secured and the final liberation of Zeeland was held at bay. It was not until several years later that the sword of the elderly but undaunted Mondragon was no longer to be wielded as the emblem of the power of ruthless suppression. Later still it had the humbler and more humane if ignominious occupation of lightning conductor on the spire of Wemeldinge church.

Through the lock at Wemeldinge the traffic swarmed out into the Ooster Schelde, with the *Commodore* following in the rear. Occasionally some small vessel would desert the main throng to head off westwards to North Beveland or northwards to Zierikzee on the now united island of Schouwen-Duiveland, but the main body of transport turned northeastwards into the Keeten channel separating Duiveland from the promontory of St Philips Land. On either side the islands devastated in the flood of 1953 lay hidden behind the banks. On that terrible night Schouwen-Duiveland was submerged from end to end and the streets of Zierikzee were tangled with dead cattle, overturned vehicles, and the floating debris of furniture and planks and rafters which only a few hours before had been the homes of Zeeland families. More than two hundred people were drowned on the island, whilst across the channel the little town of Stavenisse on the island of Tholen was practically wiped from the map.

From Tholen an expedition similar to that of Mondragon's crossing of the *Verdronken* land was planned by the Spaniard Requesens in 1575. Once again three thousand picked men were to attempt an assault through the waters by following a submerged sandbank, this time towards the coast of Duiveland, their object being to secure control of Zierikzee, which had been freed from Spanish rule. A thousand Spaniards, a thousand Germans and a thousand Walloons were selected to plunge into the water in the early hours of the morning, followed by a force of more than two hundred military engineers who were to convert Zierikzee into a fortress after it had been captured. Once again the Spaniards were in the van, led on this occasion by another veteran commander, Ulloa, 'whose greatness of mind equalled the valour of his followers.' After inspiring the troops with a fervent speech he rushed ahead into the water, and the long cavalcade set off.

Though successful, the expedition did not pass over as easily as that of Mondragon. The Zeelanders had received warning of the Spanish plan, and the waters on either flank were crowded with their boats, many of which were brought to anchor on the very edges of the submerged spit along which the Spaniards were to pass. Boissot, the determined leader of the Zeeland sailors, had even constructed a temporary fort from flat-bottomed craft beached half way along the bank which the invaders had to follow, and from this a heavy fire was poured on the column. So narrow was the raised strip that many of the soldiers stepped off it in the dark and were drowned, whilst the remainder had to fight their way through the dim forms of the ships of the Sea Beggars, and the whale-men and seal-hunters of the islands hurled their barbed harpoons into the breasts of any of the advancing horde who came within reach. Others leaned out over the gunwales, snatching at Ulloa's men with their long boathooks and dragging them from the sandbank to

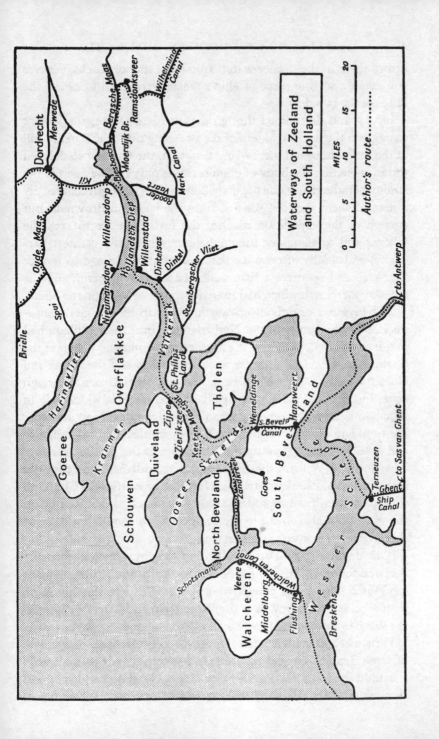

Waterways of Zeeland and South Holland

MILES
0   5   10   15   20

Author's route............

drown them in the deeper water. Iron bars, anchor stocks, sheaves and every available piece of ship's tackle were used to crush the heads of the invaders.

Strong and disciplined though the Spaniards were, the violent struggle in the narrow waters of the sweeping tide took a heavy toll of the three thousand men. More than that, the fighting so delayed the advance that the body of engineers was only halfway across the strait when the rising tide began to flow in such strength that hardly a man of them was not washed from the spit and drowned. But enough of the expedition reached the further shore to sack the villages and to slaughter their inhabitants with the greatest barbarity, and finally after more than six months of siege to reduce Zierikzee and so drive a firm wedge between Walcheren and the cities further north which had risen in support of William the Silent.

The invasion of Schouwen was however to have a vital consequence for the future of the Netherlands. Until then William had nominally been governor of the northern provinces on behalf of the Spanish crown, elected under ancient privileges of the towns and cities themselves. There had been no Dutch nation as a sovereign state, but only a part of the Spanish dependencies which was in rebellion against the tyranny of an infamous ruler. Now however the time had come to throw down the gauntlet in final defiance and to tear off the last vestiges of allegiance to the hated sovereign. The words of William the Silent when he addressed the deputies after the loss of Zierikzee strangely foreshadowed those of Churchill in 1940. 'Even if we should not only see ourselves deserted by all the world, but also all the world against us, we should not cease to defend ourselves even to the last man.'

The deputies of South Holland in solemn session formally declared the end of their subservience to Spain, and at that moment the Dutch nation was officially born, even if it was then no more than a collection of towns and villages scattered from Flushing in the south to the coasts of the Zuyder Zee.

Perhaps some rusted anchor-stock or the corroded breastplate of some Spanish trooper or German mercenary still lay buried in the mud beneath the *Commodore*'s keel as she plodded ahead through the narrows towards the coast of North Brabant, but even on the land on either side there was little to be seen from her deck except here and there a line of trees tall enough to overtop the sea wall, and very rarely a distant spire or windmill. At Dintelsas however a gap in the bank to starboard led through into a vast enclosed area of water, the Vluchthaven, in which barge trains might lie up and wait if the state of the tide was such that they could make little headway against the pent-up river waters which poured down the channels on the ebb. We too put in to the harbour, not from necessity but out of curiosity.

Dintelsas is nothing more than the outlet for Dinteloord, a village a couple of miles inland, but its name suggests that it is the site of a *sas* or lock. And so it is, for here the River Dintel flows out. Further inland the course of the Dintel connects with a series of waterways by way of which a boat can pass through to Breda or to the Wilhelmina Canal which passes across the flatness of North Brabant to join with the Zuid Willemsvaart, which in turn leads through to the Upper Meuse and then to Wallonia.

Moored against a barge alongside the jetty the *Commodore* lay far below the top of the Dintel lock gates, and yet on the night of the storm these gates themselves had been completely submerged as the sea drove over them and forged up the river. With the land behind the dykes now so prosperous and green it was not easy to imagine the terror of that night, but the barge against which we now were moored was a regular visitor to Dintelsas and it so happened that on the day before the tragedy the bargemaster had put into the Vluchthaven for shelter from the rising gale, and the boat was one of many which had spent the night there, held out from the land on anchors lest the tops of the tall mooring piles now high above us should have damaged their bottoms. The skipper could never drive that night from his memory, he said. More than half a mile of the dyke beyond Dintelsas had been carried away, and of those who lived in the farms behind it very few were saved. Intermittently throughout the night the families on the barges had heard in some momentary lull of the wind the cries of people perched on tottering houses, and the frantic bellowing of the cattle plunging and slipping in the roaring water. Every now and then a groaning and cracking amid screams of despair told them that one more house had crumbled to pieces beneath the onrush of the water. Yet the boatmen had been unable to reach the land behind the dyke, or to do anything to save the families trapped in the swirling flood. No, not many had escaped, and those fortunate enough to survive the first onrush of the wild waters had spent days and nights clinging to the ridges of their roof-tops before they could be rescued.

Just round the point beyond Dintelsas and on the extreme tip of North Brabant lies the attractive little town of Willemstad. Little of it is visible from the water except the sails of a windmill projecting into the air, for Willemstad lies hidden not only by the dyke but by the massive fortifications which surround the town. On one of our voyages through Zeeland however we were tempted to turn out of the shipping highway and to make over to the narrow cut which curved towards a gap in the fortress wall. Like others of the Zeeland harbours the Willemstad entrance can provide a fine eddy at certain states of the tide, and just when we were passing inside the mole the *Commodore* disregarded her helm and made straight for the shore as though in a hurry to land. We were obliged to put her full speed astern to stop her and then we waited whilst the eddy swung her through the rest of the circle like a locomotive on a turn-table. When she had completed her slow pirouette we put her ahead again and she chugged happily up the slack water beyond the swirl to draw in at the quay beside a delightful sixteenth century town hall with diamond shutters, and a golden mermaid poised on the weather vane.

Willemstad is no longer a fortress, but it still preserves its geometrical structure intact. It was built in 1583 by William the Silent in the form of a seven-pointed star and at each point the high walls broaden out into a massive bastion. Their names — Holland, Zeeland, Utrecht, Friesland, Overijssel, Gelderland and Groningen — recall some of the estates of the Netherlands which at that time had rallied to his cause and revolted for ever against the cruelties of the Spanish monarchy and the papacy. Outside the walls a moat forty yards broad surrounds the town and follows the same geometrical outline, and this in turn is enclosed in a lower outer wall, defended on its exposed side for most of its length by a second somewhat narrower water obstacle. Beyond this the rich fields and small holdings and orchards of fruit stretch inland to the horizon.

Because of its elaborate array of walls and moats Willemstad is compact within its boundary. Today the walls are edged with rows of trees, and from the walks beneath them one can look far out over the prosperous land of Brabant behind the town, or northwards across the channels to the dimness of the distant smoke lying over Rotterdam. Or one can look inwards across the orange-tiled roofs of the little houses to the Prinsenhof, the pretty country residence built by Prince Maurice early in the seventeenth century.

The fortifications are cut in two places only; on the landward side by the Landpoort — now a mere bridge instead of a gateway — and on the water side by the Waterpoort, through which the harbour cut passes into the shipping channel beyond. Beside the Landpoort the fortress wall at either side of the road is provided with a vertical slot, and the same arrangement is found on the corner of the town hall and on the hotel which faces it across the top of the main street. Into these grooves massive boards can be lowered to keep out the dreaded invader — not in this case the Spaniards, but the rising waters of a flood — and as an extra precaution the entire street and market place along the line of the town hall and hotel is raised into a formidable hump. This ridge forms a barrier high enough to protect the town from all but very exceptional floods, and it can be raised still further by setting emergency boarding along the top.

The great moat, originally dug to keep attackers at bay, has another very practical use too. It is connected by way of culverts with the inner end of the harbour and during the flood of 1953 careful judgment of when to open and close the sluices enabled the people of Willemstad to maintain their town in a relatively dry condition. Only two of the townspeople lost their lives, whereas sixty were drowned in Numansdorp, the ferry terminal on the opposite shore of the Hollandsch Diep, and across the fields beyond the Landpoort sixty more were lost in the farmsteads and cottages swept away by the water which streamed from the broken sea wall to flood the country as far back as the second line of dyke four miles further inland.

Had it not been for the stout ramparts of William the Silent the fate of Willemstad might well have been disastrous, but the walls which were built to withstand an army were well able to hold out against the water, and the only weak place in the defences was at the boards capping the hump of ridge between the town hall and the hotel above the harbour quay. Here the driven water succeeded in forcing an entry close against the hotel, and it ran down the reverse side of the hump in such strength that it washed away the corner of a house in the main street and began slowly to rise against the doors and walls of the lower-lying houses beyond. But on the ebb tide the streets were drained through the sluices into the moat, and this reservoir could in turn release its surplus water out through the harbour, so that at the end of two days Willemstad was almost the only piece of dry ground amid a watery waste which extended for miles in every direction and remained inundated for months. The land of Brabant and Zeeland being below sea level, the water once admitted could not drain off again of itself, but had to be pumped away or in some cases released little by little by temporarily opening again at the time of lowest water the same gaps through which it had forced an entrance.

How fortunate Willemstad had been in its possession of walls and moat we could see from other evidence too. Beside where the entrance channel opened out to the harbour basin a modest guardhouse stood back from the quay. On the wall beside the door we noticed five plaques at different heights from the ground, and on examining them we found that each marked the level to which the water had risen on the occasion of some notable flood during the last few centuries. The mark for 1953 was perhaps a foot higher than even its nearest competitor, and on that winter's night the sea had risen half way up the walls of the guardroom. Yet this building — the only one apart from the shipwright's house at the top of the slipway to be situated outside the fortifications — stood considerably higher than the streets of the town itself.

The quayside of Willemstad was as happy a place to lie as we could have wished, but the depth of water alongside was somewhat restricted at low tide, and as we had arrived at Willemstad during the springs we considered it prudent to move across and lie instead

against the flat side of the *Zeehond*, a family barge of a hundred tons which was awaiting its turn on the slipway of the local shipwright. The fair-haired, stocky young skipper welcomed us alongside and introduced us to his wife, and to a golden-haired baby of eighteen months who was tethered to a running lead above the hold covers. The ship was in for careening, he explained, and until another barge had left the slipway they had little to do but lie on the hatches in the sun, patiently awaiting their turn.

The captain of the *Zeehond* had served his apprenticeship on a Rhine barge carrying bulk cargo from Antwerp to Basel. Every seventeen days the ship had reappeared to load in the Antwerp docks before making the long haul through to Switzerland to un-load, turn round, pick up more cargo, and set off on the speedier return journey with the Rhine current on the fat stern. Then after five years his father had died and it was his own turn to take over the *Zeehond* for a generation.

That he loved his boat, the traditional home of his family, there could be no doubt. And yet it was easy to see that he was worried, and before we had been long in his company he turned from showing us his photographs of the Rhine castles to tell us that he could see no future for the *Zeehond* under the changed conditions of modern water transport. It was not that there were too many boats, but just that the *Zeehond* could not compete with the Rhine giants and the smart new diesel ships the throbbing of whose engines carried to us continually from the channel outside the fortress walls. The *Zeehond* carried eighty tons of cargo and she could travel at a shade over five knots with her thirty horse power oil engine. Once this had been sufficient but nowadays it was not. A barge three or four times the size could earn more money on each trip and because it could travel half a knot or a knot faster it could make more trips in the year than he could. Such a boat could cover the voyage to Paris from Rotterdam in two days less than the *Zeehond*, and could afford to tender keenly for the cargoes. Yes, a ship of even four hundred tons could clear a net profit of 25 gulden a day — about £900 a year — and with this margin there was ample money for repairs. If only he could afford a new diesel engine then the *Zeehond* too could be made to travel fast enough to earn a good profit, but her small capacity and lack of speed prevented him from earning such profits that the money could be laid aside. And even if the cash could be saved, would it really be worth spending it on machinery for a boat which could carry no more than eighty tons of pay-load? No, the *Zeehond* could never hope even then to compete against the larger ships, he said. On the big waterways the massive craft of the big transport firms had all the advantages, and they could always raise capital from shareholders to make their fleet even more efficient. The only advantage on the side of the *Zeehond* was that she could enter the innumerable smaller canals of France and the Low Countries and load wheat straight from the thresher or take flax from some remote farm jetty to the factories of the River Lys. There was still plenty of trade to be had in such ways, but return loads were not always easy to arrange, and he could not afford to have his ship travelling light or lying idle. Even the two days waiting for the slipway were serious. One had to face the fact that the heavier and faster motor barges were gradually ousting the smaller privateers from the main bulk transport. He could keep going and make a modest living, but no more. And if one day the *Zeehond's* oil-engine should chug to a standstill from old age, what then?

We asked him how far afield he took the boat, and were surprised to find that he had just returned all the way from the south of France. During the last year he had been to Friesland and north-west Germany, to Ghent and the coalfields of northern France. And more than once to Paris, too. Yes, he liked Paris, but it was expensive. There were many fine things there that he could have wished for his wife, but the old *Zeehond* could never earn them. Besides, the money had to be saved for something else, for the future of the little boy who crawled over the hatches, trailing behind him the line which ran on a steel safety-wire stretched fore and aft from the wheelhouse to the mast. Until he was nine years old the boy would stay aboard, returning to Willemstad once a year when the *Zeehond* put in for slipping. After that he would have five years at school, a good boarding-school it would be, and whilst he was there his parents would be away on their endless voyaging through western Europe. The schooling would cost money, too. The state? Yes, the state would contribute five gulden a week towards the cost, but what was five gulden? The *Zeehond* would somehow have to earn all the rest. Then there would follow the years at a skipper-school — for it was inconceivable that the lad could be trained for any other occupation than that which his forebears had followed for generations. Finally he would go into the army.

But why, why spend a year or two training the lad as a soldier, the young skipper wondered. How long had Holland held out against the Germans in 1940? A day or two only, for all the long and expensive training in mechanized warfare. And if war were to come again it would be even more efficient, and defeat would be there not in two days but in two hours at the most. Then why waste the time and money of the nation upon making them ready to achieve no more than a deferment of the inevitable result for a matter of hours, or even of minutes?

War however was not his chief fear for the future either of his boat or of his infant son. A much more real danger lay in the fact

that eventually the lad could be expected to fall in love. Many a
family ship had been ruined by love, he said; then, seeing the
puzzled expressions on our faces, he laughed. Oh yes, he wished
the boy a happy love and just such a marriage as his own. There
could be nothing finer. But he himself had been lucky, he assured
us. His wife came of skipper stock, and a husband and a family
aboard a barge was what she wanted. She would never have been
happy on land in a box of a house. But it did not always turn out
that way. Many girls seemed to think a boat was not a home; they
were always hankering after a house, with electric cooking and a
refrigerator. Yes, he had seen it happen among his own friends.
From boyhood they had been brought up on ships, like himself.
They had gone to the skipper-school, and year by year they had
been prepared for the day when they would take over the boats
which were the homes and livelihood of their families, and in
which all the money of their parents was tied up. Yet in spite of
this it was a gamble, for however much a boy might belong to the
water a girl could come and sweep him off his feet and carry him
away to a life on land where he was just like a fish out of water and
had neither knowledge nor skill. The parents were left, ageing on a
faithful boat with no young master to take it over in their old age
or if they should be sick; and when they died — well, that was the
end of it. The boat would perhaps be put up for sale, but nobody
would want it. Not if it were like the *Zeehond*, a good boat but too
slow for the modern age. Yes, it was a strange thing that a good
honest girl — by land standards, of course — could be more of a
danger to a barge than the maidens who were said to have sat in
olden days on the Lorelei cliffs below which he had often passed on
the Rhine barge of his apprentice days, combing their golden locks
with golden combs. Not that there might not be a few Lorelei here
and there in such cities as Antwerp, but bad girls were not so
dangerous as love. It was a strange fact that without love there would
be no wife and no son, and therefore no future for a family privateer however many knots its motor could deliver, yet many a fine
craft had been wrecked on the fascination of a boy for a girl whose
feet were planted on dry land.

Turning from the problem of love we enquired what had become of the *Zeehond* during the war, and the skipper explained that his family had been fortunate — far more so than many. When the country was over-run a few inland ships managed to escape to sea, but most of them were trapped. The *Zeehond* was one of hundreds of barges commandeered by the Germans and taken with their family crews to Norway to replace the coastal shipping which had escaped to England. They had made their way in convoy up the country to Friesland, and thence across by the Ems and Weser and Elbe to the Kiel Canal. Arriving in the Baltic they had skirted the Danish Islands and crossed the Skagerrak, bound for the fjords. It was more of a sea voyage than the old barge was used to, but there was no heavy sea and she had reached the Norway coast along with the others and had settled down to five years of carrying food and cement and grain from one little Norwegian port to another. The Germans had paid them well and fed them well, and the Norwegians had always befriended them. Yes, the *Zeehond* had indeed been lucky. Many Dutch craft had merely had their bows summarily cut off with oxy-acetylene plant to prevent their making a desperate run for England. Many more had been taken from their skippers, cut lengthwise in two, and then railed to Russia for assembly and use on the waterways of the Soviet Union. None of these ships had ever been heard of again, he said, but he imagined that a few of them were now in use on the Russian canals under different names, though most had probably been abandoned or scrapped.

IV

The signor's equipment — Dordrecht — The theological dispute — The Rhine traffic — Canals of the Romans — The Geldersche Ijssel — Zutphen — A surprise on the bank — Buying a chart

The *Commodore* seemed to be in no hurry to leave Willemstad, and so when the evening began to draw in and the water which had filled the harbour at high tide turned to run out again, we set to work to put out our fishing devices in the hope of picking up some eels.

Nothing can be more delicious than a fresh eel lightly fried, and so the *Commodore* carries in her hold an impressive if not always very effective variety of gear with which to catch them. Sometimes in a big harbour we have baited sea-lines with juicy pieces of bacon fat and dropped them over her side, and just occasionally this simple system has brought in a fine specimen. Steak is said to be an even better lure and it is the favourite bait on the lines hanging from the sterns of the Dutch coasters in any harbour in Europe, but we rarely carry a supply of it aboard, and if ever we do then we cook it for supper rather than offer it to eels which so often have a way of remaining in the abstract.

Besides a variety of lines and hooks the *Commodore* also carries an eel-trap once built for her by an old Italian net-maker who lived in a shack in a remote corner of Essex far from the sea. We discovered Signor Barbagli by chance as he stood in an orchard stringing a trawl between a couple of apple trees, but he was very willing to apply his mind seriously to the problem of eeling. He made for us a collapsible trap on a framework of cane hoops and all we had to do, he said, was to hang some bait in the narrow end, preferably the dried skin of a lemon sole — a commodity which in practice we never happened to have on board — and lower the thing on a rope to the bottom. Any eel slow-witted enough to swim in through the funnel at the broad end would, he assured us, be unable to get out again.

I doubt if we really expected the device to work, particularly when we had substituted bacon rind for sole-skin, but it certainly did. Small crabs, starfish, and foolish young fish two or three inches long were admittedly our most usual customers, but every now and again an eel actually proved sufficiently stupid to nose its way inside and become imprisoned there just as the signor had prophesied. Indeed, if there were eels about, we could almost rely on having one of the D-stream for breakfast. But we had also asked the Italian to make us a dropnet. In principle this was the same as those which the fishermen on the jetties of Calais and Dunkirk lower from their little cranes and wind up again with bicycle pedals, but it was somewhat smaller. We swung it out from the side on an improvised derrick.

The basic assumption of this method of fishing seemed to be that fish did not stay still, and that there was therefore a definite if rather small chance that one of them would actually happen to be passing over the eight foot square of net at the very moment when the hauling up began. Admittedly this seemed very improbable, but when lying in French harbours we had been surprised to see that fish were indeed caught in this way — not very often perhaps, but now and again, and just occasionally in twos and threes. We had happened to notice too that at certain particular states of the ebb tide, when the fish were presumably moving from a part of the harbour which was drying out, the catches were more frequent. There was another run of fish on the inward flow of the tide too, whereas at both high and low water the dropnets yielded very little beyond an occasional starfish and a few wine corks.

We accordingly rigged up our dropnet and swung it out to the side to lie in the channel where the water from one of the moat culverts streamed out as the tide began to fall away in the harbour. The net was dropped, left down for a minute or so, and then hauled up by hand-over-handing the rope on the derrick. The skipper of the *Zeehond* was politely sympathetic as time after time the net broke surface entirely empty, but we persevered.

After dark there came a time when things suddenly changed

Perhaps the moat was becoming too shallow, or it may have been that the fish just enjoyed making a midnight excursion into the harbour or out to the Diep beyond it, for throughout a period of perhaps an hour and a half we never once hauled up an empty net. Sometimes there was a single fish flopping in the bottom, whilst at times we had three or four together. With plenty from which to choose we soon became selective and only pulled on board those which we considered to look particularly appetizing. There were half a dozen eels, but we only wanted big ones and so we dropped them back again and concentrated on the other fish.

The water backing up the Hollandsch Diep with the flood tide was no more than brackish, for it consisted mainly of the substance of the Rhine and Meuse which had run down on the previous ebb. Much of our catch consisted therefore of freshwater fishes, including some handsome perch, but as none of us was inclined to a dish that would taste of little more than mud these too were allowed to swim off again in thankful relief. But there were other species too, and before the run of fish had ceased we had managed to scoop up a dozen specimens of some type which in the dim light of our lantern appeared nearly related to herring, and in the morning we cooked them for breakfast. Admittedly they fell a trifle short of delicious, but they were certainly not unpleasant and we had had the pleasure of discovering that such an improbable method of fishing could really be successful.

All the while, by day and by night, the procession of Rhine traffic rounded Willemstad close inshore as the ships turned from the Volkerak into the Hollandsch Diep. By day we could bathe at the edge of the sandy shore and see-saw over the wash of one boat after another as the transports filed by, and in the night the stillness of the sleeping town was broken by the beating of their screws under the water, the sound carrying in as a soft rhythmic thudding to where we lay in our bunks in the *Commodore*. If we happened to awaken we could pick out the different craft as they passed outside the walls. The slower surging, accompanied by the hollow note of a broad exhaust-pipe, came from single barges, but the more urgent rushing with an overlying faster engine note in triplets indicated an express Rhine boat. Sometimes there would be a sound of water swashing against the bows, but no mechanical noise other than the faint hiss of steam, and then we knew that a steam tug was hauling a train of heavy lighters round the point from Antwerp.

At first light the captain of the *Zeehond* was to be ready to take his craft on to the slip, and as we ourselves got under way the shipwright's men were winding at the hand winch and two thirds of the barge was already clear of the water. The skipper and his wife and a shipyard labourer were standing at the water's edge, scrubbing the steel plates clean as they emerged from the surface, and before the morning was out the first coat of paint had no doubt been applied. Meanwhile we were far on our way towards Amsterdam.

It was still early when we slipped out of Willemstad — early by land standards, that is, but not according to the *Commodore*'s habits. Four in the morning was a time of day which appealed to her, and she preferred a departure at about this time to any other except three o'clock or half-past two. Originally we thought that her preference for voyages at sunrise was connected with the calmer sea usually to be found at that time, but this was not really the case. On the contrary, she invariably enjoyed what a sailor once described to us as 'a bit of a puffle', and if she elected to start early it was just because she knew that we could sleep no longer. Holidays are for some people not only a relaxation but an opportunity to lie in bed whilst the loveliest part of the day slips by unseen, but though we had plenty of relaxation on the *Commodore* it lay more in the thrill of the beauty of the places to which she took us than in lying late on the comfortable mattresses of her bunks. Sometimes she would see to it that we had less sleep in a week than we would have had in a couple of nights at home, but at the end of it we were fresher and more rested than if we had slept each night through to the traditional time of hotel breakfasts. Sleep on land might be welcome, but on the *Commodore* it always seemed unnecessary and a sad waste of the opportunity to explore the beauty of the creeks and rivers and harbours and cities around us — a loveliness which is at its most glorious in the golden side-lighting of the first sunshine when a film of pale mist hovers over even the most polluted water and all is quiet except on the water and in the hedgerows and bushes beyond the banks.

E

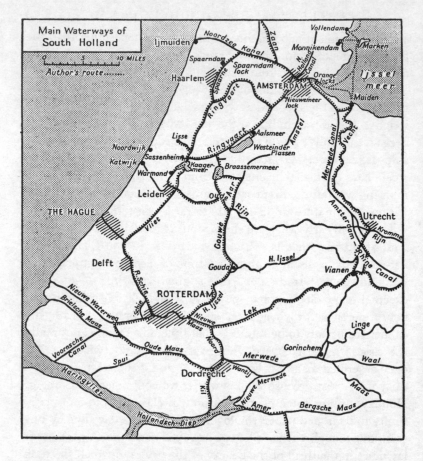

Soon after leaving Willemstad we saw the long line of the distant
Moerdijk bridges breaking dimly through the haze which lay over
the broad sweep of the Hollandsch Diep. Completed in 1871, the
railway bridge is a fine feat of engineering with its fourteen great
spans stretching from bank to bank at a point where the Diep is a
mile and a half across, and beside it there has since been added a
road bridge to carry the traffic on the road from Antwerp and Breda
to Dordrecht and Rotterdam. For us the row of spans marked the
end of relatively open water and we turned to port just short of
them, following the main flow of traffic into the River Kil. Some
of the shipping continued ahead, passing under the bridges towards
the swampy archipelago of the Biesbosch — a name which means

'reed-forest' and accurately describes the maze of hundreds of diminutive islands and beds of sedge which suddenly came into being on a November night in 1431, when the waters of the rivers rose to wipe out seventy villages and drown a hundred thousand people. Those ships which left the forlorn waste of the Biesbosch on their starboard side would be bound for the Nieuwe Merwede river which led through to the River Waal just short of Gorinchem (or Gorcum), whilst those passing round its southern side were aiming for the Meuse towns and perhaps for the Juliana Canal in Limburg, or might be turning in by Ramsdonksveer towards Tilburg, Helmond, and the Zuid Willemsvaart route. The main trade route however lay not through the bridges but northward up the Kil, and we had plenty of company as we turned in at the Willemsdorp point light. Forty minutes more brought us into the Dordrecht, five hundred miles distant from the Swiss frontier upstream.

Dordrecht has its own claims to historical fame. It was here that the meeting of representatives was held which founded the Dutch nation. It was at Dordrecht too that the brothers Jan and Cornelius de Witt lived, those two great patriots who were later to be dragged out by a crowd worked up to fever heat by the crafty allegations of pamphleteers, and torn to pieces. Here too in some unrecorded alley stood the printer's shop where the tracts of Barrow were running through the press when Johnson came from Middelburg to destroy them, and here was held in 1618 the great Synod of Dort (the alternative name for Dordrecht) at which the long and bitter disputation between the supporters of Arminius and Gomarus was fought out.

This dispute, which began on matters of theology between two professors at the University of Leiden — Hermans (or Arminius) and Gomar (or Gomarus) — was centred round predestination and divine omniscience. Arminius held that all those who of themselves renounced sin and trusted in Christ were granted forgiveness, whilst the intransigent and impenitent were punished. The fate of man depended on his own choice, and God did not compel him. Gomarus on the other hand held the strictly Calvinist doctrine that by the almightiness and omniscience of God a man was predestined to be saved or damned, and therefore his fate was in no way influenced by his own free will. He declared that the tolerant humanism of the followers of Arminius elevated man even higher than did the doctrines of the papacy, since they refused to give God the sole credit for the one thing that mattered above all other — 'a righteous disposition of spirit'. The Arminians wanted to see the Calvinist doctrines and books reformed in the light of criticism, but to the Gomarists this was sheer heresy. As the argument became more bitter, the dispute split every town and village and church from top to bottom, and it became allied with politics too. The Arminians formally presented to the States of Holland a 're-monstrance' setting out their views, to which the Gomarists replied with a 'counter-remonstrance'. When the Arminians were finally expelled from the Church at the Synod of Dort the forces of intolerance had won a notable victory, and the heat of feeling involved in the wordy struggle between remonstrants and counter-remonstrants was to leave a deep and regrettable scar on the history of Dutch protestantism.

But Dordrecht has a beauty of its own, a charm which does not depend upon historical memories. Nor are the simple stateliness of the Groote Kerk and the renaissance elegance of the doorways of the merchants' houses along the quays of the basins its chief ingredient. Without the shipping the town would lose nearly all of its extraordinary fascination, for it is at Dordrecht that the Rhine first meets the highways of the sea. Openings in its quaysides lead through to basins of great beauty in which row upon row of tall funnelled steam tugs and their more racy diesel descendants lie moored between tall white-capped piles, whilst outside in the river the water is heaved into a seething turmoil by the wash of heavy traffic and the thrust of the deep-set screws of further battalions of tugs. For though at first sight the Nieuwe Haven might appear to be a pool in which these stately craft are laid up for retirement they are there only for a brief respite from the heavy duty of shepherding the cargoes of the fairways beyond. And appropriately enough the doors of the houses on the quays and in the alleys beside the tidal creeks running through the town bear little brass plates announcing the occupation of the inmates. Skipper, tugmaster, tug-owner, charterer, ships agent, towing agent, chandler, fuel agent, pilot, master engineer and shipwright — the men of Dordrecht are men of the water.

To say that Dordrecht is on a river is an understatement. It lies at the junction of four massive waterways. The River Kil by which the *Commodore* had reached the town on the shoulder of the tide runs out to the southward and forms the highway for shipping from Ghent and Antwerp; the Oude Maas, with a depth of more than thirty feet, leads westwards to Vlaardingen and the Hook of Holland; the impressive Noord Canal runs north-west to the docks of Rotterdam and to junctions with other routes which lead to every part of Holland lying to the northward, whilst from the east there flows in the Merwede River which at Gorcum metamorphoses to the Waal and further upstream changes its name yet again to be known as the Rhine. The Rhine barges trans-ship their cargoes to ocean vessels not only at Rotterdam, but at Dordrecht too, and from these two ports, connected by the Noord, the long trains head slowly upstream, strung out for half a mile or more on the hawsers

radiating from the hooks of the massive river tugs. Whichever of the two ports may be their origin or destination they must necessarily pass in ceaseless procession round the bend at the northern edge of Dordrecht where Kil and Merwede and Noord unite.

The size of these barge-trains came as a surprise to us. We were familiar with the tugs of the Thames hauling a quartet of seventy-ton lighters of coal or esparto grass up river to Brentford or Kingston, but as we approached the town we had to wait until a tug and its barges had passed upstream before we could cut across the river to the quays. First came the tug, a stream-lined diesel boat of more than a thousand tons with power in every line of its sleek body and a bubbling mass of heaving water driving backward from its stern, whilst ahead of the bows a huge anchor hung on a derrick, ready for release in a split second. A hundred yards astern came a long low-laden black lighter flying the Belgian flag and proclaiming from the carved oaken board ahead of the wheelhouse that it was registered in the figure of 2,654 tons. An equal distance behind it another barge appeared round the bend, this time a Dutchman, but still hitched to the same tug and linked with a hawser to a third not yet in view. We held the *Commodore* in the current and waited patiently as one after the other the Rhine-carriers glided slowly past us on the ends of their tow-lines, and by the time the eighth and final barge was clear of us the tug was already far round the bend at the edge of the town, and long since out of view. We had been adding the tonnages of the tows as they came level with us and with this final barge the amount hauled by the one great tug reached its total of rather more than sixteen thousand tons.

Shipping on the Rhine is nothing new. The Romans had at times a fleet of six hundred vessels on its stream, and even if these craft were not carrying ores and cement, coal and oil, iron and steel and chemical fertilizers, they were even then used for transporting supplies to the towns as well as for more direct military purposes. Throughout the centuries the river continued to handle trade, but the swift current in its middle and upper reaches made a return journey very difficult. But in 1816 steam power made its first appearance on the river in the graceful form of the London-built *Defiance*, and this

event marked the beginning of the rise of the river to its position as the greatest traffic artery of all Europe. No other stream approaches the Rhine in the quantity of goods which it carries, for upstream of Dordrecht the shipping is swollen by the traffic from Amsterdam, and further up again it receives small contributions from the eastern areas of Holland. By the Convention of Mannheim international carriage of goods on the river is open to the shipping of any nation, and quite apart from the Swiss boats and the large numbers of Dutch barges the Rhine fleet includes more than fifteen hundred Belgian boats, mostly of the 2,000 ton class, two thousand German ships which ply on the river and its connections, and a number of French ships which for the most part ply to Strasbourg or Basel. The Rhine is the gateway leading from the Benelux seaports to more than forty inland harbours and industrial centres on its own banks or those of its larger tributaries and canals.

At Emmerich, where the traffic crosses the Dutch-German frontier, the customs records show that the cargoes carried up to Germany from Antwerp, Rotterdam, Dordrecht and Amsterdam are around the figure of 20 million tons a year, of which more than half is metal ores. The figure for downward traffic is not much smaller and includes more than 6 million tons of Ruhr coal for export, but it is one of those inexplicable mysteries of economics that many of the ships which take coal from Germany to Rotterdam will return upstream again with another cargo of coal. We talked with a German bargemaster who told us that his craft of 1,999 tons — not 2,000, which by law would have involved employing a larger crew — was engaged year in and year out carrying

German coal between Duisburg and Rotterdam, and American coal from Rotterdam to Duisburg — not that this was anything new, for on the Grand Union Canal near Watford we had often seen narrowboats laden with coal passing each other in opposite directions. To anybody but an economist such a practice would seem to be unnecessary, but perhaps the cost of journeys which cancel each other out is less than the expense of maintaining a bureau of planners and officials by whose masterly transport strategy such a state of affairs could be avoided. And perhaps the coal is of some subtly different quality; or again it may all be part of some vaster system of international adjustments which would collapse in ruins if coal-producing areas used their own product instead of importing it from elsewhere.

Though ores and coal are the two chief cargoes borne on the Rhine stream others too reach large proportions. More than a million tons of grain flows up the Rhine from the Benelux ports in a year, and three million tons of oil are carried up by tanker barges to Duisburg, whence a twenty-five mile pipe-line runs to the refineries of the Ruhr. Other traffic is destined for the Wesel-Datteln and Rhine-Herne canals, or for Frankfurt and the River Main, or Mannheim and the River Neckar. Nor has the Rhine yet reached the peak of its use, for ambitious work is being undertaken to make through navigation possible as far as the Lake of Constance, and the Main and Neckar are each being redesigned and extended by canals, which will provide through routes to the Danube. It may not be many years more before the flags of Jugoslavia and Austria are seen fluttering from the sterns of the river barges lying against the wharves of the Dordtsche Kil or clustered around the sides of the ocean cargo-liners in the river roadsteads of Rotterdam, and when that day comes the *Commodore* may be pushing her inquisitive nose under the bridges of Vienna, bound for Belgrade.

To speak of the Rhine as though it were a single permanent stream is of course an error, for although the German section has remained in the same bed during historic times the part of the river nearer the sea has greatly altered its form. Today the Rhine river branches immediately below Nijmegen, the southern branch being that which becomes the Waal and forks again beyond Gorcum to form the Merwede, which flows to Dordrecht, and the Nieuwe Merwede which cuts round behind the city to join the Bergsche Maas above the Moerdijk bridges. The northern branch, or Neder Rijn, forks once more on the outskirts of Arnhem, the one part flowing northeastward through Zutphen and thence onwards to reach the Zuider Zee half way up its eastern shore. This, the smallest branch of the Rhine, is known as the Geldersche Ijssel. The remainder of the original Rhine water flows westwards through Arnhem as the Lek, and joins the Noord Canal at Krimpen on the outskirts of Rotterdam, but in former times the bulk of its water flowed through Utrecht to reach the sea outside Leiden. This waterway, the Oude Rijn, is still in existence even if it no longer carries the water from the distant Alps of Switzerland, and it is the only branch of the original river to reach the sea with the word *Rijn* in its surname. In fact it leaves the Lek at Vreeswijk as the Vaartsche Rijn, and at Utrecht yet another branch divides to the northward to form the beautiful and meandering River Vecht, which reaches the Zuider Zee at Muiden, a few miles east of Amsterdam, whilst the remainder carries on as the Oude Rijn towards Leiden.

Virgil wrote of the 'two-horned Rhine', and the two horns were those streams which today we know as the Oude Rijn and the Waal, between which lived the Batavians — whose name persists today in Indonesia. He certainly cannot have been referring to the Geldersche Ijssel as the northerly of the two arms, because at that time this river did not connect with the Rhine stream at all. The modern junction was made much later in an effort to provide an additional outlet for the springtime floodwater from the melting snows of Switzerland, but the change was disastrous and parts of Gelderland were inundated.

Today canals lead from the Dutch branches of the Rhine in every direction, but as early as the first century A.D. there were artificial waterways in the area, for the Romans cut a canal link from the Rhine towards the area where the Zuider Zee now lies — or rather, the remains of the Zuider Zee; because, as we shall see, it is rapidly disappearing from the map. Mark Antony's son-in-law, Nero Claudius Drusus, was responsible for this waterway. The Canal of Drusus was navigated by his son Germanicus when taking his troops on the second of his expeditions to Northern Germany, in A.D. 16, and the quays where they embarked have been excavated at Vechten, outside Utrecht (Trajectum). When describing the canal Tacitus uses the singular, suggesting that one waterway was involved, whereas in reporting the engineering schemes of Drusus another author, Suetonius, writes of *canals*. Tacitus also mentions a mole constructed by Drusus in order to regulate the waters of the Rhine, and there was also the Drusus Dyke, a bank built to prevent the inundation of the Island of the Batavii by the spring floods coming down the river from its upper reaches.

The Island of the Batavii still preserves its name in the Betuwe, the land between the Lek and the Waal rivers, but classical experts have long deliberated over the exact situation of the Roman engineering works. It seems highly probable however that there were two Drusus Canals. The one mentioned by Tacitus would have been a navigation canal to link what was then the most northerly branch of the Rhine with the course of the Vecht, but there would also have been another which led from the same branch of the Rhine near Vestervoort across to the River Geldersche Ijssel, and served to prevent inundations on the lower reaches of the Oude Rijn by diverting the flood water into this other stream.

The complete picture would therefore be that Drusus reclaimed the swampy area of the southern side of the Island of the Batavii, which then lay between the Waal and the Oude Rijn, by planting a mole or groin in the fork in such a way as to send the bulk of the waters round the northern side. This structure would be the *moles* of Drusus which was later broken down by the Batavian leader Civilis — an action which returned the southern side of the area to a swampy condition. The *agger* or dyke seems to have been a bank close to the same point, extending along the left bank of the river from near Cleve to the junction. This too would have had the object of keeping the southern side of the Betuwe dry by preventing the floods from overspilling the banks and streaming into the Waal course. The Oude Rijn would have been connected to the Vecht for navigation purposes by the Drusus Navigation which joined it at Utrecht, whilst to restrict the overflow during spring floods the Drusus

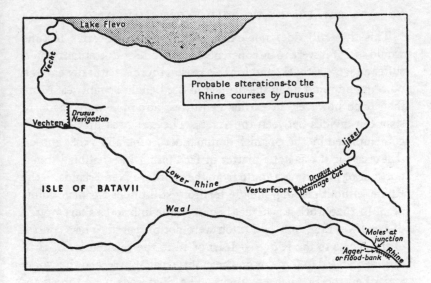

Within the map:

Lake Flevo

Vecht

Probable alterations to the
Rhine courses by Drusus

Vechten

Drusus
Navigation

ISLE OF BATAVII

Lower Rhine

Vesterfoort

Drusus
Drainage Cut

Ijssel

Waal

'Moles' at
junction

'Agger'
or flood-bank

Rhine

Drainage Canal was cut to link the river near Arnhem with the
Ijssel at Doesburg — the two streams being comparatively close
to each other at that point. If in this account there is no mention of
the Lek, which today is one of the two main Rhine branches, that is
because in Roman times it was not yet a Rhine channel. Later,
when the Pannerden Canal was cut to carry into its course some of
the Waal water, the Lek came into its own and replaced the Oude
Rijn as one of the two main streams by which water from the Black
Forest hills and distant Switzerland covers the last seventy miles of
its journey to the delta channels.

Although the Rhine and Meuse and Scheldt converge as they
approach the coast of the Low Countries to merge finally in the
channels of Zeeland and South Holland it has long been a dream
that a link should connect them at some distance from the sea.
Traffic bound from Germany to Antwerp still has to run down the
Waal to the Hollandsch Diep and thread its way among the Zeeland Channels to pass through the South Beveland Canal and turn
inwards again up the Scheldt estuary. A canal from the Rhine near
Cologne to the Meuse north of Liége, from whence the fine Albert
Canal carries 2,000-tonners across the Campine to Antwerp, would
cut hundreds of miles off the route of ships running between Germany and Belgium or Northern France.

This link still does not exist, and though Antwerp's fortune would soar if it were to be constructed the trade of Rotterdam would suffer a severe setback, and for this reason there is naturally enough no common mind upon the project in the Benelux countries. More than once however, in earlier centuries, attempts were made to span the divides between the rivers. The task was first seriously contemplated by the Spanish commander Spinola in 1598, and on that occasion it was not a matter of facilitating international transport but of providing a route from the southern Netherlands to the Rhine without passing outside territory still under Spanish dominion. In 1626 work was in fact begun on the link and a short stretch of canal was dug, but the Dutch were not prepared to lose control of the access to the Rhine — least of all to the Spaniards. In 1628 they descended in force upon the embryo canal, wrecked the works and killed the Spanish engineers. The Spaniards were forced reluctantly to abandon the scheme, but even today the remains of their works are still visible.

It was these same ruins which were seen by Napoleon in 1804, and which inspired him with the similar idea of building a barge-route along which his supply ships could pass from Antwerp to the conquered Rhineland without touching Dutch territory. His engineers surveyed the course and selected a slightly different route for the Emperor's proposed Canal du Nord, running by Weert and Venlo to reach the Rhine at Neuss. Once again the work was put in hand, but in 1810 it was rendered superfluous by the simple expedient of taking Holland into the Empire instead. A section of the canal at the German end of the line was by this time already completed and it continued in use until 1848, when it was finally filled in and used as the bed for a railway track.

In 1834 however the Rhine was indeed linked to another of the great rivers, but this time it was neither the Meuse nor the Scheldt. It was to the Rhone that the Rhine was now successfully wedded, but although the Rhine-Rhone Canal is still in use it has never carried much traffic. More than 200 miles in length, it cuts through the Belfort gap to reach the Saone at St Symphorien, with 161 locks on its course.

The ambitious project of a through route from the Rhine to the

Danube has for centuries been another dream of engineers and politi-cians alike. Napoleon was by no means the first water-minded ruler to consider it as a possibility, but he went so far as to have the route surveyed by his generals Desolles and Moreau. Goethe too advoca-ted the waterway, and thirteen years later the energetic Ludwig I of Bavaria put the work in hand, and the link via the River Main at last took shape as the Ludwig Canal. Unfortunately its dimensions were too modest for the larger barges of our own century, and the Ludwig Canal was finally closed in 1950. Finally, that is, for the moment; for a great reconstruction of this route is now projected.

So the Rhine is not a simple stream but a highway connecting with other routes which lead all over Western Europe, and it ends in a maze of channels in which its water is mixed with that of the Maas. And at the centre of the complex of rivers and deep water-ways weaving through southern Holland towards the North Sea lies Dordrecht, with its army of tugs.

On a voyage back from Friesland we ran up the most easterly of the Rhine branches, the Geldersche Ijssel. We found this river to have sufficient current for considerable shoals to be deposited on the inside of its many bends, and it had not the depth of water of the Waal branch. There had been a serious lack of rain in Central Europe during the previous weeks and so the water was exception-ally low — the gauge boards set up at intervals on the bank inform-ing us that in places the depth in mid-channel was reduced to about five feet. The drought had of course also reduced the bankside depth in the towns, and as the water had fallen to such a degree that the stones and bedsteads and perambulators were often only just awash, to draw alongside the quays was virtually impossible. We arrived at Deventer before supper and found a temporary berth outside a beached barge, but as the locality seemed to offer no attractions sufficient to offset the heavy odour of cake which hung in the hot evening air we decided at nightfall to leave the city of the Royal Gingerbread factories and to move on upstream. Ahead of us lay Zutphen, once the scene of a particularly horrible Spanish massacre, the screams from which were heard far across the Gelderland countryside. It was Alva's son who had the privilege of attacking the city and carrying out his father's holy command that not a single man was to be left alive, nor a house unburned, and Don Frederic was certainly a suitable son for such a father. The defenceless citizens were murdered in the streets, hanged alive on the trees which lined them, or stripped and driven out into the snow to die. Five hundred were tied back to back in pairs and flung to drown in the Ijssel, whilst those who dared to try to escape were hung by the feet from the branches to endure days of torture until death released them.

Such deeds, undertaken under the name and warrant of the temporal representative of the Christian Church of the time, are so frightful that one is left wondering how men can have been found to execute them, yet it seems that in any age, however enlightened by arts or science, there is no lack of servants ready to carry out unspeakable orders. Zutphen and a dozen other towns of the Netherlands only foreshadowed Lidice and Oradour, and the burghers imprisoned to die in their blazing homes or hanged naked by the feet in their doorways have their counterparts in those who in our own day have fallen under the more refined tortures of brain-washing and concentration camp. Such love of cruelty must always astonish us, yet in reality the power of the spirit of freedom and conscience which has enabled men and women to endure the worst that Alva or his modern disciples can do is far more astounding. And not only to endure, but to found even amid the terror of Zutphen a new order, not of hatred and violence, but of tolerance and kindliness. Whether such values can only be born out of tyranny, and whether the qualities of the Dutch nation could never have been forged except in the heat of the ashes of the Spanish fire and fury perhaps even a historian cannot say for certain, but in our own times it is not altogether discouraging to look back upon the days of the Spanish occupation of the Netherlands and to see how a people who had known neither freedom nor national entity, and who were almost unarmed and for many years quite unaided, broke the power of a system which ruled by absolute terror of mind and body and spirit backed with a mighty and disciplined military force.

As we swung the *Commodore* out into the current to head for Zutphen we remembered the sack of the city, but we recalled too that it was there that the gallant Sir Philip Sidney showed the remarkable sense of fair play which cost him his life when in 1586 a small English force under the Earl of Leicester attempted to capture the city, and free it once more from the Spaniards. The English had set up their camp on the opposite shore of the Ijssel when news came that a relief column was on its way to attempt to bring supplies into the city. Leicester ordered a force of three hundred horse to be ferried over and to ride to cut it off, and the gay and romantic Sidney accompanied it for the sake of adventure. On his way he noticed that another knight, Sir William Pelham, had forgotten to put on his leg armour, and thinking it unfair that he himself should be better protected Sir Philip took off his own and gallantly flung it away.

Fog soon descended on the band of horsemen and when the mist cleared again the English found themselves pressed back against the walls of the city by a greatly superior Spanish force. Sir Philip's horse was shot under him, but he leapt on another, charged alone into the enemy ranks, and succeeded in cutting his way right through the enemy formation. He then turned and cut his way back again, but this time he was wounded in one of his unprotected thighs, and after a month of pain he died. The words with which he declined a drink of water and offered the bottle instead to a wounded foot soldier were to become his most famous epitaph.

Running up the Ijssel in the dark we had no chart, nor even a survey map, but we kept in the centre of the stream where it ran straight and we took the bends well to the outside, though not so close inshore as to risk fouling the breakwaters and training walls which ran out to divert the current from undercutting the banks. Now and again we passed a pair of barges lying at anchor in the stream, slowly swinging under the lights of their tall masts, but not once did we meet another vessel — and this surprised us, for the Dutch bargemasters are not men to waste time in sleeping. We carried cautiously onwards however, and by comparing the upper and lower edges of the dark shadows towards which the river led us we were able to distinguish those which were river bank or islands from others which were no more than the reflection of lines of trees lying inshore and sometimes far beyond the winding course of the stream. Dry land and reflections look identical at night except for the fact that a reflection is necessarily accompanied by a similar but reversed contour immediately above it — an outline of the landscape of which the darkness on the water is the mirrored image.

The *Commodore* always appreciated a night run, perhaps because it gave her the opportunity to show proudly her port and starboard lights and the white glow from her masthead. She felt her way easily up the current under the moonless sky and soon after midnight we heard a clanking ahead of us and a glowing caterpillar moved noisily through the air above the horizon. It was accompanied by a similar but shorter trail of lights below it where the water reflected the illuminated windows of the train, and we knew that we were approaching the Zutphen railway bridge. Soon we could see the lights of the quayside houses on the port side beyond it.

Feeling for the arch, we saw a swirling in the water just at the entrance to it, and noticing a buoy ahead of it we realized that a wreck obstructed the channel. But there was room enough to slide cautiously past outside it and then to steer close beside the square bulk of a houseboat moored in the stream just ahead. We ran within a few feet of its side, and as we did so a light was turned on and the face of a man appeared at the window, staring in obvious surprise at the *Commodore*'s smooth flank as she thrust past in such presumptuous disturbance of the midnight quiet of a life afloat.

The waterfront of Zutphen did not look very promising, for in the light of the street lamps we could now see that a somewhat crumbled wall fell away to a mass of debris at its foot. We cruised slowly up past the whole length of the quay without detecting any place where it might be possible to draw in, and soon we had passed the town frontage to reach an area where there was no more street lighting and the shore lay in the shadow of a high bank crowned with trees. We brought up from below the searchlight which we carried for use on such occasions, and rigged it up to a bracket on the bows which in the *Commodore*'s previous existence had held the admiral's pennant. Then we slid closer inshore across the current, directed the lamp towards the bank just abeam, and switched on.

As the patch of bank beneath the trees burst into illumination, our surprise at the scene so suddenly floodlit was probably only exceeded by that of the pair of lovers. Out of modesty we at once switched off and did not turn on our spotlight again until we had moved some little way further ahead, and this time we slanted it downward to the water and worked it politely and by degrees up to the shore and the trees, to give adequate warning of its approaching beam. This time we discovered a narrow creek leading through into a derelict basin, and sounding with the boathook we squeezed through the entrance; but the lack of water forced us to withdraw into the river again and we had no choice but to drop back close to the railway bridge and swing gently round to float in on the current and moor silently against a pair of barges anchored off the bank close beside something which we took to be a large advertisement hoarding. Safely moored, we were soon in our bunks, and it was not until the light of the following morning that we looked out of the cabin windows and discovered that the hoarding was not one which bore the expected advertisements of beer or cigars, but a vast notice-board painted with red lettering a couple of feet in height. There, in Dutch and German and French, was the warning:

'Night Navigation of the Rhine Stream Strictly Prohibited'

— a statement which explained satisfactorily enough why we had met no shipping all the way up from Deventer.

After breakfast we went ashore for shopping and it occurred to us that it would be useful to try to obtain some kind of map so that we might at least know where the river was leading us. We sought out a bookshop and asked the proprietor for a large-scale map, preferably one which showed details of the rivers. Best of all would be a water-map if he had such a thing, we said. We wanted it for a boat.

The bookseller stared. 'You are a *schipper*, yes?'

'Yes.'

'Would you be on the *scheep* which came to Zutphen in the night?'

F

Wondering whether we were about to have our attention drawn to some dire penalty we admitted that we were. But the bookman grasped us by the hand.

'Wonderful, wonderful!' he exclaimed. And then, 'There is no navigation by night — you know that?'

'Really?' We tried to sound surprised.

'Yes, it is forbidden. It is very dangerous. Very, very dangerous. The Ijssel is full of banks and sand, and now with so little water. . . .'

We said that the river did not look particularly dangerous. In fact our journey had been very simple. It had just been a matter of keeping in the channel.

'And did you see a houseboat, near the bridge? You did, of course, for you came past within one metre. That is where I live.'

'Then we saw you, when you turned on the light and looked out of the window.'

'Yes, that was me! I had to look, and I called my wife too, and I said to her "Ei! Look at that! There is a *schipper* who knows the river like his own children. Many many times he must have been through here, to come up so in the dark. And at new moon too!" Yes, I said that to my wife and she too ran to the window to see, for she could not believe it either. Our Dutch *schippers* here — not one of them would do it. Not one. Yes, I said to my wife "See how he moves over to avoid the wreck in the centre of the bridge there. Ah, what experience of the Ijssel he must have to know every foot of the stream!'

Perhaps the course might have been difficult for a fully laden barge with a draught of several feet and with bluff bows which did not answer well to the rudder in the current, but for the *Commodore* the passage had been easy enough — even if prohibited. The shop-keeper came to the end of his praises however, and turned to the business in hand. Of what area, he asked, did we wish a *Water-kaart?* And suddenly we realized that we could hardly admit that it was a map of the Ijssel around Zutphen that we had in mind, and we hastened to say that a chart of the Lek was what we wanted. The bookseller took us to a rack of maps and we selected one which took in the River Lek as suggested, but at the same time we made a quick mental note of the number of the sheet which covered the Ijssel. Then we returned to the *Commodore* in the satisfactory glow of unearned admiration, and despatched Rene the Swiss into the town to buy the map by number only.

V

The bridge of Arnhem — The Noord Canal — The Oude
Rijn — Rotterdam and its tide — The smoker's will —
Treckschuyts

Any waterway is attractive from a boat — even the Grand Union
by Brentford gasworks — but apart from the very lovely section where the stream curls along the edge of the wooded cliffs of
the Hooge Veluwe the Geldersche Ijssel above Zutphen is not of
itself a river of any special interest or beauty. Nor is it a busy waterway. It leads through no places of any size and almost the only
traffic to use it is the shipping bound from western Friesland to the
towns of the Rhine or Maas. A few hours upstream however lies
the confluence with the River Lek, and when we reached the junction we turned the *Commodore* to point down that river. In half
an hour or less we were galloping on the useful current into the
outskirts of Arnhem, and ahead of us lay the newly built bridge
which replaced the one which had been the scene of such a desperate
struggle.

As we approached the bridge we noticed a crowd of men and
women gaily dancing in the roadway of its span and we assumed
that they were the townspeople celebrating on the occasion of some
local festival or holiday, but when we had drawn in to the quay and
walked in to the town we discovered that what we had seen was a
most remarkable phenomenon of Social Tourism. We could not
conceal our surprise to learn that the dancers were not Dutch, but
a party of German visitors from the Ruhr who had come in coaches
to view the scene of a notable victory. That the battle of Arnhem
was indeed a German victory there could be no doubt at all, but
that the visitors should exult so unashamedly in the presence of the
long-suffering Dutch who had endured such horrors and starvation
during the occupation of their country seemed to us to suggest an

extraordinary lack not just of manners and tact but of the most ele-
mentary decency. Nor did we appear to be alone in this opinion, for
throughout the town we found the local people murmuring with
resentment. They had certainly seen more than enough of the
Germans only too recently and did not wish to be reminded of
characteristics better forgotten.

During the afternoon the party left in its coaches to return to the
Ruhr, and this we thought was wise. Had they remained until after
dark there might have been some unpleasant encounters on the
quayside, and it would not have been altogether surprising if one
or two had ended their lives among the rocks at the foot of Arnhem's high and tree-lined waterfront.

Arnhem must always evoke memories of tragedy. Beside the
bridge on the right bank is the plain but moving lump of charred
and shell-torn stone which forms the memorial to the men of the
First Airborne Division. Behind it is the van Limburg Stirum
school where that band of men was stationed who managed to hold
the bridge for four days before they were annihilated. Across the
road are the ruins of the once lovely church of St Eusebius, a new
building in the days of the Duke of Alva but now a desolate memorial to the savagery of the fighting.

Such a mixture of destruction and memorials is of course something which is repeated in a hundred cities of Europe, but where
the river Lek flows out of the town to wind between the rich pastures on the left bank and the rising ridge of the Veluwe on the
right the quiet beauty and sheer peacefulness of the countryside
makes the memory of the battle all the more poignant. The cliffs
of the German Rhine further upstream, the rocky crags and the
ruined forts of the robber barons — these provide a setting in which
bloodshed and battle are natural enough and it needs little effort to
call up the ghosts of the warring armies, whether of Roman times
or of Remagen. But the Lek is no Wagnerian river. Frank and open,
its stream glints in the sunlight and the heavy cattle stand knee-
deep in the sandy baylets between the training walls, flicking away
the flies with casual sweeps of their tails. Marigolds bloom in the
marshy meadows, and loosestrife and forget-me-not flash along the
water's edge. Ringed plover strut on the narrow beaches, and pee-

wit and oyster-catcher and redshank pipe and call across the damp
ground beyond. Occasionally a small tug creeps upstream round
the bend, a bright blue flag held out to one side or the other on a
short staff to show according to the Rhine code that that is the side
on which down-coming craft are for the moment requested to pass.
The Lek is not spectacular, but it is charming with a beauty which
seems to lie in no special feature. Certainly it is not a river tragic in
mood.

As we slipped down the broad stream beyond Arnhem we passed
close by a little church, alone in the meadows to starboard. It was
just such a medieval church of stone as we had often found beside
the Thames, still standing humble and age-old, long after the
village to which it belonged had moved elsewhere. Yet this church
was the last point held by the rearguard of British and Polish
soldiers in the short days which began so full of hope for the people
of Oosterbeek, but which ended in disaster. A little lower down on
the opposite shore, lay the church tower of Driel, and we knew that
where now the *Commodore* cut through the ripples of the current
the last exhausted remnants of the airborne army had struggled
into the water. Forming human chains, some had reached the far
shore and the track that led through the meadows to the hamlet of
Driel. Many had been less fortunate.

In less than an hour Arnhem and Oosterbeek were far behind us
and although on our way towards Rotterdam we passed several
pretty water frontages of small river towns, there was no place of
any size between ourselves and the great port. With very little
traffic — the main Rhine route is by the Waal — the stream flowed
on as before, a country river, gentle and soft, yet with just enough
power to remind us that some of its water had plunged over the
Schaffhausen falls and swept between the reefs of the Binger
Loch before smoothing out to carry the *Commodore* down to the
tug-churned waters where inland and ocean shipping met to exchange the cargoes of Europe for those of America and the Orient.

To give a precise description of the arrangement and configuration of the canal network of the Netherlands would be a formidable
task. Throughout the provinces of Zuid Holland and Noord
Holland in particular the waterways are so abundant that to enu-

merate them would be as endless as to retail the streets in the West End of London, and when the *Commodore* nosed her way out of the Kalkhaven and past the gabled merchants' houses into the Kil she had a wide choice of routes ahead of her on her voyage to Amsterdam. Each course had its own attractions, but most of them led out of Dordrecht by way of the Noord Canal, and so it was by this route that she chose to continue her first trip northwards from Dort.

The Noord is a fine waterway ploughed by the Rhine traffic and crossed by a massive span at Alblasserdam, where the smooth hulls of new cargo vessels lie cocked up on the stocks, brilliant in the orange red of priming paint. The air vibrates with the rattle of mechanical hammers, and white sparks fall in showers from the metal as the acetylene flashes of countless welding-torches move over the plating. Ferries laden with shipyard workers bustle from bank to bank and everywhere there is hurry and ceaseless activity. Beyond Alblasserdam the Noord makes junction with the Lek, and a short way further on with the River Ijssel — not the Geldersche Ijssel but the Hollandsche Ijssel, a tidal stream edged with banks of thick black mud at low water. A few miles up this stream lies the Juliana lock on the edge of the city of Gouda.

At the Juliana lock the *Commodore* had to pay, but the sum was only nineteen cents — about four-pence halfpenny. Though further small dues would be levied before she reached Amsterdam the trip was not expensive and when she later arrived at that city she was pleased to know that the entire voyage from Ostend to Amsterdam had cost less in fees than the use of any one of the forty-five locks on the Thames. For each passage of a Thames lock she had to surrender five shillings — and this over and above fees of £15 levied on herself and £4 on her insignificant dinghy for the mere right to move through the Conservators' water at all. The reaches of the Upper Thames are certainly lovely, but the cost of visiting them is not inconsiderable even if its full impact is only appreciated the moment a boat leaves the river and visits foreign waterways instead. The same is to a certain extent true of the canals under British Transport Commission management; they may be sweetly picturesque, but to travel ten miles on them is more costly than to traverse a couple of countries elsewhere. In fact the crossing of Belgium cost the *Commodore* ninepence, with an extra threepence for the use of the sea-lock in Ostend harbour. The locks at Bruges and Ghent were free, and so was the Ghent Ship Canal. No charge was made for the South Beveland Waterway, nor for the Noord, and not until the Juliana Sluis did the navigation authorities want even such a pittance as nineteen cents. On a later voyage the *Commodore* was to travel from London to Norway through more than twenty canals and a dozen rivers and yet pay less than the amount required by the Thames Conservancy for the passage from Maidenhead to Teddington which preceded her departure, even after the initial 'registration' had been paid. No doubt there are reasons for the heavy dues charged on the Thames, the chief of which may be that the river is not a public transport highway but a stream which derives its main income from the sale of its contents to waterboards and which will tolerate boating for a suitable consideration. The same explanation can hardly apply to British canals, however, and it is a pity that their facilities are not offered to the public at a more reasonable price.

We did not find Gouda a particularly attractive place—at least in a country where superb towns existed on every hand — and apart from the famous glass of St Jan's Church we met little to keep us there. The town had become industrialized, and what must once have been a beautiful frontage on a branch canal was now very backstairs, so we continued onwards across the countryside of Zuid Holland. The Juliana Sluis had led us into a waterway named the Gouwe, and a few miles farther north this canal or one-time river led to a crossroads with the Oude Rijn at Gouwsluis. Here we turned to the left down a course which certainly bore no resemblance at all to the proud name it bore.

The Oude Rijn is among the loveliest of Dutch waterways. Winding and comparatively narrow it flows westwards towards the sea and all the way to Leiden one or both of its banks is lined not with modern houses but with a jumbled string of village homes, cottages, small timber-yards, brickyards, horticultural concerns and one-man businesses. Each house tumbles away towards the water at the rear, and gardens sometimes no more than a few feet square

are gay with begonias and roses and above all with pansies. Zuid Holland seems to grow pansies all the year round. The *Commodore* has nosed through the Dutch waterways in early spring and late autumn alike, and always the pansies have been blooming in the beds, in the windows, and in the rows of pots stacked in racks in the open barges which carry them into the towns for sale in the market.

The Oude Rijn is enchanting all the way from Gouwsluis to where it enters Leiden at the Spanjaardsbrug, a distance of only a few miles but one in the course of which no less than eighteen minor canals and cuts used by farm barges and floats run off from its sides.

The Spanjaardsbrug could be reached by other routes too, and one year the *Commodore* decided to turn from the the Kil into the Oude Maas just below Dordrecht and to follow this less busy stream round into Rotterdam, and pass up the River Schie to reach Leiden by way of Delft and the Rijn-Schie Canal.

When the Italian author Edmondo de Amicis approached Rotterdam by packet boat in the nineteenth century a Dutch passenger on the ship explained to him that when the river was frozen 'the currents coming unexpectedly from warmer regions, strike the ice that covers the river, break it, upheave enormous blocks with a terrific crash, and hurl them against the dykes, piling them in immense heaps which choke the course of the river and make it overflow. Then begins a strange battle. The Dutch answer the threats of the Meuse with cannonade. The artillery is called out, volleys of grape-shot break the towers and barricades of ice which oppose the current into a storm of splinters and briny hail.' De Amicis also recorded that when Bismarck was at Rotterdam he wrote home to his wife and told her that at night he saw phantoms on the roofs.

It happened to be the brilliant daylight of an August afternoon when the *Commodore* swung slowly out of the Oude Maas to plough against the downcoming tide of the Rotterdam river and so neither of these startling phenomena were in evidence. Instead, there was an endless vista of row upon row of ships at the quaysides against a background of the skeleton forms of cranes and the pretty gables of

ancient warehouses tucked in between the smooth lines of their modern neighbours. Ahead of us a Greek and an American were steaming slowly in the stream, waiting for the tugs which would haul them alongside or to buoys in the fairway, whilst behind us a smooth-bowed Russian was racing up the centre of the river as though determined to show that she was as good as any other. A Missions to Seamen launch cut across towards a cargo-ship from Sydney, and ferries criss-crossed the water to the jetties and ship-yards, refineries and customs posts, cold stores and coaling wharves. The air was full of the toots and blasts of barges, tugs, and even our own humble hand-trumpet.

Mrs Radcliffe, on tour in the year 1794, described the sail up this waterway as delightful. 'The river flows here with great dignity and is animated with vessels of all countries passing to and from Rotter-dam. The huge Archangelman, the lighter American, the smart, swift Englishman, and the bulky Dutchman, exhibit a various

scene of shipping upon a noble surface of water, winding between green pastures and rich villages, spread along the low shores where pointed roofs, trees, and masts of fishing-boats are seen mingled in striking confusion. Small trading schuyts, as stout and round as their masters, glided by us, with crews reposing under their deep orange sails and frequently exchanging some salute with our captain.' All in all, the scene a century and a half later was not essentially different, except that perhaps the Americans were heavier and the crews of the schuyts were no longer reposing beneath their sails — though perhaps at the base of a mast where canvas might still be hoisted on the broader waters of the Zeeland channels or the Zuyder Zee. Pointed roofs, trees and masts still mingled in striking confusion and certainly the voyage into the city was as delightful as could be.

Rotterdam is the busiest port of the whole mainland of Europe and it owes its success not only to its position at the edge of the great delta but also to a fortunate freak of the plan on which nature and the erosions of the Ice Age had laid out the shape and dimensions of the North Sea. At Le Havre the difference in water level between the highest high tides and the lowest low tides is twenty-five feet, and at Liverpool the range is twenty-eight. Even on the eastern shores of Britain large ranges crop up here and there — sixteen feet at Ramsgate, twenty at Grimsby, seventeen off the Tay — and nowhere in the whole of the British Isles is there a port in which the water level varies within such modest limits as at Rotterdam, where the greatest range even on spring tides is only a few inches over six feet. The explanation is that the tides of the North Sea appear to be in the nature of a series of more or less stationary waves. The Atlantic tide provides a push off the northeast of Scotland, and the water of the whole basin swings up and down in clearly defined sections.

Every see-saw has a point in the middle where there is no vertical movement, and the North Sea is the same — except that it is not so well balanced as a well-constructed see-saw and so the movement at the pivot is not quite absent. In fact there are two lines of very little vertical motion across the North Sea, and one of them runs approximately from Great Yarmouth to near the Hook of Holland, the entrance to Rotterdam's harbour. The rotation of the Earth complicates the business still further, but it has the effect of reducing the range at the Dutch end of the line and providing Rotterdam with the smallest tidal range to be found anywhere in western Europe except at ports such as Gothenburg and Copenhagen which lie in areas of sea too small to respond appreciably to the great swayings of the oceans which the Sun and Moon together induce.

A six-foot range is worth millions, and to the Dutch it means that even the biggest ships can lie alongside the wharves or out in the river roadsteads of Rotterdam at any state of the tide. Long floating landing-stages such as those of Liverpool or Tilbury are not needed, and dock-basins closed off from the fairway by gates and only accessible at high water are unknown. Nor is there any need for the skipper of a large vessel to calculate the hour of his arrival in order to clear the bottom of the approaches, for Rotterdam is

open at any hour even to ocean giants drawing thirty-six feet of water.

There being no docking, the turn-round of shipping is more speedy than in some other ports, and Rotterdam's loading and unloading facilities are stream-lined to match. A grain carrier from Canada or the United States can moor between dolphins in the Nieuwe Maas (as the Rhine is rather confusingly called where it passes through the city) and within minutes the pneumatic elevators are moored alongside to dip their elephant trunks into the holds. Thirteen tons of grain surge through their pipes in a minute, pushed up the flexible tubing by the pressure of the air outside to cascade down chutes on the outer side of the suction floats into the holds of Rhine barges. Blown free of dust, sifted, and weighed automatically as the grains fly through the machinery, eight thousand tons of wheat can be transferred in ten hours, and on the same evening a cargo just arrived from overseas may be creeping round the bend in Dordrecht where Waal and Kil and Noord unite, bound for the Rhineland cities or for Switzerland.

In such a harbour the *Commodore* shrank into insignificance as she crept up the fairway, steering between the ships of Ecuador and Greece, Sweden and France, Argentine and Liberia and Panama.

Every hundred yards or so an opening led off on the northern side of the river and we knew that one of them connected at its upper end with the Schie. The Wilhelminahaven, the Wiltonhaven, the Vliethaven, the Koushaven and St Jobshaven, one by one we ticked them off with a pencil on a plan of the town until at the twenty-first opening we turned out of the Nieuwe Maas into the Parkhaven, at the top of which lay the lock.

No doubt we should have stayed in Rotterdam to view the magnificent modern architecture of which the city is justifiably proud, but to us the place was on this occasion no more than the junction with the water-route to Leiden and beyond. At the same time we could not pass through the town canals without wondering whether it was in one of the waterside houses that Mijnheer van Klaes had lived, whose cheerful last will and testament had provided him with a somewhat unusual funeral and a permanent place in the history of the city.

Van Klaes was a wealthy burgher engaged in the India trade, and he was such an enthusiastic smoker that by the time of his death at the age of ninety-eight he had run through nearly four and a half tons of tobacco — a quantity which, we are told, might be unravelled and 'laid down over a distance of twenty French leagues'. In his ninety-seventh year he summoned his lawyer and dictated a will which instructed that every smoker in the country should be invited to his funeral, and each one who attended was to be presented with ten pounds of tobacco and a pair of pipes on which the name, arms, and date of death of the testator were to be inscribed, whilst every poor person who walked in the funeral procession was to be given a large package of tobacco on the anniversary date every year during his own lifetime. The only condition was that all who wished to secure their gifts had to smoke without interruption throughout the funeral ceremony.

There followed a few detailed instructions. Mr van Klaes ordered that his coffin was to be lined throughout with the wood of the boxes of Havanas which he had smoked, and his favourite pipe and a box of matches were to be placed at his side. Finally, when the bier was laid in the vault and the guests took their departure they were to knock out the ashes of their pipes on the coffin.

Today such a will would probably lead to endless litigation and a judge would be confronted with a phalanx of psychiatrists who would declare that the testator was psychotic. Or the will would simply be declared as against the public interest. Mr van Klaes however was fortunate enough to live and die in an age when character and individuality were accepted at their face value rather than as manifestations of obscure tanglings in the subconscious, and his instructions were splendidly obeyed to the last detail. The cheerful procession filed through the streets beneath a cloud of *caporal* and cigar smoke, and year by year thereafter the poor received their annual bounty of tobacco. Even his cook, who had been a defiant non-smoker, threw up the resolution of a lifetime and chose to accept the considerable sum of money which he left to her on the sole condition that she should take up smoking. She took her place in the cortège, puffing dutifully at one cigarette after another.

Though war and the internal combustion engine have altered the appearance of Rotterdam it is still a city of water transport not very different from when J. Phillips described the commerce of the Dutch canals in his *General History of Inland Navigation*, written a century ago. The canals, he wrote, 'may be compared in number and size to our public roads and highways; and as the latter, with us, are continually full of coaches, chaises, waggons, carts, and horsemen going from and to the different cities, towns, and villages, so on the former the Hollanders in their boats and pleasure barges, their treckschuyts and vessels of burthen, are continually journeying and conveying commodities for consumption or exportation from the interior part of the country to the great cities and rivers. An inhabitant of Rotterdam may, by means of these canals, breakfast at Delft or The Hague, dine at Leyden, and sup at Amsterdam, or return home again before night. By them also a most prodigious inland trade is carried on between Holland and every part of France, Flanders, and Germany. When the canals are frozen over they travel on them with skaits, and perform long journeys in a very short time, while heavy burdens are conveyed in carts and sledges, which are then as much used on the canals as in our streets.'

The *trekschuyts* to which he referred were express packet-boats, and though the last of them had vanished many years before the *Commodore* passed through Rotterdam on her way towards Delft it was not difficult to picture the graceful craft with their loads of country people going to market, of business men bound for the capital, and of tourists from other lands travelling by what once was the main form of transport. Harry Peckham, the Recorder of Chichester, travelled the same waterways in the eighteenth century and he sent home a letter which described in some detail his journey by *trekschuyt* from Maassluis to Delft. There were six sailings daily, and the ship resembled a livery barge on the Thames, but was smaller and less ornamented, he wrote. 'It is drawn by one horse, and goes with the greatest ease four miles in an hour, which is the Dutch method of computing distance — so many hours to a place, not leagues like the French, nor miles as the English. In fine weather this method of travelling is absolutely delightful; for a mere trifle you may hire the *roof*, which is a small cabin at the end of the boat, with two sash windows on each side, a table in the middle, velvet cushions to sit on, and good room for six or eight people. The motion of the boat is imperceptible, and you may read, write, eat, or sleep, with as much ease as in your chamber. If this is not agreeable, you may get on the top of the boat, which has almost a flat roof, on which you may walk without danger, and as there is not a hillock in the country you have nothing to intercept your view. It is a most agreeable journey. The number of little gardens and pleasure houses built on the banks of the canal, the little village of Overschie, which is about mid-way, and a fine avenue of trees above half a mile in length, all conspire to fill the mind with pleasure.'

The fare from Maassluis to Delft was one guilder and four stivers, and for the benefit of those who found the contemporary Dutch currency hard to understand he explained that one doit corresponded to an English half-farthing and there were eight doits to a stiver, two stivers to a dubliky, five-and-a-half stivers to a sestehalf — unless it had arrows on the reverse, when it was worth three dublikys. A guilder was twenty stivers, and seven guilders made a ryder. Five gulden and five stivers made a ducat. That was all, except for the goode skelling, which was six stivers — like the sestehalf with arrows on it.

The fare included the *roof*, but on his seventh journey by *trek-schuyt* Peckham was too late to get a seat in this part of the boat, and he had to travel in the public saloon. He paid three guilders and four stivers for the non-roof fare from Amsterdam to Utrecht and sat below decks writing another letter.

'As it rains hard we cannot walk upon the top,' he wrote. 'We therefore have no other alternative than to sit in the body of the boat with upwards of twenty persons of both sexes, from whose mouths nothing has hitherto issued but volumes of tobacco smoke, which has made my friend sick and me sulky.'

Greater detail of the arrangements on board a *trekschuyt* was given a few years later by Frederic Shoberl. 'These vessels, like our stage-coaches, set out from all the towns in Holland at fixed hours several times a day, at some places hourly, and at others every two hours. They carry goods as well as passengers, and proceed at the rate of something more than three miles an hour. Each of them is divided into three parts. That in the middle, which is the largest, is covered with a wooden platform only just high enough to permit a person to sit under it. Along each side of this division is a bench for fourteen or fifteen persons; the passengers can lay their luggage on the floor, or on a third bench running longitudinally through the middle. At the head of the vessel is the hold for the stowage of goods and other bulky articles. The space between the central division and the stern is occupied by another cabin, capable of accommodating eight or ten persons. Here passengers are less confined than in the great cabin and they enjoy the privilege, when the weather is fine, of going out and sitting on the benches on each side of the stern.' Seats could be booked at about a sou per mile, and the passenger might 'either converse with his companions or read by himself; if the passage is long he may take such refreshments as he has brought with him; if he has secured a place in the best cabin he has a mattress to sleep on at night.' There was in fact a sleeper-*schuyt* running from Leiden to Amsterdam, arriving early in the morning. Only the boats of Western Flanders were smarter. There one had plush seats and gilt fittings, and the Bruges-Ghent *trek-*

schuyt served a three course dinner and was fitted up with a liqueur bar.

Mrs Radcliffe too was fascinated by the *trekschuyt* when she travelled in one from Leiden to Haarlem, and she described how the passage under a fixed bridge was not delayed for an instant. The horse was of course uncoupled to go round the edge, but often there was an attendant specially placed on the arch to catch the rope and throw it back to the skipper as the boat emerged from the other side. At bends in the canal the inner edge of the tow-path was flanked with posts supporting vertical rollers round which the rope could run without friction.

Until the coming of railways the *trekschuyt* was almost the only means of travel from place to place, and such canal-boats were in regular use long before inland transport by artificial waterways was so much as contemplated in the more difficult and hilly country of Britain. When Holger Jacobaeus, a Danish student, first visited Holland in 1671 he travelled right across the country by *trekschuyt* from Delfzjil in the north-east to Leiden in the south-west, and for much of his route he followed the very same waterways along which the *Commodore* was to carry us. He wrote a *Rejsebog* or Travel Book, in which he noted fifteen distinct classes of ships which he encountered in Holland. Among them were sea-going vessels of up to five hundred tons, fly-boats and cod-fishers, Buysen '*pro captura harengorum*', yachts, *Turfpotten* (or peat carriers) of twelve to twenty tons burden, and water-boats which carried drinking water to the breweries. And there were the '*Scaphae, Traeckschoiter, quae ob rivorum et fossarum frequentiam, equorum ministerio protrahuntur*'.

Jacobaeus drew delightful little sketches in his diary, and coloured them. One of these shows a man in purple breeches standing by the front of a house and tolling a bell with a rope. The caption explains that the bell is rung at the departure of the *trekschuyt*. Of the boat itself there is a very handsome sketch too. A man in brown is carried by a white horse and seated side-saddle on a cloth of red and gold. The boat has sharply pointed bows and a mast set fore, through a hole in which a double rope passes from the harness to each side of the stern. A bowman is standing on the foredeck, and a steersman sits aft in an open seat against a massive scrolled stern-post. The cabin is roofed over, and through the windows one can see the passengers seated along the sides, chatting and eating and drinking, for all the world like first-class passengers in a modern railway dining-car.

VI

If on her way out of Rotterdam the *Commodore* met no *trekschuyts* she had an encounter of a very different kind. She very rarely had trouble with youths in Holland, but on her way up the Schie she was obliged to carry on a running fight for several miles. It was not that the young people had any vicious intentions but simply that the *Commodore* came to be used as a public facility in the same way which on earlier occasions had caused her embarrassment on the Thames. Her dinghy was towing behind, closely hauled up to the stern, and as the weather was very hot the prospect of being towed along the canal was irresistible to the swimmers in the water. One after the other, young lads would dive in, catch hold of the dinghy or its painter and float happily along under our stern.

We had no merely possessive objection at all to giving lifts in this way, but anyone who hangs on the stern of a boat is only safe provided that there is no undertow and that the craft does not have to go astern. Swimmers seem to be very obtuse about such matters and we have never been able to make them understand the danger, even when able to speak their language. They just cannot believe it — unless perhaps they see a curious object floating in the wake behind and realise in annoyance that it is one of their own feet neatly severed above the ankle by a swift slash from a propeller blade.

Running through the suburbs of Rotterdam we were infested with cheerful bathers, and the danger to them was very real. The *Commodore*'s propeller caused a powerful forward and downward run of water at the transom and there was the added circumstance that we had frequently to put her astern to wait for a swing-bridge to open. We had no wish to amputate the limbs of any of such a kindly people, but all attempts to persuade them to keep clear were met only with friendly smiles, and we were obliged to station somebody on the quarter with orders to keep them off by every possible means. Flourishing a boathook had no effect, for they knew as well as we did ourselves that we would not contemplate harpooning them, and they just laughed. All except one, that is, who was only saved from having his feet entangled with the propeller by a hard blow across his knuckles.

But before long we discovered a means of defence which would remove even the most adhesive of these amiable limpets without causing grievous bodily harm. The guard stationed on the quarter was provided with a bucket on a rope, and he had only to fling a pail of water in the face of a floating passenger to make him leave go immediately. The procedure caused some spluttered abuse — and considerable laughter from those on the bank — but at least it prevented unfortunate accidents.

A less sociable form of amusement for smaller boys is to spit on a boat passing under a bridge, and though this sport is much rarer in Holland than in London we provided a convenient target when we rowed in the dinghy beneath the low bridges of the city canals of Delft. But this nuisance was easily dealt with, too. No lad given to spitting on boats could resist the temptation of having a first spit at one side of a bridge and then crossing to the other to take the boat unawares when it emerged from the shelter of the arch, but it did not occur to him that he might himself be taken by surprise. We always carried a bucket or bailer in the dinghy and affected not to notice the first expectoration, but out of sight under the arch the pail would quickly be filled and held in readiness. Then, as the bow of the dinghy came gliding into the field of fire once more the spitter would lean out from the bridge ready for a second shot, only to be drenched by a shower of not very clean water flung from within three feet of him. Such retribution always delighted the bystanders — and indeed everyone except the shame-faced urchin who had to slink home and account to an angry mother for the sad state of his clothes.

Perhaps the city of Delft was not without its spitting urchins in

the days of Vermeer. Certainly there are other features of the town
which even today appear much the same as in his delightful domestic pictures, and the narrow canal running beside the Oude Kerk
is one of the loveliest medieval waterways in the country. Across
the cobbles and behind the limes which flank the Oude Delft *gracht*
or canal lies the Prinsenhof, where the bullet marks are still shown
at the foot of the stairs where the founder of the Dutch nation fell
to the most ingenious and patient of assassins.

It is an astonishing testimony to Prince William's courage and
to the loyalty and affection in which he was held by his countrymen
that he was not killed earlier. The Spaniards promised the most
lavish rewards for his assassination, and between 1582 and 1584
five attempts organized with the assistance of the Spanish Crown
had failed. It remained for Gerard, a fanatical catholic, to intro-
duce himself into the company of William in the guise of the son
of an executed protestant. Once within the circle of the Prinsenhof
he waited patiently, and although he was more than once alone in
the company of the Prince he stayed his hand until by representing

himself as too shabby to go to church he induced William to make him a gift of money. With the cash he immediately purchased a pair of pistols, and two days later as the Prince came up the stairs from the dining-room Gerard stepped out of an alcove and fired three poisoned bullets into his stomach.

Gerard was caught as he endeavoured to escape from the battlements into the moat and he was subjected to the most excruciating and prolonged tortures, which he endured with nothing but defiant pride, further infuriating his captors by raising his bleeding head from the rack to utter the words '*Ecce homo*'. The Spaniards had every reason to be proud of him, and they rewarded his parents with three of the estates formerly taken from the Prince, and with a permanent place among the landed aristocracy — permanent, that is, until the area of Franche Comté in which the properties were situated became united with France, and the French governor tore the papers of the award to pieces and trampled them under his foot. As for Prince William, he was buried at Delft, 'amid the tears of a whole nation. Never was a more extensive, unaffected, and legitimate sorrow felt at the death of any human being.'

Delft is rich in history, and in the tombs — not always very beautiful — of great men. The Nieuwe Kerk, named 'New' in the fourteenth century to distinguish it from the 'Old' church of the thirteenth, contains not only the memorials of William the Silent and later members of the house of Orange, but also the tomb of a Dutch theologian and politician to whom, in his role as jurist, the *Commodore* owed a particular debt, and now that she had brought us safely to the city of Hugo Grotius we could not decently depart from the city without paying tribute to the man who wrote not only *De Jure Belli ac Pacis* but the *Mare Liberum*, a work which established maritime law and laid down the principle of the freedom of the seas from his day to our own. The doctrine of freedom of navigation through the seas and oceans is now so thoroughly accepted that one tends to think of it as an axiom, but it was originally argued by Grotius in an age when the Dutch were endeavouring to expand their trade to the East and West Indies and push their prows into waters appropriated by the Spanish and Portuguese either on the basis of their occupation of the adjacent land, or because a Pope had once split the oceans between the two powers just as though they were his own to give away. Such proprietary rights greatly hampered the expansion of Dutch trade, and it was Grotius who attacked them. 'Can the vast, the boundless sea be the appanage of one Kingdom alone, and it not the greatest?' he asked. 'Can only one nation have the right to prevent other nations which so desire from selling to one another, from bartering with one another, actually from communicating with one another?' Of course not. The sea was free and open to all.

It is interesting to recall that England was one of the opponents of this new theory. Less enterprising than the Dutch in maritime commerce at that time, our own country still maintained that the sea could be the property of a nation, and that in fact 'the King of Great Britain is Lord of the sea flowing about, as an inseparable appendant of the British Empire'. This point of view inevitably led to difficulties with the Dutch over the North Sea fisheries off the Scottish coast, but by 1700 British ships too were roaming far afield in considerable numbers and the country found it more profitable to drop the older outlook and fall into line behind the Dutch in claiming a *mare liberum*, free for all.

Scholar, theologian and statesman, Grotius was also the hero of an escape romantic enough for a tale of Dumas. Seized by his political enemies and sentenced to life imprisonment in the fort of Leuwensteen in the Biesbosch swamp, he set himself to the task of writing his monumental work on the Law of War and Peace. But he was to be rescued by his courageous wife who smuggled herself into the castle in a chest believed to be filled with books for his researches, and then took his place whilst he was carried out concealed in the same chest — a deed which earned her the praise even of his enemies.

If Grotius laid the foundations of freedom of the seas, he had less success with a second doctrine of perhaps even greater importance, for it was he who insisted that an International Court of Justice should be set up to deal with disputes between the nations. Three hundred years were to pass before this institution was brought to birth by the League of Nations and sited appropriately enough within the province of the Netherlands where Grotius had carried on his life's work. It is only to be hoped that three further centuries may not elapse before the International Court is equipped with that which Grotius declared to be an absolute essential — the power and force to ensure that its decisions are binding, and are carried out by the states on which it sits in judgment in the name of all the nations.

The Rijn-Schie canal is an undistinguished but pleasant waterway leading from Delft to Leiden, skirting the edge of The Hague on its way, and at the Spanjaardsbrug it makes a junction with the Oude Rijn, which runs right through the city of Leiden to reach the sea through a drainage sluice at the fashionable resort of Katwijk. For much of its course it runs in the bed of an older waterway, the Vliet, and this in turn replaced a navigable canal older than any other in the Netherlands with the exception of the canals of Drusus. The scholars are unanimous in identifying the Vliet with the canal of Corbulo, built about A.D. 47, and mentioned by Tacitus and by Dio Cassius. Tacitus gave its length precisely as 23,000 paces (34 kilometres), and Dio Cassius as 170 stadia (31·4 kilometres), and it was described as dug by Corbulo between the mouths of the Rhine and Meuse. The present length of the direct waterway from Leiden to Nieuwsluis, west of Rotterdam, is between these two figures.

The classical authors stated quite clearly that the object of the canal was to prevent flooding of the surrounding country, and there seems little doubt that Corbulo enlarged and improved a water channel which even then already existed. The work may well have been undertaken with the primary object of confining flood water to an embanked and deepened course, but it seems very unlikely that it can really have been of very much use in this respect. Dr Hettema, a Dutch classical scholar who has made an exhaustive study of the evidence, believes that in fact the canal was misconceived for this purpose, just as in our own times the new harbour at Haarlingen proved to be unusable because the engineers were not so fully in possession of the relevant facts as they imagined themselves to be. Yet even if it was a comparative failure as a defence against flooding, it was used as a canal navigation. Of this there can be no doubt whatsoever, for the remains of a Roman canal boat were dug up when the excavations were undertaken for the modern Rijn-Schie canal.

The Rijn-Schie canal must therefore have a long history of shipping behind it, and one of the voyages undertaken along its waters held a particular interest for us aboard the *Commodore*. It was by way of the same waterway — then known as the Vliet — that the band of emigrants sailed with William Brewster during their final days in Holland, and they were bound from Leiden to Delfshaven in Rotterdam to embark on the *Speedwell* — the not so very sea-worthy little ship which they had hopefully purchased.

Immediately before the Spaniard's Bridge we turned left and followed the course of the Rijn past the lovely turreted city gateway and drawbridge and down the centre of the Oude Vest, a street ranged half on one side of the canal and half on the other. One by one the heavy bascule bridges clanked up to let the *Commodore* through and finally we moored her at the quayside of the *Beesten-markt*, right in the centre of the city.

Leiden has many buildings of great charm, and nearly all of them face the water — for besides the two complete rings of moat there are numerous little canals which criss-cross the centre of the city and are still used by commercial craft as far as their size permits. It is in fact more of a water town than any other in Holland with the exception of Amsterdam, and there are canals enough for the city to have an aquatic version of a street-sweeping lorry. This machine consists of a flat float driven by a propeller and armed in front with a broad scoop of wire mesh with which the cabbage leaves, newspaper, driftwood and any other floating rubbish flung into the water is neatly swept up and tipped back into the boat. This simple device keeps the surface reasonably clean so that Leiden's waterways are not so cluttered with rubbish as some in the cities of Belgium, and even in a few Dutch towns.

Leiden is nowadays an industrial city with smoking chimneys and gaunt factories extending outwards from the line of the outer moat which marks the confines of the older town. There are trams and traffic everywhere too, and the main streets have lost much of their former beauty, and though any alleyway will lead through to a delightful little court of almshouses or to a group of humble sixteenth and seventeenth-century houses huddled tightly together beside a hump-backed bridge, the romance of the place lies primarily in its memories rather than in its architecture. Rembrandt was born in a mill which once stood at the Weddesteeg, whilst Jan Steen and Lucas van Leyden are only two of the host of artists who lived and painted in the city. Gomarus and Arminius began their dispute within the walls of the famous university, and the Pieterskerk contains the memorial to John Robinson, 'pastor of the English Church worshipping over against this spot, A.D. 1609–1625, whence at his prompting, went forth The Pilgrim Fathers to settle New England in 1620.'

Robinson, that excellent leader of the English émigré protestants, left his Anglican living at Norwich to join Brewster and his associates, and to go with them into exile in the Netherlands. He soon became the accepted spiritual leader of the refugees, and it was under him that they gathered together in the famous 'House with the Green Door' when they elected to leave Amsterdam and settle in Leiden. Most of them found employment to support themselves as craftsmen and tradesmen but they could not forget the cause of their flight from their own motherland and they wrote books and pamphlets decrying the persecution carried on by King James and his bishops in the name of the established Church. The energetic William Brewster set up a printer's shop, and two printers came from London to join him, and to help with the skilled work of cutting the wooden type.

One of the first volumes to come from the Leiden press was a violent attack upon James I for his relentless persecution of the Scottish Presbyterians, and the refugee dissenters packed the edition in French wine barrels and shipped them to Scotland as *vin blanc*. The books were admitted under the noses of the ecclesiastical authorities, and they caused such a stir in the northern part of his realm that King James sent orders to his ambassador in Holland that William Brewster was to be apprehended at all costs, and deported to England for trial.

It is not difficult to imagine the fate which would have awaited the leader of the Pilgrim Fathers if the agents of the King had found him, for another Scottish minister who published a similar attack and had it printed in Holland was more easily arrested and tried. He was flogged, and one of his ears and his nose were cut off; he was branded on the forehead with a red-hot iron and flogged again; finally his other ear was cut off, and he was thrown into the Fleet prison to die there. The Stuart monarch was not very far behind the Duke of Alva in the cruelties he could devise in order to prevent freedom of worship.

Brewster undoubtedly knew and accepted the risk he ran, but he was a resourceful and ingenious man. The moment the book had been smuggled into Scotland he sailed over to England, correctly guessing that his home country was the one place in which the King's men would not expect to find him. Meanwhile, the hue and cry began in Leiden, and the remainder of the party dropped chance remarks in shops and taverns, sometimes suggesting that they had seen Brewster in Leiden only the day before, sometimes that he had fled to Amsterdam, where he was said to be setting up another printing shop. As intended, these clues reached the ears of the King's agents and successfully confined the search to Holland, and not until the hunt was abandoned did Brewster return to Leiden.

It was however quite clear that no permanent peace could be had in a country so close to the Stuart crown, friendly though the people of Holland might be. Besides, the refugees still felt themselves strangers in the land, and they longed for a country which they could call their own. At length many of them came to the conclusion that the best solution was to pool their savings and to buy the *Speedwell*, which was lying at Rotterdam, and on a July day in 1620 the party boarded canal boats in Leiden and began their voyage along the Vliet. Sadly, they were to leave behind them their pastor, John Robinson, for he felt it his duty to stay in Holland and remain in charge of the many others among the English refugees who had chosen to settle permanently in Leiden, where newcomers from England were continually joining them.

The exiles were of course poor, and after buying the ship and provisions they had little left in the way of personal belongings. It is recorded however that one of the Leiden party took among his effects 'a great iron screw'. Certainly this man, whose name is not known but who is sometimes thought to have been Brewster himself, could never have guessed that the inclusion in his baggage of such an unusual object was to save the lives of the expedition.

Passing down the North Sea and sailing down the Channel the *Speedwell* ran in to Southampton, where in secret the *Mayflower* had been getting ready to join her for the voyage to America. Together the two ships put out to sea, but before long Captain Reynolds of the *Speedwell* had to report a serious leak below the water-line and the two boats were obliged to turn back and run into Dartmouth. Repairs were carried out quickly, for it was vital that the authorities should not get wind of the identity of those aboard the ships, and a second time the two craft set out for the open ocean. This time they were three hundred miles out in the Atlantic when Captain Reynolds again reported that the *Speedwell* was leaking, and this time so fast that the bilge pumps could not keep the water from rising. To return was dangerous, but to go on was impossible, and again the ships put back, on this occasion to Plymouth. Amid these discouragements some of the passengers lost heart and decided to return to Leiden, but the remainder were packed aboard the already crowded larger ship, and the *Speedwell* was abandoned as useless. In the *Mayflower* alone the emigrants now put out to sea for the third time, and with thirty-five men and women from Leiden and sixty-seven from England the ship headed out into the Atlantic.

Half-way across the Atlantic the ship ran into such heavy weather that it proved impossible to keep her under sail, and the skipper, Captain Jones, was obliged to heave to and let her drift rather than lose the masts and rigging. Day after day the waves pounded against the hull and the ship wallowed and pitched in the fierce sea. At the height of the storm a violent sea struck the vessel on her side, and the main beam cracked and sagged out of its position.

The expedition was now in very real danger. The main strength of their vessel had gone and the ship could hardly be expected to withstand more days and nights of helpless hammering by the storm waves. A conference was called of all on board, and many of the passengers, miserably sea-sick and exhausted from lack of sleep, urged that the ship should at once be put under sail and headed back for England. Captain Jones however was not optimistic, and with the ship so weakened he was decidedly doubtful whether they could even manage to reach England again.

It was just at this moment of doubt and despair that one of the passengers from Leiden produced from his baggage his great iron screw. It seems to have been something in the nature of a jack and in all probability it was part of a printing press, but however that may be it entirely changed the situation. Packing it tightly under the centre of the broken beam the crew were able to turn it, and with its help they managed little by little to force the heavy sagging timber back into position again and shore it in its place with a stout wooden balk braced against the lower deck.

With this main danger overcome, Captain Jones made a thorough inspection of the hull. He decided that it was now safe to continue the voyage westward, and sixty-six days after leaving Plymouth the *Mayflower* at last dropped anchor in the bay that is now Princetown harbour, and the Pilgrim Fathers set foot on the shore of the New World. It was many months before the news of their arrival reached the remainder of the exiles at Leiden, gathered under the leadership of John Robinson.

The line of the Vliet up which the *Commodore* had carried us to Leiden, and down which the English protestants had sailed in their canal-boats three centuries earlier, reaches the outskirts of the city by the Lammebrug, at a place where once the final obstacle lay in the path of Admiral Boisot and the fleet of the Sea Beggars when they sailed and rowed on their memorable expedition to relieve Leiden in 1574. What the city endured from sickness and starvation during that famous siege can scarcely be imagined, but the resistance of the burghers was to have a permanent memorial in the founding of a great university in recognition of their heroism — the same university at which, forty years later, John Robinson was to be enrolled as a student. Under the circumstances it was ironic enough that the charter of the university should be issued under the fiction of the authority of King Philip of Spain, of whom his mortal enemy William of Orange was still the delegated representative or stadholder.

'Considering that during these present wearisome wars within our provinces of Holland and Zeeland all good instruction of youth in the sciences and liberal arts is likely to come into entire oblivion ... we are inclined to gratify our city of Leyden, with its burghers, on account of the heavy burdens sustained by them during this war with such faithfulness. We have resolved, after ripely deliberating with our dear cousin, William, Prince of Orange, stadholder, to erect a free public school and university. . . .' So ran the extraordinary document which authorized the foundation.

To relieve Leiden seemed an impossible feat, but it was achieved with no help from the outside world. The Sea Beggars mounted a fleet of two hundred shallow craft armed with cannon and manned by more than two thousand veterans of the Zeeland fighting, many of them wearing in their caps the Moslem crescent with the defiant motto 'Better Turkish than Popish'. From Rotterdam to Delfshaven the sluices were opened, whilst the ladies of Holland gave over their silver and plate and their jewellery to aid the villagers whose fields and farms were inundated. Amid scenes of wild enthusiasm the country people shouted 'Better drowned land than a lost land', in counterpoint to the defiant slogan of the sailors. As the waters swept over the fertile fields, reclaimed from the same sea at the cost of so much patient labour, the strange armada of outlawed fishermen and sealers, farmers and men whose lands had been seized by the Inquisition, floated on its way.

Each of the dykes further inland was seized and torn down as the waters carried the rescuers ever onward, with the *Ark van Delft* in the van — a massive fortified ship propelled by paddle-wheels turned by a great crank inside the hull.

In sight of Leiden the rescuing fleet was halted. A strong east wind drove back the waters and stranded the ships a mere three miles from the city walls. Already without food for two months the famished citizens had stripped the trees bare of their leaves and bark, and now this setback brought murmurs of despair. It was at this moment that the brave burgomaster, van der Wert, haggard and scarcely able to stand, rose up in the corner of the market place, waved his hat for silence, and fired the citizens with fresh courage by his famous speech.

'My own fate is a matter of no moment to me, but not so that of the city entrusted to my care. I know that we shall starve if not soon relieved, but starvation is better than the dishonoured death which is the only other choice. Your threats cannot move me. My life is at your disposal. See, here is my sword; plunge it into my breast and divide my flesh among you. Take my body to assuage your hunger, but expect no surrender whilst I am still alive.'

Nobody stepped forward to accept the challenge. Instead, the citizens replied to the overtures of the Spanish commander, himself beleaguered by the shallow floods, with fresh defiance. 'So long as ye hear dog bark or cat mew within the walls, ye may know that the city holds out. And when all has perished but ourselves, know that we will each of us eat our own left arms in the defence of our families, our liberty and our religion against the foreign tyrant. Should God in his judgment doom us to destruction and withhold us all help, even then shall we endure to the last against your entrance. And when the last hour has come we will set fire to our city with our own hands and die, men, women and children, together in the flames, rather than suffer our homes to be polluted and our liberties crushed.'

In this spirit, and with their wives and children dying of famine in the streets, the burghers held out through those grim weeks during which the fleet of the Sea Beggars lay stranded within sight of the walls. Then quite suddenly the wind veered and a gale from the north-west drove the equinoctial springs up from the delta across mile after mile of inundated land and Boisot's fleet sailed onwards in the darkness. Among the branches of the fruit trees the cannon roared, and as the Spaniards fled slipping through the mud on the tops of the banks the Zeelanders once more hurled their sealing harpoons, dragged the soldiers from the dykes with boat-hooks, or leapt into the water to stab them with daggers and hold them down to drown. Only the fort of Lammen now remained, but it was heavily fortified and held by a strong force of Spaniards, and it covered with its powerful artillery the whole of the approaches to the city. Once again the Sea Beggars were halted, and the promised relief to the citizens was frustrated within sight of the walls.

And then in the darkness, a strange thing happened. The high tide driven by the wind had been surging against the fortifications of the city, and without warning a great length of the wall itself collapsed, falling outwards with a crash which shook the darkened countryside. The burghers trembled, for they believed that their dreaded foes had at last carried the fortifications by assault; but the Spaniards for their part believed that the citizens had sallied out to the attack, and at the moment when in fact Leiden lay defenceless and at their mercy — of which there would certainly have been none — they abandoned their positions and fled. When next morning Boisot's ships surged past the fortress of Lammen it was utterly deserted, and within an hour van der Wert and his emaciated citizens were kneeling with Boisot and the crescented Zeelanders in the nave of the Pieterskerk to give thanks for the relief so long awaited. The very next day the waters which had borne the ships to Leiden's rescue rolled back from the land towards the sea.

It was a peaceful and prosperous landscape across which the *Commodore* had carried us as she followed the Vliet towards the city, and only the names on the map remained to tell of those fatal weeks. To our right lay Zoetermeer and Zoeterwoude, villages past which the *Ark van Delft* had floated impelled by its man-turned paddles, and Noord Aa, where the fleet lay stranded for two whole frustrating weeks. Ahead lay Leiderdorp, where Valdez had planted his headquarters, and here at the Lammebrug had stood that last redoubt so providentially abandoned on the final night without the firing of a single shot. Now there was merely a bascule bridge like any other on a Dutch waterway, and the uniformed man in his control box was there to pass the shipping through on its way into Leiden, and no longer to keep it at bay with cannon. He pressed the switch to drop the barriers across the road from Noord Aa to the city and the span rose slowly upwards to tilt on end and so allow the *Commodore* to proceed on her voyage.

H

VII

*The Lake of de Kaag — The water police — Warmond —
Delights of Dutch — The draining of the Haarlemmermeer —
Boat travel is leisurely — Canals by night — Equality on
the water*

Our course northward from Leiden lay under the Spanjaardsbrug, at which the Rijn-Schie canal metamorphosed into the
River Zijl, a stream which slowly but continually broadened out
until two miles beyond Leiden it opened into a wide and sprawling
meer, and it was here at the Lake of De Kaag that the Holland of
the story books and picture postcards and coloured Christmas
calendars lay in front of us. Though the chimneys of the Leiden
gasworks were plainly visible beneath a dark smudge of smoke, the
city itself seemed far away and the scene was one of meadows and
dykes and copses of trees, with white sails gliding behind the banks
and fat white-and-black cattle raising their heads for a moment to
stare at each busy barge as it chugged round the curves of the watercourse and past the flashing point-lights into the broader waters of
the lake. Where the Zijl ran in there was a hospitable harbour of
jetties belonging to the Yacht Club, and it was there that we pulled
in for the night.

Throughout the short summer darkness we could occasionally
hear the beating of the motor of a barge making for Leiden or up
towards Amsterdam, and as the sound grew to a peak and then
began to fade away the ripples of the wash would run through the
jetties, swashing softly against the piles and rocking the *Commodore*
sleepily where she lay. None of the craft were very large, for by
whichever route they left the lake they would reach after a few
miles a bridge which did not open until six or seven in the morning,
and only if they were low enough in the water to glide underneath
was there any purpose in their crossing the lake at night. Most of
them were in fact craft with no accommodation or wheelhouse,

laden with produce from the countryside and bound for the markets in one or other of the big cities.

Early next morning we heard the creak of oars, and peeping out of the windows at first light we saw the lake dotted with clumsy craft with wedge-shaped bows, each rowed by one man and sometimes carrying a passenger too. Across each boat stood an erection which at a distance we took to be a chicken coop, but as the rowers drew nearer and passed into the channel leading out between the point lights towards Leiden we could see that the structures were the folded sections of market stalls, and that the bottom of every boat was piled with lettuce and cabbages, leeks, onions or potatoes, with perhaps a pot or two of begonias as an extra. This was the route by which the stall-holders went to market, rowing their goods and scales and paper bags and trestle tables the several miles from their small-holdings to the streets and quaysides of busy Leiden.

Before long another craft passed close to where we lay. It was a clumsy but shallow lighter of wood, towed by a man in a dinghy fitted with an outboard motor, and it pulled out of the creek beside a farm close behind the canal bank to set off across the lake. The man in the dinghy was evidently the ploughman, for the passengers in the float were a pair of heavy dappled horses with shining brass on their harness and wearing straw hats as gaily as a couple of beach beauties. No walking to work for them, it seemed. They travelled to the fields across the Kaagemeer with all the dignity of company directors gliding down Lombard Street in the firm's Rolls Royce.

The Lake of de Kaag is an irregular mass of water with here and there an island and a flashing navigation light, but it is something of a traffic junction too, for besides the Zijl leading in from Leiden there are a number of other waterways radiating outwards from its various corners. The River Leede runs out — or in, for Dutch rivers have a way of flowing in either direction — at the south-west corner to connect with half a dozen canals, one of which cuts back to the Zijl again under the dismal name of Stinksloot. Further up the lake is a canal called the Plomp, and in the north-west corner the Sassenheimer Vaart. On the eastern shore the lake connects with the Zijp, the Zomer Sloot and the Boeren Buurt — to mention only a few of the strange waterways which meander away between the buttercups and cows, but to the north the mere breaks through in three separate places to a very important waterway, the *Ringvaart van de Haarlemmermeerpolder*. Though all these canals and rivers are navigated either by commercial craft of moderate size or by farm craft, they also serve for land drainage, and all of them deliver water into the lake with the exception of the Leede and the Ringvaart and perhaps the Zijl — the function of these being to conduct the water away to the distant dykes and sluices of the sea.

The Leede is delightful. From its mouth it narrows gradually inwards until the river is some thirty yards broad where it passes into Warmond, a village set back from the edge of the lake but one of the main yachting centres of Holland — even in London's Shaftesbury Avenue it is possible to book cruisers and sailing-boats at its yards. From where it leaves the lake, the one bank of the Leede is open to the pastures except for a single windmill of exceptional beauty set right on the edge of the stream, but the other is fringed with weeping willows interspersed with the sheds of boat-builders, sailmakers and painters, and by the gardens of cottages. Warmond is a place that lives on the water. When he has completed that part of his morning round which is on land, the postman steps into a little boat and rows down the Leede from house-boat to cottage and creek to deliver the letters. Manure for the gardens is delivered by boat too, and shovelled ashore from a heavy punt poled along the river. Even the pigs and cattle go on business voyages, and every morning we would see a flock of sheep standing in their boat as unconcerned as ferry passengers whilst a proud sheepdog balanced himself on the gunwale like an experienced sailor and kept an eye on his charges to see that there was no rocking the boat.

Even the police are amphibious at Warmond, and one of the neat little houses with a healthy garden of summer flowers and vegetables is the station and boat-shed of the Waterpolitie. There could not be a more enticing place in which to live and work as an aquatic policeman, for here there is no battling with waves or with dock thieves, but an idyllic life floating comfortably on the lake in summer time, watching the regattas, helping to tow becalmed sailing boats out of the dredged channels of the barge routes, rendering occasional assistance perhaps to some racer capsized in the thrill of sailing even closer hauled than its rivals, and exchanging friendly greetings with the bargemen and the stall-holders bound for Leiden market. What happens in winter we did not discover, but as the lake is often frozen several feet thick — in fact right down to the bottom over much of its shallow area — and the ice-yachts emerge to take the place of their slower summer counterparts then perhaps the men of the Waterpolitie in their handsome uniforms become Ijspolitie for the duration of the frost, skimming from Warmond to Leeghwater and Zevenhuizen at an exhilarating sixty miles an hour on a framework carried on long runners of shining steel.

Aboard the *Commodore* we always had the greatest regard for the Dutch police. There can be no country where the authority responsible for the public observance of rules and regulations acts with more gentility and sense, and even the 'courtesy cop' of Britain's roads is brusque compared with the Dutch *Politie agent*. Once we lay moored for five days to the wall connecting the central piers of the two Meuse bridges at Maastricht, and at either end of this wall a flight of steps led up to the bridge, where there was a locked gate over which we had to climb to the pavement. A policeman stood on one of the bridges, watching with interest as the *Commodore* drew in, and when we began to scale the gate he gallantly saluted and helped the ladies down. On the succeeding days we exchanged greetings as he walked past, but on the fifth morning he stopped and chatted to us for a while about the weather before turning to the matter of the moment. At length he apologized for troubling us, but he had to tell us that boats were not allowed to moor on the wall. They could moor against the wharf lower down, or in the canal, or by the park, but not there. It was *verboden*. No, no, no, he did not wish us to move, not unless we were going to be there for many days more. But it was his business to see that the wall was kept clear. Ah, we were in any case going later that day? Then he hoped we had enjoyed Maastricht. Perhaps one day we would come back. . . .

At Willemstad too we had been bathing in the harbour during

three whole hot days before the policeman, who had been present on the quayside almost all the while, stepped over the hatches of the *Zeehond* on to our deck to open a conversation which was designed to lead up gently to the information that bathing in Willemstad harbour was *verboden* too, and that we should greatly oblige him by going to the beach instead. In Amsterdam also we were invariably met with the same mixture of tolerance and apologetic request to conform with the regulations if it would indeed not be too inconvenient to do so, and always there was the same open smile, the courtesy, and the genial preliminary conversation. No doubt the *Politie* were highly efficient and forceful when dealing with real malefactors, but in enforcing minor regulations they lacked the commanding and objectionable imperiousness which is not unknown in certain other countries.

The village of Warmond consists for the most part of a single long village street running more or less parallel to the river. It is clean and tidy and very Dutch, and the roadway is made of brick — as is usually the case in Holland, a country containing so little stone that metalled road surfaces are confined to the main highways and the chief streets of the cities. The bricks are simply set on the sand, parquet fashion, and a very good and smooth surface they make. The houses too are all of narrow brick with bright and shiny tiles of orange red or deep purple or black, and every window is filled with cyclamens and pansies, begonias and South African violets, geraniums and cacti. Somewhere behind there is sure to be a *Ficus elasticus*, and climbing plants range up to the ceiling on bamboo supports. At night — for the Dutch are happy to sit in their parlours and window alcoves without drawing curtains — we had a view of little private indoor forests of greenery and flowers.

During the *Commodore*'s explorations of Holland we often passed by Warmond, and she liked the place so much that she was allowed to spend a whole winter there, hauled up into the warm shed of one of its friendly and efficient boatyards. During the following spring we used the village as a base for voyaging, and so we became familiar with the little shops of its straggling street, and with the diminutive cafe which dealt in hot rissoles served on plates of crinkled cardboard accompanied by forks stamped out of wood.

Our conversations with the village people were carried on in a variety of languages, for although there is probably no other country in western Europe where a knowledge of English is more widespread, in Warmond it seemed almost confined to the manager of the boatyard and to the clerk in the post office.

Young people in Holland learn English at school, but others sometimes have a very surprising fluency gained entirely from listening in secret — and often in great danger too — to B.B.C. wartime broadcasts. We found too that lock-keepers and bargeskippers usually spoke English well, but for a different reason; they had served for a time in British merchant ships, or in ships which used English as a *lingua franca* among a polyglot crew. Many Dutchmen had of course learned German through the force of such circumstances as deportation for slave labour during the war, but they had a strong dislike of speaking it, and sometimes pretended not to understand it at all until they were thoroughly convinced that we ourselves were not Germans — for even among such a tolerant and friendly people as the Dutch the resentment born of cruel memories is not quickly overcome.

Where people spoke no English it seemed to us sensible to address them in German, for many of the words are identical with the Dutch and others very nearly so. Yet at our first visit to one of the village stores we seemed to make very little progress in making our wants understood. In desperation we eventually pointed at a handsome smoked eel, and enquired its price in German. The creature cost two and a half guilders, but it did not seem a bad bargain and so we bought it. Whilst the woman was silently wrapping it up for us we happened to talk among ourselves in English, and when she heard us use the words 'Yes' and 'No' she stopped wrapping the eel.

'*Niet Duitser?*'

'*Nein. Wir sind Engländer,*' we confirmed, but still in German.

'*Van Engeland, ja?*'

'*Ja. Van Londen.*'

At once the woman unrolled the paper, took out our eel and hung it up again in the window. Then she lifted down its neighbour, a beautiful specimen of twice the weight, and wrapped it up instead.

She was sorry to have made the mistake, she said. It was just the
language. . . . And whereas before she seemed to have had the
greatest difficulty in making out what we wanted to buy in her shop
she now appeared to have no difficulty whatsoever in interpreting
our wishes.

A voyage by canals and rivers inevitably took us to many localities
where tourists were not expected, and as we often came to hamlets
where there was no person who had even the most rudimentary
knowledge of any language other than Dutch we were obliged to do
as best as we could in that tongue. I doubt if Dutch could really be
termed an attractive language, and Harry Peckham was very definite about the matter. In Rotterdam he went 'to a barn, to see a
Dutch Tragedy and Farce. Two of the actresses were tolerably
pretty; but Dutch, even from the mouth of beauty, would be an
antidote to love'.

Dutch lacks the chronic bronchitis of German and is probably a
less impressive tongue in which to swear, but at least it is quite
easy to understand when written, for nearly every word is either
German or English modified in a particular and quite regular way.
Water is *water* (pronounced *wahter*), milk is *melk*, bread is *brod* and
butter is *boter*. Nor does one need to be much of a linguist to dis-
cern that *Onderwaterbottompeint* is what should be applied to the
underside of the hull when a boat is slipped for the winter. There
are of course a few traps, but one soon learns that an invitation to
start a meal with *soep* is not just a suggestion to wash one's hands.

The most obvious aid to conversation with the people of another
country is in theory the phrase book, and a friend in England even
went so far as to provide us with such an article, expecting that it
would help us out of many a difficulty. Yet it seems that the authors
of conversational guides must be men used only to unhappiness in
all their experiences from childhood onwards. They are a shade
self-indulgent too — quite apart from being hypochondriacs.
Never once when drawing in to a lockside was it of avail to us to be
able to call imperiously 'Waiter! Take the soup, the chicken, the
fish, the meat away. It is too hot, too cold. Send for the manager,
the chambermaid, the police. I shall complain to the British Consul.
I shall write a letter to *The Times*. Bring me approx. one quart of

light ale, a glass of Genever gin, two, three, four, five, six glasses of Genever gin. The bill is ridiculous. You are overcharging. My blankets are wet. The window will not open. The sheets do not look clean. Take my bags upstairs, downstairs, to the coachman. He looks an unsavoury character. I am moving elsewhere. Which is the way to the palace? Don't interrupt me!'

The *Commodore* could of course compile an international phrase book of her own, but to the usual tourist abroad her own useful sentences might seem just as inadequate.

'When does the bridge open? I am glad, sorry, to hear that the bridge-keeper is looking for his keys, in hospital, deceased. No thank you, we do not require any more eels. I regret having disobeyed the regulations of the *Rijkswaterstaat* but I thought that basket thing was a parrot-cage, not a lock signal. Yes, the boat comes from London. I am interested to hear that your brother-in-law's uncle visited Wapping in his youth. I wonder what made him return home again. I agree with everything you say, but please understand that it was not I who invited Mijnheer Kruschev to visit London.'

From Warmond and the Lake of de Kaag there are two routes to Amsterdam, according to whether one takes the Ringvaart van de Haarlemmermeerpolder to the right, or the Ringvaart van de Haarlemmermeerpolder to the left. For this waterway, as its name suggests, is indeed a ring and it is the watercourse into which the drained water from the reclaimed land within its loop is pumped. Today this area of silt and sand, more than twenty-five miles in circumference, is one of the most fertile in all the world, but once it was a collection of lakes. In fact it was on the vanished waters of the Haarlemmermeer that the fierce naval skirmishes took place during the terrible siege of Haarlem.

The Lake of de Kaag joins the Ringvaart at Leeghwater, a hamlet named after the Dutch engineer who in the middle of the seventeenth century put forward a plan for enclosing and draining the lakes, not merely to increase the area of cultivated land but because their waters connected with the North Sea and during times of gale and storm constituted a very real threat to the country further west and south. His plan was left in abeyance, but at the end of the

Napoleonic wars the matter was reconsidered, and once again a decision was deferred. In 1836 however the Haarlemmermeer threatened both Leiden and Amsterdam, and the government decided to remove the danger once and for all.

The project was to surround the entire area with two high banks, which in fact are the banks of the Ringvaart, and into the reservoir thus formed the water was to be raised by three giant steam pumps. The banks were completed by 1849 and the first of the engines was installed at Leeghwater. When the two other pumps were added the level of the lake was lowered by nearly half an inch in a day, and in just over three years the Haarlemmermeer had vanished for ever and Holland's land area had been increased by more than forty-five thousand acres.

The new land — the Haarlemmermeerpolder — is crossed by a grid of drainage canals running from north-east to south-west and from north-west to south-east. Seen from the air it is laid out in perfectly regular rectangles and down its centre runs an extra-large drainage course, the Hoofdvaart, which joins the polder villages together in a straight line and runs at its southern end to the Leeghwater pump and at the northern to a second engine at de Lijnden. A similar great ditch on the western side of the polder carries water to the remaining pump at Halfweg, half way between Haarlem and Amsterdam, at which place a sluice voids the overflow from the whole of the Ringvaart into a branch canal connecting with the North Sea Ship Canal. The system is really very simple, in that the water drains itself into ditches and thence into the grid of canals, along which it is drawn by the continual action of the pumps. The Ringvaart serves as a reservoir and shipping channel combined, and gets rid of the water from the polder into channels connecting with sea-sluices which can be opened at appropriate states of the tide. The reservoir capacity is further increased by the Kaag, Braassem, and Westeinder lakes, all of which lead directly off from the Ringvaart.

The land of the polder, which also contains the airport of Schiphol, is for the most part some thirteen feet below sea level, and for this reason alone a boat travelling round the ring has an astonishing view of the country enclosed within the banks. The converging

lines of perspective of the ditches stretch almost to the horizon, and a profusion of healthy crops grows in the neat rectangles. For the most part these crops are cereals and potatoes, celery and maize and beets, but here and there in springtime a crowded field of daffodils or deep purple crocuses stands out brilliantly among the young wheat or the furrowed fields of black silt which contain not a single stone.

The main bulb-growing area however lies immediately outside the western edge of the ring, in the strip of land in the lea of the high dunes of the Holland coast, where, as Goldsmith wrote:

> *the pent ocean, rising o'er the pile,*
> *Sees an amphibious world beneath him smile;*
> *The slow canal, the yellow-blossomed vale,*
> *The willow-tufted bank, the gliding sail,*
> *The crowded mart, the cultivated plain,*
> *A new creation rescued from his reign.*

And that was just how it was when following the Ringvaart round towards Haarlem we looked out across mile after mile of fields striped with the scarlet brilliance of the early *Fosteriana* tulips, the short-stemmed *Kaufmanniana*, or white and gold narcissi, blue hyacinths, and patchwork plots of crocuses, each variety of bulb being planted in long beds sufficiently narrow ^for every bulb and flower to be accessible to the bulb farmers from one side or the other. Here and there a particularly brilliant spot of colour flashed from a compost heap; for the heads of the blooms were quickly cut from the bulbs soon after they had opened, in order that the energy of each plant might be concentrated on the bulb rather than on seed. Piled up by the cartload to rot for manure, the heaps of blooms of Jan Bos and Lady Derby, Bismarck and La Victoire, were so dazzling as to be almost blinding in the intensity of their glow, but as amateur gardeners we could not help feeling somewhat sad to see the same blooms which at home we grew in proud but expensive dozens consigned here by scores of thousands to no better fate than decay.

The heads of the larger daffodils and narcissi suffered a different fate. Often we would meet a barge bearing on its bows a heavy loop of intense orange gold, formed of a long string threaded through the seed-boxes of each of a thousand blooms or even more. Perhaps another string of daffodil heads would cascade down the mast or be looped round the outside of the wheelhouse, or it might be secured as a handsome wreath of gold on the stern. Sometimes we would see the bargemaster's family sitting on the hatch covers beside a bushel or two of blooms, laboriously assembling them like mammoth daisy chains for no other reason than that they made their ship gay and colourful. Occasionally the canal itself would glow ahead of us, turning from sombre blue or grey to a fantastic yellow where the workers in the fields had shot a cartload of unwanted blossoms into the water.

Sassenheim, Hillegom and Noordwijk, Voorhout and Benne-broek — the names of villages familiar from the coloured autumn catalogues at home now became the spires of the churches lying close beside the Ringvaart, flanking the route to Haarlem. Being in no hurry — for a voyage on inland waters can never be an impatient journey — we allowed the *Commodore* to take the third turn to the left a mile or two beyond the Leeghwater pump and to feel her way cautiously up a narrow cut towards where it ended in an ornamental flight of steps in the centre of a village, part old and part new. Quietly she drew in to the wall opposite an auction hall from which in the autumn the bulbs of Holland would go by barge on the first stage of their journey to gardens all over the world. The place was Lisse, and within a mile of the *Commodore* there were more tulips than in all the gardens and parks and florists' shops of Britain.

It may seem to the reader that to travel by boat is a slow business. And so it is, but for that very reason it may be all the more rewarding. The waterborne traveller is rarely infected by that virus which breeds in the upholstery of the motor-car and which may so easily infect the occupants with a strange and insidious malaise, the symptoms of which include a determination not to stop until the town beyond the next one. And besides this irrational desire to reach just one more city before midnight there is the disease which manifests itself in a strange longing to achieve a superiority over others in the speed at which one can flash across a couple of countries without even pausing for breath.

'I suppose you stayed overnight in Paris?'

'My dear, we didn't want to waste time like that! We never stopped at all. Charles and I took it in turns to drive and we just kept going all through the night. Do you know, we were at the frontier outside Menton exactly twenty-eight hours and fourteen minutes after leaving Calais? What do you think of that?'

What indeed! And yet perhaps they did not miss very much, for had they stopped in one of the towns or cities on the dusty route to the South they would have met only the people professionally skilled in attending to the needs of travellers and relieving them quietly and obsequiously of as large a slice of their currency allowance as possible. The waiter is all smiles and English spoken, the table-cloth is turned clean side up, there is an air mail copy of *The Daily Telegraph* on the counter of the reception desk, and except

for the smell of garlic and the thickness of the slices of bread it
could all be in England.

'We might take a short stroll around after supper, dear. It seems
quite a place.'

'Don't you think we had better go straight up? I don't expect it's
very exciting here. It looked pretty dead when we came in. Let's
ask them to have our bill made out tonight. Then we can get away
early in the morning.'

'I see they have bacon and eggs on the breakfast menu.'

'Mm. Seven hundred francs. Still I suppose it's worth it. After
all, this is our holiday. . . .'

On a boat it is very different. With a speed of six or seven knots
there is no temptation to put back another forty miles before supper, and if one travels at night it is not in order to cover the distance but because a voyage in the dark may have a thrill all of its
own. It is not the excitement of danger — of which there is probably none — nor of achieving something which will provide a
cocktail party topic for the next winter, but a delight unknown to
the more conventional traveller — though perhaps one who has
walked over the mountains or moors at midnight may have an
insight into something of the same beauty that persists whilst the
world around is asleep.

To voyage at night on the *Commodore* was always to experience
the world in its essential loveliness. Beyond the low line of the
river bank the pastures might merge into the darkness of the horizon, but in the starlight the dewy grass glistened and the reeds
would nod low towards us as we passed, throwing back from their
moist leaves just the faintest shine caught from the port or starboard lamp. Often the water itself would be entirely hidden beneath a layer of steamy mist no more than an inch or two deep, but
here and there a black dot moving over its surface would indicate the
head and neck of a duck or a *waterhoen*, and a stilted shape at the
edge of the meadow a heron — or if we were in Friesland a stork.
Or the air might be dry and the water clear and smooth as plate-
glass except where a little wedge of ripples moving hurriedly towards the bank told us that a *waterrat* was returning to his hole
with a mussel dredged from the bottom. In the stillness we could

hear his footfalls in the grass, and the drip of water from his tail before he disappeared into the silence of his burrow and left us alone on the canal.

A town too would be transformed. From the land the glare of a sign for Heinekens or Amstel Bier might be no more than an ill-judged intrusion into the calm of a line of crooked gables, but the same electric colours could make a canal dance with fire as the breeze stirred the water into row upon row of tiny ripples of just the right steepness to catch the glow and spread it over half a mile of water towards us. The pall of smoke drifting overhead from a power-station would glow in the bottom lighting of the chimney-stack beneath, and ahead by the jetties the orange flame of a paraffin lamp dangling from a mast would pick up a score of brass fitments in the dark curved shape beneath, which by day might be seen to be no more than a dirty old tug.

Whether by day or by night, the voyager on inland waterways will by-pass tourist Europe without consciously attempting to do so. He may go to famous cities or to the same popular beauty-spots which offer themselves in gay brochures to the patrons of inclusive coach tours, but the places themselves will be utterly different in nature. Only the names remain the same. Perhaps we were to appreciate this most of all at the island of Marken; but at Ghent too, where the story of this book begins, the city in which the *Commodore* lay beneath the lime trees opposite the Law Courts was far removed from that seen by the procession of cars and buses hurrying on the first lap of their race from the Ostend ferry quay to Germany and crossing the bridge ahead of her bows. They had everything from A.A. town plans to meal vouchers and lists of hotels and the dates of foundation of the churches, but I doubt if Ghent was more to them than a possible place for a bed or a momentary halt in the square whilst the coach guide told them that this was Ghent and their beds were booked and supper was in ten minutes, tips were included, and would they please have their luggage outside the bedroom door by seven next morning. Of the loveliness tucked away alongside the waterways where barges had unloaded their wares below the same hoists for seven centuries, they would see nothing. They might catch a brief glimpse of the floodlit gables of the Quai aux Herbes, but not one of them would discover the incomparable loveliness of the reflection of those same buildings framed in the span of the bridge over the Lieve. They might already have had to wait, impatient at the delay, whilst the barriers held up the traffic to allow a bulky barge to pass from the Verbindingskanaal towards the Upper Scheldt, but they would not have seen in the straight line of that same back-street waterway a hint of the struggle for an outlet to the sea upon which the history of the city had hung in each succeeding century. But aboard a boat, history and beauty flow silently past in a never-ending stream.

I would not wish to tell others how they should take their holidays. After all, there are plenty of people to whom the mere notion of going by boat would be for a variety of reasons unattractive, and others may have neither the time nor the opportunity to travel in this leisurely — though at times very energetic — way, but the difference in the aspect of places as visited from the land or from the water is a very real one. In the case of Ghent I have experienced it myself, for in the days before we began to allow the *Commodore* to take us through the countries of Western Europe we ourselves once travelled that same route which leads from Ostend to Germany, and we covered it by car. We spent the night at Ghent and thought it a very dull place. After a very slight but costly supper, we took a conventional stroll in order to stretch our legs and straighten out the bends in them which came from the driving, and it was then that we made a discovery. In the course of our wanderings we happened to look over a bridge, and there below us was a boat which we recognized by its name as one we had seen on the Thames. We stepped aboard, and at that instant the whole of Ghent became astonishingly transformed. Perhaps the thought of visiting the same city ourselves by boat did not actually take shape in the same moment, but at least we were acutely aware that these people were spending the night in Belgium, whereas we had beds in what might just as well have been Birmingham — although our hotel was only a hundred yards distant from where their ship was lying.

The greatest difference of all may be in the way in which one is accepted. The motorist or the member of the guided tour is not really a person in his own right but a unit of the national tourist industry, a cow to be tended and fed and quartered — and milked. And the better the fodder, the richer the yield of cream. His every wish may be catered for, provided it is not troublesome, but he can rarely hope to penetrate further below the surface of the life of the country than the pictures on the postcard stalls and he is forced to remain a *Fahrgast*, a *Bezoeker*, a contribution to the statistics which the Ministry of the Interior will later issue and which will be plotted on a wall chart in the office of the Director of the National Tourist Traffic Association, and which may also perhaps cause a small advance or weakening in the ordinary shares of hotel companies. But the boat tourist is regarded quite differently. He has no dealings with head porters and couriers. He meets the people on whom much of the prosperity of the land ultimately depends — the bargemasters and farmers, the lock-keepers and harbour-masters. His boat is a common denominator, and he is accepted on terms of frank equality and of confidence. It is not very likely that a lorry-driver in a Paris street will walk cheerfully up to an English family in their saloon car and ask in the most natural way in the world where they are going or whether he may take a peep at the engine out of mere curiosity, yet the men on the barges will talk to a boat-owner as though he were one of themselves — which in fact he is. A continental policeman may be courteous and helpful in the extreme, but he will hardly draw up his motor-cycle alongside a visiting motorist solely in order to chat, and he would certainly not run home to fetch his wife so that the party could all sit round and talk over a glass of beer or a cup of coffee. But on the waterways it is different and people are drawn closer together, because they are engaged in an activity which is fundamentally the same. The *Commodore* might be voyaging for pleasure and the *Zeehond* or the *Twee Gebroeders* or the *Drie Gezusters* for their livelihood, but they chugged down the same canals, waited at the bridges, helped each other with the locks, took each other's lines, and saw and loved the same beauty in the villages through which they passed. Particularly was this the case in Holland, where an appreciation of line and form and shape and colour seems fundamental. It was not a travel agent but a waterman on the Ringvaart, a man in all probability

I

scarcely able to write his own name, who insisted that we should go to Haarlem and see the Frans Hals paintings. Yes, certainly we should see the Halses, but particularly the Ruysdaels, which were his own favourites.

I believe that the success of the Dutch in the floral trade is not entirely due either to the climate or to the soil, but to an innate affection and care for everything that is inherently beautiful. Yet however that may be, they have brought bulb growing to a very fine art indeed, and when the *Commodore* drew in at Lisse she had brought us to the very centre of that colourful industry.

VIII

We had not been long at Lisse before a car drew up beside the *Commodore* and a quiet and unassuming man introduced himself to us as Mijnheer Lindhout. We very soon discovered that in fact he was a grower whose business was conducted on such a scale that a thousand bulbs was the smallest quantity of any variety for which he would quote. Forty varieties of hyacinth, two hundred and fifty of tulips, and narcissi without number, the firm of Groeneveld and Lindhout had field upon field of every bulb and corm from scilla and muscari to begonias and Madonna lilies, and Mr Lindhout thought we might spare the time to see them.

In Mr Lindhout's car we turned and twisted through the lanes and over the ditches towards the high row of the distant dunes which flank the western coast of Holland with a belt of sand a couple of miles from side to side, and at each corner we would gasp at the beauty of the massed blooms in the fields beside the track.

'Madame Lefeber. Quite a fair crop,' our host would say. 'But what do you think of the one over the ditch there? That is Alfred Cortot, a new variety. Cortot should be one of the best, though Caesar Franck and Johann Strauss are popular. Cortot has more red of course. You would like to try Alfred Cortot? Then I can find you a man who has them to sell in small quantities. You would not want many I think, as they are thirty-three or thirty-five shillings a dozen. Fritz Kreisler is the same price. Fair Lady is more — forty-five I think.'

One after another the fields would flash by — Vivaldi, Praestans Fusilier, President Lebrun, William the Silent, L'Innocence and Ostara and Holland's Glory. Before we reached Noordwijk our eyes were physically tired with the intensity of massed colour, but our journey had only begun. Mr Lindhout wanted us to see the freesias. It seemed that Groeneveld and Lindhout only grew freesias for seed, but there must have been a great demand for it, for in the lee of the dunes stood a double row of oil-fired glass-houses, each of them larger than a tennis court. Two greenhouses were given over to each variety of freesia and they were planted so thickly that hardly a single bulb more could have been squeezed into the beds of rich black soil within them. We were lucky enough to have arrived just at the time when they were in full bloom, and the lovely spikes of flowers formed a dense and gorgeous carpet from end to end of the space, whilst the air hummed noisily with the thousands of bees streaming in and out of the skep-hives slung from the roof as they hustled to collect another drop of the precious nectar and incidentally to undertake for Mr Lindhout the vital task of pollination.

'There are half a million freesias in this house,' said Mr Lindhout modestly. 'Of course we grow more seed of the most popular colours.'

Some years earlier we had visited a perfume factory in France, but the vats of essence which we had met there had nothing to compare with the heady scent of a few hundred thousand freesias in the warm and damp atmosphere of the Noordwijk greenhouses. In fact we had already picked up their scent half a mile away as we drove across the fields, but though in the glass-houses our own eyes were streaming, Mr Lindhout hardly seemed to notice it.

Bulb-farming is now one of Holland's major industries and it brings a great quantity of foreign exchange into the country, particularly from Britain and Germany and from France too, where formal municipal gardens are laid out on a scale which is rare in Britain and which demands a great many bulbs for its execution. A massed bed of hyacinths can be quite expensive, and when we computed the cost to ourselves if we were to have in our own garden even one of the smaller patches of Ostara which we saw in the squares in the villages beside the Ringvaart the cost came out at about thirty-five pounds. Nowadays the prices of bulbs of different varieties are mostly within a limited range, but in the early days of bulb-growing there was a mania of speculation in new forms. It was in the early seventeenth century that the tulip became popular and fashionable in Holland, and as the wealthy merchants sought for new types with which to be superior to their neighbours and rivals the growers were encouraged to try every conceivable cross. The prices of new forms soon reached fantastic heights.

The market reached its peak in 1636 and 1637. A single bulb of Semper Augustus is recorded to have fetched 13,000 guilders — there were only two bulbs of this variety in the country at one period — and many others were sold for prices which today would correspond to hundreds or thousands of pounds apiece. A single bulb of Viceroy was sold for 25,000 florins — the sum being paid in cheese, corn, cattle, wine and other goods, for want of ready cash — and a price-list of the favourite varieties of the time shows a dozen tulips quoted at more than 1,000 florins a bulb, whilst of the 'cheaper' varieties one might purchase a pound bag for between 1,800 and 5,700 florins. With such prices current, it was not surprising that jobbers and brokers arose who dealt in the open market in bulbs which they did not even possess, and at times the forward purchases exceeded the quantity of bulbs which the entire country could produce. Inevitably the crash came, and whilst a few city men retired with vast wealth and many more were ruined the Semper Augustus continued to flower without the least concern — though with a value of only fifty guilders. Today it is not even in the list of tulips which Mr Lindhout sends to his wholesale customers in England.

Later it was the turn of the hyacinth. The fondness of Madame Pompadour for Dutch hyacinths brought them into vogue and though the prices never reached quite the same heights a number of varieties figured in a grower's list of 1730 at prices of several hundred florins for a single bulb.

We learned from Mr Lindhout that the hyacinth differed from other bulbs in a very important way in that it did not naturally reproduce itself by splitting off smaller bulbs at the base in the familiar manner of a tulip or a crocus or daffodil. For the growers this had meant that propagation could only be done by seed, and this was a serious disadvantage in lengthening the time of nursery care. It had taken as long as seven years or more to raise a top-size bulb in this way, and everything had been tried — or so it seemed — to induce hyacinths to conform to the practice of the rest, but without avail. And then one day the problem was solved, not by a grower but by a rat. It happened that a grower inspecting his crop had pulled up as usual any stray bulbs which had somehow become mixed up in a bed of another variety, and he had flung one of them away into the ditch. There it was subsequently found by a rat, which nibbled away at the base of the bulb. The hyacinth survived, and the effect on the bulb which had lost its pad of roots was to make it throw off bulblets all round the base. On finding the bulb again by chance, the grower at once noticed what had happened and he checked his observation by cutting off the base of a further set of bulbs with his knife. In due course each of them produced a family, and at last the industry was provided with a technique for speeding up the development of hyacinths to a degree which cut years off the production cycle. Mr Lindhout thought that in all honesty a monument should have been erected by the Growers Association in gratitude to the rat, but no doubt its other depredations have weighed too heavily against it. And besides, it was not only rats which had from time to time eaten bulbs. During the last winter of the Second World War there was little other food available in Holland, and Mr Lindhout was only one of many thousands who had kept starvation at bay with stewed tulips and hyacinths. Not that he ever really liked the dish, he said. He still thought that the colours of the blooms were infinitely preferable to the taste or tastelessness of the bulbs themselves.

Though the country around Noordwijk and Lisse was brilliant with bloom it was the slack season for the growers. There was little to do at the moment but lop off the heads and pull out strays which had become misplaced, and although there was a certain amount of work going on in the coloured fields the warehouses were deserted. Later in the year the great activity would begin as scores of millions of bulbs were lifted from the ground, cleaned and shaken down moving lattices of wood so that they sorted themselves out into sizes. Then they would be dried with the greatest care, not too fast and not too slowly, and every day the temperature of the air driven through the warehouses by the big propellers on the ceilings would be adjusted to the exact degree necessary to ensure the best results. So many days at one temperature, so many at another, the bulbs lived through a climate which had only been perfected by centuries of experiment and experience. It was easy enough to produce good bulbs if one knew all the details of this treatment, but the secrets were not worked out in a day. Not even in a lifetime. That was why there were good bulbs and bad bulbs, Mr Lindhout said. It was not the actual strains that were at fault when bulbs were poor; it was merely that their grower did not happen to know how to get the best results. And why should anyone tell him? In a couple of centuries his descendants would master the business for themselves — if they were still in it.

Mr Lindhout asked us if we liked gerberas, and we told him we did. Could we grow them at home? Certainly not, he said emphatically. These exquisite luxury flowers with their star of long thin petals in strangely modern hues might grow easily enough in Africa perhaps, or in Madeira — at Funchal there are beds of them in the open — but outside the subtropical areas it was a matter of great skill. We had seen gerberas in Bond Street, had we not, and perhaps one or two blooms as a window dressing in Piccadilly? And in Paris? Well, they came from near Noordwijk. There was only one gerbera farm in Holland and probably only one in the world. He would take us to see it.

We climbed into his car again and soon we were being introduced to the gerbera-farmer, a tall thin man in a trilby hat who met us at the door of one of his glasshouses. He did not shake hands, nor were we allowed in without walking through a shallow pool of disinfectant immediately inside the door, for gerberas are the next thing to botanical hypochondriacs. If there is any disease about, they will catch it, and if there is not then they will invent one for themselves. And as the gerbera-farmer was explaining this to us and begging us not to stray from the disinfected duckboards a young man in a mask and rubber suit advanced slowly between the rows, filling the air with just one more complex organic chemical which would keep some virus or rust or bug at bay.

The gerberas were to a certain extent in an experimental stage.

Hundreds were cut every day and left the farm by car for Schiphol airport on the first stage of their journey, each with its head carefully shielded by a little cone of paper surrounding the petals. Even the grower received a shilling a bloom, so they must certainly have been expensive by the time they reached their high-class destinations, but they really represented little more than rejects. The farm was engaged in long-term breeding and crossing, and the flowers on many of the plants would not be sold at any price. They carried the hope of the future in the blooms which would set as seed. It was only the comparative failures which were cut for the florists.

Beside each of the thousand or more plants in a single house stood a cane to which a wire hook was attached, and from the hook dangled a collection of rings and discs. Each plain wire ring represented one bloom grown on that plant, and the colours of the discs indicated particular cultures and treatment. Every gerbera was numbered too, and its characteristics were entered in a private *curriculum vitae*. One had a magnificent hue of reddish maroon but it flopped as though it had no strength. Another was stocky, but there was no point in preserving such a washed-out yellow. And here was one of a salmon pink, tall and thin but with petals of superb elegance. It was a matter of crossing and combining and selecting afresh in each generation, of knowing one's Burbank and Mendel and Morgan and seasoning the lot with careful tending and absolutely rigid control of humidity and heat. Even then there were unaccountable failures, and for every really good plant there were half a dozen wasters. It would take time, yes certainly, but what a prize was to be had when in ten or twenty years the stocks had been established, improved and stabilized. Already the plants could just about pay for their keep if he sold the blooms that were not wanted. No, he did not just cut them and send them to market. People only bought gerberas to order. If there was a milliner anywhere from Berlin to Manchester who wanted half a dozen for display with the spring fashions, then sooner or later their wish would be translated into a ringing of the telephone bell in his office. 'A dozen, mixed? On the Skymaster flying out at 12.30? Yes, yes. *Dank U wel.*'

However startling the colours of the massed fields of tulips through which we drove back between the dykes to Lisse, there was no doubt that Mr Lindhout had done wisely in showing us the production side of the industry first, for even the finest mass of colour we saw was to pale beside the spectacle which he had reserved for the next day, when he called on us once more with complimentary tickets for the Keukenhof. This park of seventy acres of woodland and lake, of lawns and formal bowers and borders, is famous enough to attract many thousands of overseas visitors during the few short weeks of springtime when it is open to the public. It is the shop window of the Bulb Growers Association of the Netherlands, and it would be worth going to Holland just to spend half a day at the Keukenhof alone — provided of course that one was prepared to realize that even a single bed of Keukenhof's glorious massed hyacinths or tulips could only be reproduced at home if one had centuries of experience and a hundred pounds or two to lay out on each variety. I doubt if there can be a floral display in the world to match it, particularly just at that short time when the late daffodils and the early tulips bloom along the lakeside with the scillas and the hyacinths, as they happened to be doing when we visited the place. Perhaps our envy, and our despair too, reached its height as we entered the single glasshouse, a building large enough to contain under its glass roof a row of tennis courts, but which in fact housed the massed plots of the seven hundred best varieties of tulip, each kind represented by the huge blooms of several dozen superb quality bulbs planted in a compact mass. We would have liked such a glasshouse at home, but our garden could not quite have contained its area of 24,000 square yards — and perhaps that was just as well, for Mr Lindhout computed the cost of the bulbs alone as between two and three thousand pounds.

Outside, in one of the hedged and formal gardens we came upon a party of English visitors. They wore the shapeless berets and the black stockings and brown blazers of a London school, and they were huddled in a circle with their backs to the Bismarcks and the Delft Blues and Myosotis and La Victoire, intent on earnest whispered discussion. Passing slowly by, we heard that they were discussing the mistresses. Some way further on we came to a gorgeous bower of daffodils, and there on the grass with their backs

towards the Edward Buxton and the Daisy Schäffer and the Golden
Harvest were three women, seated on their mackintoshes. They
were the mistresses, and they were discussing their dentists. Where
the dentists were we never discovered. Perhaps they were not in the
Keukenhof at all, unless they were some of the simple-minded
men we saw who appeared to have nothing of great moment to
discuss and were just wandering about, drinking in the dazzling
loveliness of it all.

The Keukenhof is not the only show garden in the bulb land.
There is the Linnaeushof too, at Bennebroek, and the *Commodore*
took us to see it also. Perhaps it is indeed Europe's Most Beautiful
Garden, as it claims to be, and certainly its woodland show of
miniature irises is very fine. It was there that we met the charming
dwarf *Iris danfordiae*, which thereafter took up its residence in our
own garden as a humble reminder of·what we too might do if only
we had a few hundred acres of woodland and a staff of men who
knew all the tricks.

The Linnaeushof was once the scene of the researches of Carl
von Linné, for it was in Holland that he studied as a doctor, and he
soon became physician to the Lord Mayor Clifford of Amsterdam
who resided at Bennebroek. He could not have chosen a better
patron, for Clifford was himself a great gardener and at Bennebroek Linnaeus had the opportunity of studying the rare and exotic
plants under cultivation, and of laying the foundations of the classi-
fication of living things which even today is the backbone of systematic biology. Many of the thousands of species which bear the
proud L after their Latin tags first received it in the books which he
wrote at Bennebroek.

The Linnaeushof had its glasshouse too. It may not have been so
large as that of the Keukenhof, but we could not have wished for a
more delightful place in which to have lunch than beside the indoor lawns where tulips bloomed in the grass and the walks were
gay with the scented blossom of prunus and azalea and forsythia.

The bulb country which lies along the western side of the Ringvaart van de Haarlemmermeerpolder is a springtime attraction
only, but on the eastern side of the loop the same canal leads by
another horticultural wonder. Turning right instead of left at the

end of the Lake of de Kaag a run of an hour and a half led us past the end of the Braassemermeer and the long water-bisected single street of Oude Wetering, where the shops identified their trades to passing boats by the plain words *Melk, Fruit, Groenten, Brod* and so forth painted on the water-frontage of the quay, and on towards the largest of the lakes of the area, the Westeinder Plas. The canal passed along the edge of this lake and the distant view was broken by the countless tall and thin stovepipes and chimney stacks of Aalsmeer. And at whatever time of year we might pass this way we turned out of the Ringvaart just before the Aalsmeer bridge and let the *Commodore* nose her way up a hundred yards of cut so narrow that she could not hope to turn in it. There she came to another lifting bridge, but instead of blowing three times to summon the village *brugwachter* to come with his keys she crept in quietly between the piles to a corner where there was just room and no more for her to lie for the night, with her bows on the village street and her stern held out with a rope from trespassing in the pansy-bed of a silent old eel-fisherman. She always arrived at Aalsmeer in the twilight or after dark, for it was important to be there in time for the early morning.

Aalsmeer is an astonishing place, and a perfect example of a flourishing industry which has almost all its requirements to hand. The only things lacking are a sheet-glass factory and a gusher of heating oil, for apart from these everything is there on the spot.

On one side of the Ringvaart a pottery turns out an endless supply of orange-red flower-pots, but they have only to cross the canal in a float to find their way by water to any one of the hundreds of growers whose establishments lie within a mile at the most, and many of which are no more than a hundred yards from the pottery. Not bulb-growers this time, but nurserymen whose blooms and pot plants find their way into every corner of Europe and even to America.

Aalsmeer is not exactly dry land. From the Ringvaart and the Westeinder Plas narrow cuts run away to disappear invitingly round corners, and they are separated by strips of ground only a foot above water and often no more than twenty feet broad. These myriad islands are generally reinforced along their edges with an underwater palisade of willow stakes, and where their ends meet the Ringvaart the defences are further bolstered with a mass of broken flower-pots to break the force of the wash of passing barges. A nurseryman keeps his little channels dug out and dredged by means of a metal scoop on a long pole, and the rich humus from the bottom is swung inshore and tipped on the land to form beds of the richest quality. In the plots so constructed he will set a packed mass of plants, or perhaps plant serried ranks of standard lilac trees which will be taken inside under glass during the winter, cropped of their fine white spikes, shorn down once more to pollarded top-knots on three-foot stems, and planted out again in the bed of mud. All this cartage is done by punt or float, and if a grower needs more soil than he can grub from his channels he poles out into the lake to scoop up a ton or two from the bottom into his boat. So the lake and the little cuts between them provide the growing medium, the transport routes, and an assurance that even on the hottest of summer days the plants will grow with wild exuberance in a soil that is kept always moist from below.

A little way up, each cut usually ends at a glasshouse, for it is towards indoor cultivation that Aalsmeer's activities are directed.

From a plane coming down to Schiphol airport a mere four miles away a traveller will see little but a sea of glass, with bright colours shining through it in the sunlight, but even then he can have little idea of the sheer quantity of flowers produced beneath the panes.

We had been told that Aalsmeer was the largest flower market in the world, and when we drew in for the first time beside the village bascule bridge we perhaps imagined that in the morning we would just see a great number of old women sitting at stalls along the kerbside offering bunches of carnations to chance visitors. But as early as four o'clock in the morning we awoke to the plop-plop of boat engines, as one after another the craft brushed past us to squeeze under the bridge. From stem to stern the little green barges were packed with colour, and if their hatches were closed we could see the calceolarias and cyclamens peeping out of the portholes like stateroom passengers whilst the humbler plants rode tourist class on the deck. And all the while smart wooden trucks and vans in the style of horse-boxes clanked over the bridge beside our bows, bound for the auction.

By six o'clock the traffic had ceased, and we jumped ashore to walk through the village to the hall of the Centrale Aalsmeerse Veiling. Our way led through side streets of little brick houses, each of which bore a single coloured tile beside the door to indicate its name in picture. Each house was a bird or a beast or a flower. *Tortelduif* and *groenvink*, *beer* and *tijger*, *vergeet-mij-nietje* and *pimpernel*, their identities were not difficult to understand even without the help of the accompanying sketches in clay.

Round a corner we came on the great hall of the *bloemenveiling* or flower auction, and through the door was a scene of astonishing brilliance. On big three-deck metal trolleys the carnations, cut that same morning, were drawn up in ranks ready to be wheeled into the selling rooms. We hesitated on account of the warning notice that entry was forbidden, but a porter bustling by with an armful of early tulips gave us a friendly nod. 'Go in. Go where you will,' he said. And wherever we wandered during the whole of the morning it was always the same. We were never made to feel that we were in the way and interfering with busy men about their work. If we paused to admire the roses which a grower was unloading from his van he would stop to tell us their name. If a porter could not identify a flower for us he would find somebody who could. If there was anything we might have missed, somebody would go out of their way to tell us about it and show us where to go.

The Aalsmeer auction is magnificently organized. A broad canal runs right into the hall so that growers can unload onto the trolleys without risk of damage to the blooms by rain. Whilst they are unloading, other consignments are being driven in from the roadway, and everywhere flowers are being assembled in procession to pass through to the sale-rooms. The first consignments sold will be in the florists' shops of the cities within a matter of hours at the most, and as these earliest lots have something of an advantage in price the procedure is made fair and equitable by conducting a ballot to decide the order of sale among the growers. In any event the sheer quantity of flowers is so great that an auction by conventional methods of bidding would be much too slow, and the Dutch auction system is used.

We found that there were several sale-rooms and we climbed the stairs into a gallery in one of them to watch the proceedings. The room itself was almost exactly like a science lecture-theatre at the Royal Institution or a university, with row upon row of desk benches rising steeply up towards the back of the hall. About a hundred wholesale buyers sat in their numbered seats, smoking cigars or drinking tea, but always with one finger on the bell-push in front of them. Down below, where the lecturer's table would be, a trolley of blooms was displayed and others queued up at a door just behind it to take their turn. A porter lifted a sample of the flowers to be sold, called out the quantity, and just occasionally commented on the quality too, but if he did so it was not in praise, for the standard of Aalsmeer flowers was so high that to make no comment indicated absolute perfection whereas a spotted leaf or the least stain of raindrops on the petals had to be pointed out.

In a flying box projecting from high up in the wall sat the auctioneer and his clerks. The auctioneer called the lot number and within a couple of seconds the blooms would be sold. On the wall opposite his audience was a dial on which a great pointer swung round past a series of numbers from 100 to 0, representing cents per bunch. The auctioneer pressed a button to release the hand at the figure of 100 cents, and the finger ran quickly round the arc of descending value until some buyer pressed his own button. This stopped the hand at the price to which it had fallen, and an indicator light flashed on to give the number of the bell-push which had intervened. There were no second thoughts, no subsequent or higher bids. The first man to press his bell-push was the buyer, and that was that — a healthy system, which no doubt made for quick thinking if a thousandth of a second could make the difference between winning and losing a possible purchase.

'Ten bunches. Thirty-two cents. Seventy-four. Ten bunches. Thirty-three cents. Fifty-nine. Twenty bunches, thirty-one cents. Forty.' As fast as the clerks could enter the figures under the buyers' numbers the blooms were sold off at the touch of a button, and as each trolley was disposed of another rolled into its place.

The first hour or two concerned carnations, lilac, and roses — those roses which are at once recognizable in florists' shops all over Europe by the long stems which represent just one of the arts of Aalsmeer culture. There must have been several boatloads of lilac that morning, for towards the end the pointer swung round the dial in vain. There were no buyers for lilac by this time, and the lovely sprays were wheeled away to be thrown on the rubbish heap or dropped into one of the canals where they would rot and return to the mud which had grown them, and so begin once more the cycle of soil and growth and pruning and bloom which would lead eventually to another early morning journey by boat or truck to the sale-room.

With the cut blooms disposed of, the pot plants took their turn, and begonias, giant calceolarias, cyclamens, and a wealth of strange exotic species came proudly into the hall in a blaze of colour. Here too the standard was strict, but a guest we had with us aboard the *Commodore* was decidedly saddened. He was quite an expert with his greenhouse at home, where indeed he had showed us with very justifiable pride a cyclamen plant with no less than thirty-two blooms on the one corm. It came as something of a shock to him to discover that none of the cyclamens on a barrow he was now inspecting had less than sixty flowers — except for one, which had

only a few over forty, and which the porter quickly pulled from its
pot and flung into the canal because it was evidently not of sufficient quality to grace the sale-room.

Before we returned aboard the boat the auctioneers had reached lot
9438, and as one lot represented perhaps ten sprays of roses or a
half-dozen calceolarias or a hundred bedding begonias it seemed
almost incredible that such quantities of flowers could possibly be
taken up into the households or gardens of the whole country —
particularly in a land where every windowsill already seemed burst-
ing to capacity with home-grown flowers. The explanation was of
course that much of the day's produce was consigned abroad.
Schiphol airport was less than a ten minutes journey by truck, and
from the moment the first lots were sold the carnations and roses
and tulips were being swiftly packed in tissue paper and padded
boxes and whisked away to catch an express cargo or passenger
plane. By noon they would be in London and Stockholm, Paris and
Manchester and Berlin.

Many of the pot plants were consigned abroad too by rail or
ship, and it came as a surprise to us to learn from a young grower's
assistant that whole loads of greenhouse plants would be shipped
straight to London, and that many of the loveliest flowers in Covent
Garden, even if a trifle sad after their journeying, originated in
Aalsmeer.

We asked him what had happened during the war. Fuel had been
scarce for heating, he said, and with many of its markets gone
Aalsmeer had fallen on bad times. But the growing never ceased
entirely, even in the worst of those years, for they knew that better
days would come back again, and at the end of the war the growers
speedily got back into production. Almost from the moment
Holland was freed the plants and flowers began once more to make
their way up the Thames. There were of course a hundred and one
difficulties concerned with exchange and import permits and currency and sterling, but the Aalsmeer men were not prepared to
wait on endless formalities. Flowers died more quickly than
bureaucrats, he explained, and so the consignments were shipped
even without their having been ordered.

'We knew people would want our flowers. We knew we could

trust our friends there who had bought from us before the war. So we just shipped the flowers with a note, and this is what it said: "You cannot pay for our flowers, so we send them you as a gift. If you can sell them, please send us anything you like. We have nothing here, in Holland." And what do you think happened? Everything came which we could use. Fountain pens, cigarettes, razor-blades, tins and tins of meat, and it did not matter what it was for we had nothing here at all and our friends knew it. And that was how we began to make our trade again with England.'

And then he told us another tale, which seemed an impossible story and yet apparently it was true enough. Flowers were even shipped to London during the war. It was so improbable that a Dutch cargo ship should simply sail out of occupied and wasted Rotterdam for London that it never occurred to the Germans that that could be a possible destination. Yet it happened. A motor ship was loaded with plants, she steamed down the Nieuwe Waterweg to the Hook, and next morning she was unloading in London docks. She never came back — not till after the war, that is — and nor did he or the other young men of Aalsmeer whom she carried aboard her along with their flowers on that extraordinary but quite uneventful voyage.

Day by day — except on Sundays — the auction rooms of the Centrale Aalsmerse Veiling and the similar sale-rooms of the Veiling Bloemenlust disperse the thousands of lots among buyers who will distribute them over half the world. Which means of course that day by day (and Sundays included) this prodigious quantity of flowers is matured on the islets and in the glasshouses of Aalsmeer. How was such an astonishing crop achieved?

Like Mr Lindhout, the young man smiled as he gave an answer both courteous and evasive.

'It takes generations to discover the secrets. Those cyclamens there, some have more than seventy blooms. You take the same bulb and grow it the best you can, and you may have twenty, thirty flowers. It is just a matter of knowing how to do it, and how not. And if you know how — well then, you can do it any day of the year if you want to.'

That afternoon we eased the *Commodore* out from between the

K

piles, and with the dinghy towed her stern first down towards the Ringvaart. Now and again we had to stop to let a float squeeze past her, laden with boxes and pots of blooms for Amsterdam, where the flowers are sold from the barges on the old canal of the Singel. And as we crept down the cut between the nursery beds we took the opportunity to supply ourselves with gay flowers for the cabins. The white lilac which we hauled up over the side with the boathook may have been surplus to the market, and the carnations and muscari which we pulled aboard in a bucket from the waters of the canal may have been inferior by Aalsmeer's standards of perfection, but for all that they were none the less lovely.

IX

The Ringvaart van de Haarlemmermeerpolder has two exits at its northern end, one by way of Haarlem and the other directly into Amsterdam. The latter is the shorter route from the south but whether or not it is the quicker depends on the circumstances, for beyond Schiphol airport the course leading into the city turns off through a small lake to the Nieuwe Meer lock and beyond this a boat must pass down the Kostverloren Vaart, a rather back-street but picturesque canal, to reach the harbour. There are eleven lifting bridges, many of which carry tram routes, and one of them is a main approach to the railway station, so progress tends to be in short bursts interspersed with considerable periods of waiting — particularly if a boat arrives during the rush hour for road traffic or the lunch hour for bridge-keepers.

The more westerly route leaves the Ringvaart by the River Spaarne, a meandering waterway which wanders over the meadows for two or three miles before running almost through the centre of Haarlem, and right beside many of its loveliest buildings. Haarlem is now a busy city ringed with industries, and the seventeenth-century houses of its streets have too often had their facades chopped in half to accommodate shop windows and milk bars capped with discharge-tube night-signs, but the most famous of its architectural gems have fortunately been spared.

Like nearly every other great church in Holland the massive church of St Bavo has of course long since been protestant, and though its exterior is lovely we were almost ashamed to admit as dissenters that the former glory of the interior was sadly departed. No doubt Dr Schweitzer was right in his opinion that the Haarlem organ is the finest in the world, but even this could not quite make up for the huge expanses of bare white wash and the strange lack of a focal point which so often accompanies the destruction of more catholic ornamentation and the reorientation of the pews around a row of dark diaconal seats. Frankly, we thought the place had been decoratively ruined however much it might have benefited theologically.

One night we visited the Frans Hals Museum. It may seem odd to pay a visit to an art gallery shortly before midnight, but in the case of the Frans Hals it was undoubtedly the best time. The building is a gem of a seventeenth-century brick court and was at one time a medical college. We found it exquisitely restored, and it had about it the quiet ageless spirit of one of the older unpretentious college courtyards of Cambridge. The outside was lit by the moon but the court itself was faintly floodlit and among all the soft lights and the sweet music drifting down from an open upper window the beauty of the place was greatly enhanced by the stroke of genius of whoever had hit on the idea of lighting the interior only with candles. No sweeter light than a candle has ever been produced. It may lack the brightness of an electronic flash, and dusty corners are doubtless better revealed in their nudity by tungsten wire, but no other lamp can give the same gradation from brightness near the source to a growing mystery of dimness round the edges of a room, or fill the surroundings with the slight movement which the bending of a candle flame in a draught will impart.

The only exception to the candle lighting was in the case of the pictures, but here too a flash of imagination had made the display more dramatic than we had expected. So often in a gallery one is confronted with hundreds of pictures, good, bad or indifferent covering the wall as thickly as advertisements on a giant hoarding. In the Hals Museum too there were no doubt hundreds of paintings, but at night only those of special merit were lit. In one room it might be a single canvas which stood out in the half dark, a Hals perhaps, or one of the waterman's favourite Ruysdaels, but one could stand and look at it without the distraction of feeling that each of the neighbouring paintings was continually begging for a just share of attention.

In the market place of Haarlem there stands a statue of one Costerus, and we were somewhat surprised to find that the inscription described him as the inventor of printing from movable type. We had always believed this to be the work of the clerk of Mainz who preferred the pious sounding and respectable pseudonym of Gutenberg to the name of Gänsfleisch (or Gooseflesh) with which he was endowed. The Haarlemers however are adamant about the matter — just as the Mainzers are — and it is probably one of those historical uncertainties which will never be unravelled but which will provide a subject for university theses as long as civilizations remain. The Haarlem version maintains that Costerus was walking in a beech wood outside the city when suddenly the idea of type just came to him. He cut pieces of beech bark into letters and found that he could ink them and stamp them on paper. He soon began to experiment with letters cast in lead, and then with pewter type, and after a while he set up a printing shop in his house. But one day, while he and his family were at church, his servant John Faust stole the whole apparatus and made off with it to Mainz. And of course it is true enough that a short time afterwards Johann Faust or Fust was indeed the technician in the Gutenberg establishment at Mainz.

It is curious that whereas today we think of printing as the wonderful achievement that it certainly is, Gutenberg's partners went to considerable trouble not to advertise their skill but to conceal it. Hand-copied Bibles represented years of labour on the part of a clerk, and even printing from carved blocks was a lengthy enough business to command a high price. If it were to be known that one had but to set the type and rearrange the letters for other pages the work would not be thought worthy of the same price, so the printers of Mainz went so far as to put out the famous Bibles of 1462 in the guise of handwritten copies and even added an inscription to the effect that Johann Fust, citizen, and Peter Schoiffer, clerk, had completed the copying on the eve of the feast of the Assumption of the Blessed Virgin Mary. This ingenuity brought its rewards until it began to appear to the purchasers that the eve of the Assumption seemed to be something of a bumper day for reaching the end of the Book of Revelation, and the secret was exposed.

It was at Haarlem too that the first of the great open-air meetings took place which played such a notable part in bringing the Reformation to Holland. Tens of thousands of men and women flocked on foot, on horseback, or by boat from the surrounding towns to a meadow on the edge of the city where Peter Gabriel was to preach. In vain the authorities locked the gates, for in their enthusiasm the Haarlemmers scaled over the city walls and swam across the moat. The preacher was 'a little, meagre man, who looked as if he might rather melt away beneath the blazing sunshine of July than hold the multitude enchained four uninterrupted hours long, by the magic of his tongue' as he preached on his text from Ephesians, '*For by grace ye are saved, through faith . . .* ' but his eloquence was the beginning of a popular movement which in the case of Haarlem was to lead to tragedy. Gabriel's sermon was delivered in 1566; six years later the terrible siege of Haarlem began, a siege which had a very different outcome from that of Leiden which was shortly to follow.

By the time the Spaniards began the investment of Haarlem the Netherlands had already been the scene of such wholesale butcheries as those of Zutphen and Naarden, where Alva had tortured and murdered almost the entire population. It was therefore natural enough that wild hatred fired both besieged and besiegers alike to heights of savagery hitherto almost unknown even to the Spaniards. Prisoners were hanged by the feet in full view of the people of the city, who retaliated by hurling the heads and mutilated corpses of their captured enemies into the Spanish lines. Even the women joined in the active fighting, and a band of three hundred of them armed with sword and musket and dagger was engaged in some of the most ferocious of the actions outside the walls. Firebrands, blazing hoops soaked in pitch, broken statues from the Catholic altars, every conceivable missile was hurled in the faces of the Spaniards with such effect that twelve thousand of them were slain before the walls. It was in vain however that the citizens erected a huge grave upon the ramparts, topped with the banner 'Haarlem is the Spaniards' graveyard'. The forces sent to relieve the city were routed, and when Don Frederic, the Duke of Alva's son, eventually promised to put an end to the starvation and misery by granting a pardon, the city elected to surrender. Don Frederic achieved its submission only by a solemn assurance that there would be no reprisals, but even when he pledged his word he was under orders from his father to execute the entire garrison. This he at once proceeded to do, and the Duke himself came to Haarlem to see that the work was carried out. More than two thousand of the citizens were butchered before his five executioners became so exhausted with their work that there was nothing left but to take the remainder, tie them back to back, and throw them to drown in the lake where today the fertile meadows are cropped by the sleek fat cattle. Don Frederic was evidently quite a gentleman however, for he gave a polite undertaking that women actually in labour would not be raped. A piece of lace was to be hung on the door of any house where such exemption could be claimed, and even today the passover custom just occasionally still persists here and there of hanging a strip of lacework outside the door when a newborn baby is shortly expected, or has just entered upon his life as a Haarlemer of a later and less brutal age. At least, that is the explanation sometimes offered for this rather attractive usage, but others believe the custom merely to be a request to reduce the noise of traffic; they suggest that the alternative explanation endows Don Frederic with qualities which lack confirmation elsewhere. Nevertheless the Spaniards were not always unkind; Motley recorded that pregnant women were allowed to be tortured sitting instead of lying.

Through Haarlem the Spaarne leads northwards out to Spaarndam lock. Spaarndam is not a place of any intrinsic beauty, but it has two claims to fame. On the one hand it was the place of the famous exploit of Pieter, the boy who saved the dyke — though whether in fact Pieter ever existed is perhaps another matter, even if a very handsome statue of him is to be found in the village. The other more certain fact is that the lock at Spaarndam is a descendant of the very first lock in the whole of Europe.

A publication of British Transport Waterways states that 'the ancient Egyptians were among the pioneers of canal construction and by 2000 B.C. had not only built canals of considerable size but *had devised a workable lock system*'. What the historical authority for this statement is I do not know, but we are on surer ground in recognizing that in the third century B.C. the Chinese used sluice-gates of a vertical lifting type for navigation both on rivers and on artificial canals. There was however still no lock chamber, and a whole reach had to be drained down for a boat to pass under a gate, and the boatman had then to wait until the water had made up again before he could proceed. In Europe, lifting sluices on the principle of the Chinese system are shown in an illustration in an Italian treatise of the fifteenth century, and single gates were certainly in use at Bruges as early as 1180.

The first records of genuine lock pens with gates at either end seems to have been about A.D. 825, when such structures were in use in China. Similar pen locks, with paddle sluices to let out the water, were built by Filippo Visconti of Milan from 1440 onwards and the Venetians were also using canal locks at about the same time. Yet the lock at Spaarndam certainly goes back considerably further, and as the *Commodore* is unlikely ever to penetrate as far afield as the canals of China the Spaarndam lock must be allowed to have the longest history of any that she will ever pass.

In his 'Tractaet van Dyckagie' or Manual of Dykage, the six-teenth century Dutch engineer Andries Vierlingh describes in exact detail how the lock at Spaarndam was *reconstructed* in 1567 at a cost of '950 pounds of each 40 Flemish groots', and was equipped with three pairs of mitred gates, the centre pair being for use when one of the others was under repair. The pen measured 121 ft. by 24 ft. and there was a drawbridge over the top of the lock — just as there is today. But a structure of the same breadth is mentioned as early as 1253 'to provide a channel through which the laden sea ships might pass to Sparrendamme and the neighbourhood'. This was probably already a proper lock, but we know for certain that after the structure was broken down by the storm flood of 1277 it was rebuilt with three vertical lifting gates, so at least it is possible to say that there has definitely been a lock of normal modern type at Spaarndam for the best part of seven centuries, and very likely for more than seven hundred years.

The early locks led into a channel running into the now vanished Wijkermeer, but with the changes in the face of the Dutch countryside the modern counterpart leads out into a canal which crosses broad meadows of pasture and arable land. Passing through it in the *Commodore* we had only left the gates a few minutes astern of us when across a field where the reapers were piling the stooks of wheat we saw the superstructure and derricks of an astonishingly large ship, apparently gliding along a track which ran on the top of a dyke. In fact the ship was not on the bank but behind it, and she was a ten thousand tonner which had entered by the Ijmuiden locks on the North Sea coast and was now making her way up to Amsterdam along the Noordzee Kanaal, the ship canal into which we ourselves turned a minute or two later. The Noordersluis lock at Ijmuiden is the largest lock in the world — its length is more than 1300 ft. — and as the canal itself is more than a hundred yards from side to side there are not many ships which cannot reach Amsterdam if they wish to do so.

The position of Amsterdam on the inner side of the North Holland peninsula has made its use as a modern port dependent on artificial channels. Originally access was by the open waters of the Zuyder Zee (now sealed off to form the Ijsselmeer) and though deep in its outer approaches the southern end of this great inlet of the North Sea was always shallow. Northerly gales piled the sand and silt towards the shallow end and because of the proximity of the land such gales as might blow from the reverse direction could never restore the balance. The approaches to Amsterdam therefore became continually shallower until a stage was reached at which it was extremely difficult for a vessel to run down the length of the Zuyder Zee without being grounded when the tide turned before Amsterdam had been reached. As the years went by, the sands became more and more dangerous and the losses of shipping more frequent until in 1824 a ship canal fifty miles long was opened which led through the length of the peninsula to by-pass the entire coast of the Zuyder Zee and provide a direct inland route from the Texel roads to Amsterdam. The Zuyder Zee had by this time a depth of only eleven feet on the route to Amsterdam, but the North Holland Canal provided eighteen. Forty yards from side to side it was a remarkable piece of canal engineering and though much of its route passed through soft and marshy ground its construction was entirely successful.

At first sight it may seem strange that the Dutch chose to make the canal follow a winding course of fifty miles up to the north of the country instead of selecting the route towards the North Sea at Ijmuiden, which involved only a third of the distance. In fact a canal from Amsterdam to Ijmuiden was contemplated as early as 1629, but the countryside to the west of the city presented very difficult engineering problems. Most of it was occupied by the shallow Wijkermeer, and any alteration in the level of this lake would greatly have affected not only the drainage of the surrounding land but also the communications of the villages scattered around its edges. What with these difficulties, and the varying water level of the Zuyder Zee, which was connected to Lake Ij on which Amsterdam was situated, the idea of following the shorter route was rejected as quite impracticable and when the subject of a ship canal was later raised once more it was the North Holland route which was chosen.

The North Holland saved the position of Amsterdam as a port, but as cargo ships continued to increase in size it became clear by the middle of the nineteenth century that new provision would have to be made for them. To enlarge the existing canal was not altogether satisfactory, because its course led round many bends which would have needed entire reconstruction — in Alkmaar, for instance, there were two right-angle corners. Besides, for ships bound to anywhere but Scandinavia or Scotland the length of time involved in passing fifty miles of canal which led away from the actual direction of voyage was a serious disadvantage and put Amsterdam in an unfavourable situation compared with ports more conveniently placed. When all these various factors were considered together it was decided to cut a new and larger canal across the Wijkermeer route, for it was clear that the advantages should outweigh the very real difficulties of construction. This choice was certainly a wise one.

The Amsterdam Ship Canal follows an almost straight line, and its construction involved dredging a deep channel through more than ten miles of the lake and depositing the dredgings out to either side by means of long floating tubes to form banks. The banks were then strengthened with mattresses of brushwood and faced with stone, and the remainder of the lake was pumped out into the canal. Branch canals had of course to be cut through to Spaarndam and to other places, but the amount of land reclaimed for cultivation by draining the Wijkermeer was more than 14,000 acres, and the company covered nearly a third of the whole cost of the construction of the canal by selling the new land behind the banks. The Zuyder Zee was shut off by a great dyke nearly a mile long and provided with locks (the Orange Locks) to connect it with the harbour and the ship canal, and an unusual feature of this undertaking was that the enclosure had to be done without interrupting even for a day the considerable flow of sailing barges and steamers trading between Amsterdam and the Zuyder Zee ports or Friesland. This was achieved by building the locks inside a temporary dam, so that when the dyke was ready for closure they could at once be put into service.

The locks at Ijmuiden as well as the Orange Locks had to have double sets of gates, because at certain states of the tide the canal was lower than the level of the sea, and at other times higher. The level of the canal had in fact to be very carefully planned, as it was to be the main channel into which the water of the Ringvaart was discharged, and it also served to drain the land to the northward. From the new canal this drainage water was to be voided into the Zuyder Zee by three pumps on the dyke, which were later supplemented by a fourth, and by a sluice at Ijmuiden which was opened whenever the tide was sufficiently low for the water to flow out. Up to 6,000,000 tons of water could be voided in a day by the pumps at the Amsterdam end of the canal, and this proved sufficient to prevent flooding.

There were difficulties at Ijmuiden too, for the west coast of Holland is one against which sand is continually piled up in shoals and ridges of dunes by the action of the waves driven before the dominant south-westerly wind. Piers a mile long were built out into the sea, but there was trouble with the current washing away the sand from under the foundations and a wave-breaker had to be added outside each pier, consisting of a mass of concrete blocks tumbled into the water. But it is surprising how powerful the sea can be, and how great a mass can be moved by storm waves. Even when the weight of the blocks at Ijmuiden was increased to twenty tons apiece they were still shifted out of position in a heavy sea, and though chaining them together was tried it could not entirely prevent movement. Maintenance of the breakwaters and dredging the channel between the piers to the extent of some two thousand cubic yards of sand every day has had to be carried out continually right up to the present, yet in spite of these costs the canal has been so successful that it has already had to be enlarged several times.

However ugly or sordid a port may be it cannot help being attractive when experienced in a small boat. Boulogne, Calais, even Dunkirk has a fascination undreamed of by those who snatch a cup of coffee at the Gare Maritime or wait impatiently whilst a port officer tries to discover a number stamped on the cylinder block of their car. But Amsterdam is quite in a class by itself. The entry, whether from the Noordzee Kanaal or the Kostverlorenvaart, leads into a broad *vaarweg* (or fairway, as the Dutch word is anglicized) called the Afgesloten Ij, on one side of which are ranged the dry docks and slipways and cargo quays, and on the other the barge quays of the port. Here on the port side are the yacht harbours too, and though yacht clubs in Holland as in most countries are extremely hospitable to visitors from abroad we never put in there. We preferred to penetrate right into the vast complex of medieval canals which has no equal anywhere in the world. How many canals there are in Amsterdam I would hardly like to estimate, but there are certainly more than four hundred bridges, of which perhaps half are old-fashioned fixed arches of great beauty but too low for the *Commodore* to slip underneath them. There are newer bridges too of equally restricted height, but certain canals are equipped with lifting bridges to pass the tugs and barges into the Amstel — the river which runs into the city from the south, and which provides it with the name, which may once have been written *Amstelerdamme*.

Quite sizeable boats can reach the Amstel provided that they follow a route such as that of the Nieuwe Heerengracht, where every bridge will swing or tip or turn, but progress is slow. Every hundred yards or so a ship must wait until the bridge-keeper judges that the time has come to interrupt the flow of cars and trucks and countless bicycles, and apart from waiting a boat will be required to pay. The *brugwachter* has a fishing-rod from which dangles a line ending in a child's wooden clog, and with years of practice behind him he can lean out of his window and swing the shoe right into the hand of the skipper of an approaching craft, who has then to take out a ticket from the toe and in its place put twenty-five cents, a *quartje* of *bruggeld*. The fee is certainly not expensive, but being economical by nature we decided to try to penetrate into the centre without payment, and after repeated visits we eventually discovered a route along which all the bridges had just sufficient headroom for us to squeeze underneath with the mast down, provided the *Commodore* was riding perfectly level and there was no slop from garbage lighters or water buses just as she was half way through.

The railway station of Amsterdam is built on piles, right in the water of the Afgesloten Ij, and as the size of the ships using the harbour rules out the possibility of a bridge to connect with the newer portion of the city on the other side, no less than twenty jetties stick out from the station like bristles and from among them a continual flow of ferries runs backwards and forwards across the water. At the same time the ships bound to and from Ijmuiden thrash past at right angles, and the processions of barges arriving from the Zuyder Zee or the Amsterdam-Rhine Canal, or bound for Zaandam and North Holland, come pounding through in the opposite direction. To this bustling assortment of shipping are added passenger steamers, craft with cadets in training, dredgers, water-carriers, harbour launches, fuelling craft, pilot boats, gun boats, muck boats, tug boats, bum boats and just mere boats, with the result that the Afgesloten Ij has something of the nature of an aquatic Hyde Park Corner at rush hour, but without either rule of the road or one-way traffic.

We always enjoyed every moment of this bustling approach. Taking whatever chances offered we edged gradually through towards the station side of the Ij and began to count. A bridge —

no, that one only led through to the Prinsengracht, where the headroom was too restricted. One jetty, two jetties. Warships with an
unusual flag, lying alongside, and sailors with nothing to do.
Argentinians! Were they on a courtesy visit, or just delivering the
ships for scrap? From the rusty appearance of parts of the superstructure it was not easy to decide. Three, four, five jetties, packed
with the fuelling boats of the great oil companies, and then . . . Ah!
Here was a cut leading off to dive through under the railway girders and the clanking tram-bridge beyond. No, this was not the
one we wanted; it led through to the Singel and the canals of the
old city but somewhere ahead it was crossed by low fixed bridges,
ten of them in succession. More jetties, thirteen in a row, and car
ferries playing 'touch wood'. Carefully now, Carefully. . . . Where
had that tug suddenly appeared from? It seemed to have come out
from under the end of the station. Indeed it had, and that was our
own way too.

'*Naam!*' A voice boomed through a megaphone, and looking up
we saw a man in a braided cap leaning out of a broad window in a
turret beside the railway bridge. Surely he could see the name for
himself, painted on the bows.

'*Commodorrr-re,*' we called up, through the filler funnel of the
fuel tank, which served as an improvised loud-hailer.

'*Schippers naam?*' And then '*Tonnemaat?*'

'*Vijftien,*' we yelled against the roar of an express and two goods
trains crashing across the girders of the bridge just ahead of the
bows. There would not be anything to pay if we had come by the
Ringvaart, for the twopenny harbour toll had already been levied
at the Nieuwe Meer lock, and so fifteen was a safe figure.

'*Dank U.*' He waved us on into the bridge hole.

There were half a dozen craft coming up astern, but we stopped
in our tracks nevertheless. Not more than six inches of headroom
here, even with the mast laid back flat, and until there was a short
interval in the wash of the tugs we could not run under the bridge
without a risk of being tossed up on to the girders. Then in a
momentary break when the water was calm enough, we shot
quickly into the arch, hoping to reach the other side before another
trip boat would heave the water into a bouncing commotion again.

'Sit her level. Crouch down, everybody. That's it — we're through now.'

One long blast and two short ones to warn any craft coming round the blind corner, and we wheeled a sharp angle to the left under a narrow bascule bridge into the broad water of the Oosterdok. It was quiet here, with hardly a boat on the move. A fine old wooden man-of-war lay round to the right and a quarter of a mile ahead lay the Admiralty with its creeper-clad watch-house and the anemometer spinning slowly on its graceful turret. Four more jetties on our right, and then a turn under the fixed bridge of the Prins Hendrikskade. A long, low bridge, this one — more like a tunnel.

'Kneel down. Only three inches under this one.'

Now we were in the Oude Schans, the loveliest canal imaginable. On either side the tall thin houses rose up, each with a gable unlike any of its neighbours and bearing a hook or a short girder for the hoisting block. Some had windows all down the front but a few were warehouses, just as they had been for three centuries, and each floor carried a pair of heavy dark green or black wooden doors which could be thrown back to admit the sacks of flour or bales of merchandise unloaded from the barges or from lorries on the cobbled half-street flanking the water. Along either bank there were vistas beneath the arches where the quays humped up to cross the entrance to one lovely canal after another, each with its rows of gables, straight, hipped, renaissance, severe, baroque, with here and there an extravagance of cherubs or the more practical carving of a sheep or some other creature which once had served as the trading sign of the merchant family which had lived there.

A quarter of a mile up, past five of these delightful and tempting waterways, we came to the narrows of the Sint Anthonie lock. It was open right through — except sometimes on Sundays — and the chains lay slackly wound around the drums of the windlasses with their long thin yellow wooden spokes projecting at right angles. A simple system this, but effective enough. The gates could be hauled open by the chains and closed by heavy wooden shafts from the tips of which more chains led to the same drums. Practical but very beautiful, and so too was the little house of the toll collector

leaning precariously towards the lock as though tired after the centuries of watching the ships creep slowly by beneath.

The next bridge, over the end of the lock, was the lowest of all, but we still had an inch to spare over the top of the chimney of the stove. Beyond it the canal metamorphosed into the Zwanenburgergracht, and here on the left was a pretty building of narrow bricks, greying red. Rembrandt's house this was, from the days before he died in poverty, almost unrecognized by those who had commissioned the works which now drew thousands to the Rijksmuseum seven bridges ahead of us through the maze of waterways.

Only one more bridge now lay between ourselves and the Amstel, but this particular bridge was always a favourite of ours. It was not of any particular architectural merit, a broad span of Victorian iron work neither beautiful nor ugly, but on its underside the H-girders were so placed that they scooped a quantity of coal from every overladen lighter and kept it there ready to hand. It seemed reasonable to reward the *Commodore* in some way on her arrival in the

centre of the city and so we would always ease off under the bridge
by the Staalstraat and fill a bucket for her central heating before
gliding out into the broad water of the Amstel beyond. Then we
had but to turn right, and right again, and bring her gently in beneath the trees alongside a narrow cobbled quay. This was the
Groenburggracht, and close ahead of her bows rose up the tall
yellow wooden arch which supported the bascule of the loveliest of
all the hundreds of bridges in the water city, the Gelbe Brug. Beyond it, overtopping the trees, the square tower of the Zuiderkerk
ended in a belfry of openwork and storeyed dome, and as though to
welcome us to their dreamy canal the bells burst into chime.

> *Ik verhef myn toon in 't zingen*
> *aan den Amstel en het Ij*
> *Op den geest van Hemony. . . .*

Vondel's lines could themselves have fitted the rhythm of the
chiming, and these particular bells were indeed cast by the Hemony
brothers whose lovely carillons still ring over the low countries
after three centuries of song.

> *I uplift my voice in song*
> *By the Amstel and the Ij*
> *To the praise of Hemony.*

Of the six carillons which peal across the rooftops and along the
water channels of Amsterdam five are sets of Hemony bells and
only that of the Rijksmuseum is by van den Gheyn. The Hemonys
began as cannon founders in Zutphen and it was there that they
constructed their first carillon in 1645, for the tower of the local
wine-house. That set of bells has now been replaced by a more
modern one cast by Taylors of Loughborough, but across Belgium
and Holland there are many Hemony carillons still ringing today.
The carillon of Antwerp cathedral, the famous belfry of Ghent, the
Eglise Collégiale de Notre Dame at Huy-sur-Meuse and the
chimes of Europe's most magnificent tower at Mechelen (Malines)
— these were only a few of the Hemony bells in the sound of which
the *Commodore* had lain at night on earlier voyages, dreaming amid
the perfection of their music.

L

For carillon playing 'a musician requires nothing more than a thorough knowledge of music, good hands and feet, and no gout'. So said a Dutch writer in the eighteenth century, and he was no doubt right to the extent that the keys are either struck with the fist or stamped upon with the foot. In fact the astonishingly ethereal quality of the sound depends less on the manipulator (which is usually a clockwork musical box mechanism) than on the position of the bells, the atmospheric conditions of the moment, and the absence of traffic in the street below. It might not be unfair to add that the absence of other carillons playing other folk tunes in opposing keys can be helpful too, because in Amsterdam this condition is lacking. No sooner had the first notes drifted down to us through the leaves from the Zuiderkerk than the bells of the Munt tower across the Amstel broke in, and one could just detect in the background the tones of yet a third Hemony carillon — that of the Royal Palace on the Dam — adding to the confusion. Even on the still summer's evening when the carilloneur of the Zuiderkerk treated us to a concert, the Munt insisted on breaking into the harmony every fifteen minutes as though to remind us that it too could sing the praise of the Hemony brothers.

Immediately beyond the wooden pillars which held the counter-balance beam of the Gelbe Brug lay the quayside of the Christ Church, and the *Commodore* had not long been in the Groenburg-gracht before her arrival was noted by Mr Mossman both in his

capacity as chaplain to the Anglican congregation and as chaplain to the Missions to Seamen. He introduced himself, took our washing to be laundered on the church premises, and invited us in for a magnificent tea. We were later able in part to repay his kindness by procuring for him two hundred and forty-three revivalist hymn-books which once had been used in a college chapel, and shipping them out to his mission.

As spiritual descendants of those who had suffered under King James we should perhaps have tied up nearer to the other English-speaking church, the exquisite Church in the Begijnhof, now a part of the Church of Scotland but once the building in which Brewster and his companions worshipped, and where Johnson of Middel-burg was at one time the somewhat turbulent pastor — so unruly indeed that the Scrooby party were soon obliged to leave the church and find peace and quiet in Leiden. It is in this church that the stained glass window is to be found which shows John Robinson praying on the quayside of the Delfshaven before the departure of the *Speedwell*.

The curious thing about the Church in the Begijnhof is that it is *in the Begijnhof* or beguinage, for the Begijns are a Catholic sisterhood and the church was once in fact the chapel of the convent which surrounds it. In 1578 the chapel, then nearly two hundred years old, was taken from the sisterhood in the expropriations which followed the revolt against Spain, and it became a Protestant church in much the same way that parish churches in England were transmuted at the time of the rejection of the papacy by Henry VIII. When however the English nonconformist refugees began to reach Amsterdam they constituted a Church without a church and the hospitable Dutch Protestants, deciding to remedy the matter by supplying them with a building for worship, presented the Begijnhof's chapel to their English friends.

Although the chapel was taken from the Begijns, the fine sisters of that excellent charitable order were not molested and they continued to occupy their little houses which formed the surrounding courtyard, though they were obliged to celebrate mass in their refectory. Three and a half centuries later this curious situation remains virtually unaltered. The Protestants have not sought to eject the nuns, nor have the Begijns tried to recover their chapel — even though the pious Sister Cornelia begged to be buried outside its north wall, where the rainwater would fall on her grave as a perpetual reminder of her grief that heretics were now in possession. The Protestants generously disregarded her wishes and allowed her a tomb inside the church, but it is said that three times the grave opened during the night and the coffin emerged as though trying to escape from the now heretical premises. Only when in despair the authorities finally buried her where she had requested did she lie in peace. Though this story relates to the seventeenth century, the Begijns are still in existence just as they are at Ghent, and when we crossed the cobbles of the little courtyard towards the morning service and found ourselves mingling with nuns who were bound for the mass in the dining-hall opposite the door, we almost felt that we should apologize that we were to hear the preaching of a Scottish minister in the lovely building which by rights was perhaps really theirs.

If we remained true to Free Church traditions in the morning, we always attended Mr Mossman's church for an evening which began with evensong and ended only shortly before midnight. Both the Church of England and the Begijnhof church had such overflowing congregations that those who arrived only a few minutes before the start of the service had either to stand at the back or wedge themselves in round the walls as best they could, and it surprised us to discover that nearly all of the vast congregation was Dutch, and not just made up of visitors from Britain or the United States. There were several reasons for this popularity, and one no doubt was that church-going in Holland still has a much wider hold on the people of the cities than in some other lands, but besides this the two English-speaking churches had particular attractions of their own. At the Church of Scotland one could be sure of a weighty and reasoned exegetical discourse such as was rarely met with elsewhere, whilst at the English Church the service was free from the still hated popery of Catholicism and yet at the same time was in a form not so severely bereft of beauty and symbol as the rather bleak style of worship of the Dutch Reformed Church. Another reason was certainly the great affection of the Dutch people for all things

English (and Scottish), but there was also a very practical consideration. The majority of either congregation was by no means elderly, and Mr Mossman told us that many of those who attended the Christ Church in the Groenburgwal had told him quite frankly that they did so partly in order to increase their fluency in English. Some had picked up the language from B.B.C. wartime broadcasts, others had learned it in school, and in the church they now had an opportunity of hearing the language well spoken, and of joining together in hymns and prayers in the same tongue. A hymnbook might not always be the best guide to modern English usage, but at least one could see the spelling of the words both there and in the Bible and Prayer Book, and one could hear them pronounced in faultless fashion — in English diction and not in American.

Sunday evening at the Groenburgwal was a most hospitable affair. It began with evensong and then proceeded upstairs to coffee and a snack on the top floor. This was followed by the B.B.C. 'Sunday Half Hour' programme which was then broadcast somewhat earlier in the evening than it is now, and as each hymn was announced on the wireless it was hurriedly turned up in the indexes of the miscellany of hymnbooks available. When the B.B.C. had finished it was open to anybody to nominate his favourite hymn, and those present would sing in whatever language they chose. Finally, late at night there was a service of family prayers in the church itself.

One Sunday night the congregation was swelled by a busload of Methodists from a church in Wales, and naturally enough they had brought their own hymnbooks and tune books, in fact everything but their own church organ. They had a minister too, who led the singing with all the determined charm of a conductor on the last night of the Proms, and as good Welshmen know very well indeed what are their favourite hymns the party invariably brought out one request after another before the more retiring Dutch and English had so much as drawn breath to make a suggestion. They insisted too that a hymn was not really a hymn at all unless sung in Welsh, and that we were all to sing it as they did. It did not matter in the least, they pointed out, if nobody but themselves knew either the words or the tune. Everybody was welcome to share their Welsh hymnbooks, and just sing — in Welsh.

I have never been to a service in which hymnbooks are handed round printed in Chinese characters, but I would not imagine that they could be appreciably more difficult to follow. Of course we knew well enough how far down a verse of Ton-y-botl or Cwm Rhondda the Welsh had got, but before we had even begun to decide how to tackle the conglomeration of consonants which formed the next word they would already be a line further on. 'Come on, man,' the minister would whisper between the verses. 'Just sing it as it's written.' And if in despair we lapsed into bashful English he would stop and look at us so reproachfully for spoiling the pure sound of his own language that we had not the heart to continue.

Amsterdam must be as lovely a city as any in the world, and unlike Brussels it has escaped wholesale destruction at the hands of property syndicates and entrepreneurs. Though now for the most part occupied by offices, the Renaissance houses of the wealthy merchants along the Keizersgracht, Prinsengracht and Heerengracht cannot be very different from what they were centuries ago, and though the oil engine has ousted the horse and the man with a pole, the traffic still drifts through the hipped arches of the stone bridges much as it must have done when first the spider's web of waterways was built. If the fame of the beauty of these canals has spread far and wide it is certainly not unmerited, but even without them the city would not be entirely devoid of loveliness, for the Dutch genius for beauty is seen at work in one street after another — though not perhaps in the Leidse Plein.

I do not intend to describe the famous façades of the Heerengracht, nor even to mention the many notable architectural gems which stand so beautifully preserved that one cannot always distinguish a building of the nineteen-fifties from one three centuries older. Every visitor will discover the Singel, the gently curving canal by the Munt tower along the quays of which the barges of the florists lie laden with colour, and where lilac bushes and camellias from Aalsmeer bloom in holds filled with peat. Few can visit the city without at least a short visit to the astonishing wealth of pictures in the Rijksmuseum, where every other canvas is familiar from reproductions and where one can see how Vermeer overcame the difficult problem of portraying a glass window by the simple but correct expedient of painting the panes in black. There are the Rembrandts and the Dous too, the bustling crowds of Breughel, and the stern portraits of protestant deacons and councillors, but all these treasures are already well known. Less famous perhaps is an establishment to which a few visitors manage with difficulty to find their way — the Wild Man, a most delightful sampling room belonging to the Wijnand Fockink establishment which surrounds it. No ale is served there, nor any of the dreadful bastard drinks of English clubs and bars, but only the soft syrupy liqueurs of which more than eighty are distilled by the firm. Around the walls are ranged the bulbous glass flagons and carboys in which in earlier centuries these same liquors were stored. Dark, slightly eccentric in shape but beautifully wrought, almost every one of them would be a collector's prize. And so would the liqueurs.

It was a Dutch friend of ours who introduced us to the Wild Man, and one evening he led us to a Mah Jong den. To us Mah Jong was nothing but a gentle and somewhat suburban game associated with respectable drawing-rooms and a leisurely cup of tea, but to the Chinese stokers and deck-hands from the harbour the same thing was a gambling medium, a kind of poker played with bulky bamboo and ivory cards at a speed which would have made a demon-racing expert look like a snail-watcher. We never succeeded on later visits in finding again the door in the wall which led to the mysterious basement which Piet had discovered in his search for interesting characters to draw, but the place was considered to be a café and so it contained four bare tables, three of which were provided with chairs. At one of these we sat down with Piet, whilst at the other two the sport was in full swing. In a matter of seconds the walls would be built up and the tiles taken in rotation by the players, and then there followed a machine-gun rattle as the characters were flung down on the table in lightning succession until the hand had been played out and the cash was passing across the table. And all the while the Chinamen spoke hardly a word. They just played endlessly on, swiftly but with impassive faces and with no attention for anyone or anything but the game.

The fourth table was the kitchen, on which the proprietor, a heavy half-caste Chinaman, endlessly prepared the only dish which his repertoire provided. To do so he emptied on the table a pail of dough and then took up a thin wooden roller four or five feet in length. One end of this he placed under a brass rail fixed to the wall above the side of the table opposite to him, and the other he placed between his legs. Then, springing rapidly from side to side, he swivelled the rod to and fro across the table, half crouching on the end of his roller as he squeezed out the dough until he had fashioned a square yard or more of dull white pancake. This he then cut up and fried in a syrupy fluid, and served to his customers with treacly coffee or China tea.

At that time Piet lived in a rickety house which overlooked the Zwanenburgergracht just beside the last bridge under which we had passed before reaching the Amstel. From the outside it was just one of many houses tilted slightly to one side by the shrinkage of the ground beneath, and it happened to lack an attic gable because the top floor had already decayed and had been removed. Two cheerful boxes at the second-floor windows twinkled with bright geraniums and behind them Piet's *Ficus elasticus* stood looking out through the broad panes. It was not a distinguished house in appearance, but when we had climbed the stairs to the small studio and sitting-room of the rather cramped flat in which Piet lived we found that beneath its very ordinary appearance there lay the memory of an adventure which had necessarily been known only to very few.

Modestly enough, and almost as though it had been a piece of schoolboy naughtiness, Piet told us of the secret which had lain hidden inside the wall. At the time of the German occupation he was hardly more than a lad, but he shared with many of his countrymen that same characteristic inherited determination to aid those fleeing from persecution, a desire which first arose during the great struggle against Alva in the sixteenth century. Certainly Piet was only one of thousands who came to the help of those who were being hunted down for the furnaces at Auschwitz, from which the gruesome sacks of potash fertilizer manufactured from the burned and powdered bones of Jews were distributed to farmers and market gardeners, but it was a courageous act to take into such confined premises as his two-roomed flat on the top floor a middle-aged Jew, and to hold him hidden there through month upon month of watching and searching by the Gestapo.

Piet was not without ingenuity, and he cut a cavity inside the wall of his studio, with access to it from up inside the chimney. It could not have been a very small cavity either, for Hans the German Jew was not exactly slim, but it had to be as small as his middle-aged proportions would allow. Into this hiding-place Hans was hastily stuffed whenever a knocking at the street door suggested a danger that was only too real, for on several occasions the Gestapo men raided the house under the firm and correct belief that somebody was being hidden there. By the time they had reached the top of the stairs Hans had been swiftly disposed of, and Piet himself would be alone at his work, mixing the paints on his palette whilst wondering fearfully whether every conceivable tell-tale trace of the dual occupation of the room had been obliterated.

It was of course the most natural thing in the world for an artist to be found mixing his paints, and the Gestapo men never once realized that in this lay the clue to what they were seeking. They examined every inch of the room, they pulled up the floorboards, and still not satisfied they began to sound out the walls for cavities by systematic thumping on the plaster. Yet Piet had foreseen that they would do so, and for that very reason he had hung an unfinished canvas directly covering the tell-tale hollow, because he rightly guessed that the searchers would not actually thump on the picture — particularly if he was at work upon it and the paint was wet. Time and again his sinister visitors tried to take him by surprise, but always Piet was seated at the window, sketching the view through the tree tops towards the scrap-barges on the Oude Schans below, or adding just a few more brush-strokes to the oil painting which hung, still not quite finished, on the wall inside which Hans the Jew crouched fearfully, wondering perhaps whether the faint beating of his heart might not be heard through the lath and plaster.

It is almost incredible that humans should have had the strength to endure the sheer tension of what took place in thousands of homes throughout Europe during those years, and to have lived through a terror which in other countries than Holland may still be continuing today. What Piet's feelings must have been during those long-drawn-out searches we could not begin to imagine from any experiences of our own. 'Of course I was frightened,' he said. 'So frightened that I could hardly think. But drawing gave me something to do while they were thumping on the walls, and it seemed to help me to keep quite calm.'

Later, Piet's activities became so suspect that he had to disappear. He 'dived' — that is, he lived a hunted life in mobile hiding — and some of his time was spent in painting the favourite horses of country farmers, who gave him food and shelter in return. Then at last came the astonishing, unforgettable day when he stood with others like himself on the ridge of a dyke, waving deliriously as the hundreds upon hundreds of heavy United States planes came gliding low over the land to open their bomb doors and drop not bombs this time, but a rain of canisters and crates of food for the starving people of the cities. In the roadway below the bank the German soldiers stood armed but bewildered and dejected, hesitantly offering when the last line of the planes had roared overhead to obey the orders of the hunted Dutch youths and girls and to help them as they hurdled across the ditches and meadows to gather in the food so desperately needed.

Somewhere in Amsterdam Hans the Jew too came out of the cache in which he had been hidden by others, and not long afterwards he emigrated to America, taking with him what little was left of his share of the fortunes of those of his relatives who had been unwise enough to convince themselves that Hitler would never invade Holland, or that if he did so he would surely not exterminate people for no other reason than that they happened to be Jewish.

X

Departure from Amsterdam — Terrors of the past — A run
by moonlight — The Commodore *explores the land —*
Consideration for underwriters — A useful post — Marken's
fate — A disappearing community — Edam

The Lake Flevo known to the Romans no longer exists. In the
year 1283 a storm smashed the coastline beyond its northern
edge and joined it to the North Sea to form a bay, the Zuyder Zee,
fringed on the outside by the row of sandbanks known as the West
Frisian Islands, and at the same time drowning scores of Frisian
hamlets. The Zuyder Zee survived for more than six centuries, but
it too vanished when the Dutch engineers closed the final gap in
the twenty-mile Afsluitdijk on 28th May 1932. Its disappearance at
that moment was in a sense technical only, but the sheet of water
within the dyke became known by the new name of the Ijsselmeer,
and since that date the salt water has been diluted by the drainage
of the surrounding land and by the continual inpouring of Rhine
water through the Geldersche Ijssel until today the lake is entirely
a freshwater one.

The Ijsselmeer itself is doomed to partial disappearance, for substantial areas have already been enclosed and reclaimed, and more is to vanish in the very near future. And among the features of the Ijssel Lake which no longer exist is the famous island of Marken. It has not sunk, like a possible Atlantis, nor disintegrated like Krakatoa. As late as the summer of 1957 it was still an island separated from the mainland by the waters of the Gouw Zee; but only just, for in October of that year it finally lost its intriguing insularity and was joined to the land of North Holland. I am unrepentant in regretting this, because however much the little island was exploited by the tourist trade I still think it was a place of great beauty, and once it can be approached by road instead of by water alone it will inevitably lose its charm. Marken is almost certain to become another Vollendam, for that village is as banal and horrid as Marken is (or was) delightful.

We had visited Marken by *Commodore* on several earlier occasions, and perhaps on that June evening in 1956 we would not have thought of calling there again but for the fact that we knew that this would be our last chance to see it as an island. And so, after two circuits of the unique collection of Rembrandts which had been brought to the Rijksmuseum from all over the world in celebration either of the three hundred and fiftieth anniversary of the painter's birth or perhaps of the tercentenary of his bankruptcy, and after two visits to the Wild Man — a building which dates from only twenty years after Rembrandt's death — we decided that rather than spend the night in the Groenburggracht we would move on to Marken. The island was only some twelve miles beyond the Orange Locks, and although already the sun was going down we could be confident that we should be there by midnight.

'The navigation of the Zuyder Zee is really both perilous and difficult. . . . We are struck with the configuration of the numerous sandbanks spreading in all directions, leaving between them narrow passages scarcely practicable for even a small embarkation. By the side of a narrow channel from ten to twenty feet deep, we see placed an enormous sand-bank covered with one, two, or three feet of water; the slightest false manoeuvre, a mere false turn of the tiller, a sudden gust of wind, and we are on the bank, when probably all is lost. The terrible tales of shipwreck abound in every page of the history of the Zuyder Zee, and in default of written history or verbal anecdote the great carcasses of ships, black and sinister monuments of perils past, silently but surely breaking up or rotting away, sufficiently call to our minds the dangers of this modern sea.' This information, sufficiently dismal to be a quotation from a modern Admiralty Pilot Book, is taken from the account of M. Henri Havard, who travelled on these waters in the 1860's. Had we read his account before experiencing the Ijsselmeer for ourselves we might perhaps have been discouraged, though of course it is the fashion for travellers to make the most of the slightest swell or the faintest breeze when setting down their journeys for others to read. The same, I am sorry to say, is often true of aquatic authors, and if I regret the common tendency to false heroics it is because many people will probably believe the stories and be discouraged from undertaking a similar journey for themselves.

I have read a modern book which describes the sheer terror of mooring on a barge in the nine-knot flow of the Seine below Rouen and yet this stream, which can perhaps achieve a little more than three knots on the outer edge of the sharpest bends at the very height of the downflow of equinoctial springs, is in reality a tame enough river from the navigational point of view though beautiful from any other. Hairbreadth escapes from thirty-foot waves are common enough reading in accounts of voyages on areas of water concerning which a little application of mathematical formulae will show that the largest possible wave would be an eight-footer, and even that could only be raised by a hurricane — which is a phenomenon unknown in the area. I sometimes wonder whether this longing to have bigger waves and stronger tidal streams than any previous yachtsman-author may not have its effect in making many owners of sound little ships unnecessarily nervous. On an afternoon of perfect calm I have seen a man fire distress signals within two hundred yards of Ramsgate harbour entrance instead of dropping anchor and spending a few moments investigating why the engine had stopped. At least nine people out of ten appear to think that to cross the Channel in anything smaller than the *Côte d'Azur* or the *Invicta* is about as dangerous as attempting the North-West Passage in a dinghy, whereas in reality it may be much safer (and certainly more enjoyable) than to drive from London to Hatfield on A 1. I have only once seen a yacht in difficulty in the Channel — and even then it was nothing but foolishness which had brought the situation about — whereas I can rarely drive northward from Highgate without coming within the first few miles upon the wreckage of cars in which very often people have been killed — probably also through foolishness.

We knew the way to Marken well enough. We had reached it before from Edam, from Amsterdam, and from the mouth of the River Vecht at Muiden, where the fine turreted castle stands which once had guarded the entrance to the river and which later became famous as the place where the Dutch writer Hooft gathered around him a circle of men of great intellect and ability, including Christian Huygens, the Fellow of the Royal Society who discovered the rings of Saturn with a telescope of his own construction. We had in fact already made a previous night voyage from Amsterdam to Marken, so there was nothing particularly hazardous about the undertaking. Besides, as we knew that the Dutch were continually enclosing new areas of the Ijsselmeer we did not intend to rely on our old chart but had procured one officially corrected up to twelve weeks before that very day. On this chart some chunks of new dyke were indeed marked in pencil, but they were right out in the middle of the lake and in the Marken and Gouw Zee area all appeared to be just as usual.

In the Afgesloten Ij the rush of traffic was already stilled, and only an occasional barge came plodding down the fairway from the corner where the broad Amsterdam-Rhine canal led into the harbour. We headed up the fairway to the Orange Locks, and soon we were pulling out of them again behind a pair of privateer barges into the Buiten Ij, the once tidal outer harbour of Amsterdam. Half a mile down the entrance channel the barges drew off to the side and we heard their anchors splash and the chains run out noisily over the cleats. A few others already lay at anchor, and we vaguely wondered why they were missing the opportunity of carrying ahead on their voyage when the weather was so sweet and calm. Dutch bargemasters were not usually inclined to waste much time in sleeping, and so we decided that perhaps they had business in the neighbourhood. We left them astern, ran down a mile or more to the entrance lights, and then turned slightly to port to hold in line behind us the two leading lights which marked the passage through the forest of stakes supporting an entanglement of nets, which provided the city smokeries with much of their daily quota of eels.

We did not make for Marken on a compass course. There was indeed no need to, for if we held the leading lights astern for perhaps twenty minutes we should then cross a path where two more lights were in line, that of Pampuseiland — a small fort a couple of miles off the southern shore — lying directly in front of the light marking the entrance to the Vecht at Muiden. We could already see both these useful beacons, and we knew that if we followed their combined line more or less due northward it would not be long before we saw the shine from the tall lighthouse situated on the right-hand corner of Marken. When within reasonable shooting distance of the island we would then see a flasher-buoy marking the entrance to the Gouw Zee channel, and we had only to run close to this mark and make down for the harbour.

It was a really beautiful night, calm and almost still, with just the faintest whisper of breeze under a clear starry sky, and with a cold white moon in the south-east. Nothing seemed to be moving on the waters. Away to our left we could see the lights of the villages on the shore, and on our port quarter the rosy sky-glow of the street lights and fluorescent signs of Amsterdam. We could not have picked a more peaceful hour for the run.

Everything went according to the book. We kept Pampus in line with Muiden, and sure enough within half an hour a broad intermittent flash in the sky ahead told us that the top of the Marken lighthouse was just about to lift above the curved surface of the watery earth. At midnight the island was fully in view, and a few lights were still twinkling gaily on the lamp-posts between the cottages no more than a couple of miles ahead. We turned a little to port, rounded the flashing buoy lying half a mile off the shore, and began to aim for the harbour entrance, the lights of which we could see quite distinctly some way ahead of us. We were nearing the end of our journey, and as for the 'black and sinister monuments of perils past' we had not seen a sign of a single one.

An American friend was with us at the time. He was a very competent steersman, and he was enjoying every moment of the run. He stood at the wheel, conscientiously following the course and just occasionally breaking the silence to say once again what a perfect night it was, and how lovely the village houses looked, shining dimly among the lights dotted about on the island. I was seated beside him, leaning back against the windshield in sweet contentment and gazing out astern to where the moon glistened in a broken shaft of diffuse light on the bubbling ripples of the wake which stretched away behind us to the southward. It was not only a comfortable position that I had chosen in which to take in the beauty of the night but it was a fortunate one, for after another minute or two of silence Fred spoke again.

'A funny long shadow that cloud makes on the water,' he said.

Facing the moon as I was, I could see that there was no cloud to cast a shadow, and jumping up I pulled the gear lever astern and pulled the throttle right back. The water came foaming from round the stern, but the *Commodore*'s unknown tonnage was sufficient to give **her** plenty of forward momentum and it was impossible that she could pull up completely. Quickly taking the wheel I spun it to turn her head half to port in order to give her a longer run in which to slow down, but I deliberately turned her no further. If she was going to run on the dyke I did not want her to strike the wavebreak of loose boulders sideways and tear her soft exposed flank on the hard Norwegian basalt. At the very last moment I cut out the engine to avoid possible damage to the screw.

There is a great advantage in having a boat which by E.S.P. or some other subtle sense can know exactly what to do when the time for decision and manoeuvre is unusually restricted. Probably there are ships which lack this ability, but the *Commodore* has it developed to such a strong degree that I am not sure that she might not find her way quite unaided through difficult obstacles if given full control of her movements. On the other hand motor-cars do not appear to be able of their own accord to take any active steps to preserve themselves and their owners. I remember meeting a young woman once who took a different view as far as her own car was concerned, and if ever she saw a vehicle proceeding straight towards her from the opposite direction she would take her hands off the wheel and close her eyes, but I still think the idea was a mistake. Her executors thought so too, I believe.

Perhaps the truth of the matter in the *Commodore*'s case is that she values the assistance of her companions, provided that they do not try to force her actions on occasions when, because of her superior knowledge of all the facts, she herself is the best judge of what should be done — and done quickly. At this particular moment a few yards off the island of Marken she swung a few degrees at the very last minute to select with complete confidence and excellent judgment an underwater boulder of the best possible slope and shape. Passing it absolutely centrally under her stem she surged superbly up into the air like a well-trained horse taking a hedge — with just this difference, of course, that she did not hurdle right over the dyke into the fields beyond. And there she stopped, her bows high and dry on the island and her mast-light shining cheerfully over the top of the tall bank, towards the sleeping village.

The reason for her being partly on dry land instead of in her proper element was not far to seek. A new dyke was being built out from the mainland into the Gouw Zee, and so the flasher-buoy was no longer where it formerly had lain. Between it and the entrance to the harbour the south-west corner of Marken now cut across the line of approach, and we had made a somewhat sudden landfall about two hundred yards inside the point. Obviously we could not stay there for ever, and we would have to find a means of getting her off into the water again, but at least we understood why the barges had preferred to wait for daylight. 'It is manifestly impossible that any reliance can be placed on buoys always maintaining their exact position,' the Admiralty Pilot Books declare, and we were now able to appreciate the wisdom of that statement.

Going on the rocks is an interesting experience, and it is often assumed that the first thing to do is to issue life-jackets, light a pail of oily rags to rouse the neighbourhood, and probably abandon the ship with the greatest dispatch. But there is no need to do any of these things, and the first action should surely be for the skipper to jump overboard, to inspect the possible damage. It is of course perfectly safe to do so even in the dark, because if the ship is aground

M

the water will not be above one's knees — unless of course the grounding vessel is a liner of thirty thousand tons and twenty foot draught, when the captain would be wiser to stay where he is.

At the same moment all the lights on the ship should be turned off. If farmers or other landsmen look out of their windows and see port and starboard and masthead lights dotted about over the ground they can easily become curious. They may even become anxious to render assistance, and though this helpfulness may be disinterested, it is more often than not a nuisance. Occasionally too it is underlain with the thought that underwriters may be induced to part with considerable sums of money if one can only make it abundantly clear that one has saved them the even greater expense of financing a total loss. The coast of Kent between the two Fore-lands is an area notorious for the helpful activities of men who show a remarkable willingness to render assistance to yachtsmen in diffi-culty, and once a man has learned to combine shrewd business ability with appealing charm he can make a comfortable living out of his craftiness. We had known a case of a sailor — and not a yachtsman, either — who had to sell his boat by auction to raise the four hundred pounds claimed by a kindly individual who had offered to take him in tow while he tinkered with the engine a short way off the Kingsgate beach, and though we had no reason to sup-pose that the Markenaars had similar tendencies we thought it wise not to attract attention to a position which was not without diffi-culties. Besides, there was the matter of reasonable pride. If we could take a boat ashore unaided, we ought to be able to take her off again.

Since it was dark we did not run any risk of official attention from the authorities. Such attention too may be perfectly disinterested but it can involve a great amount of form-filling and enquiry and reports, and of course there are places where the coastguards and harbour people just cannot abide the idea of ships cluttering up their imported rocks or drifting out of control down the shipping fairway. In any case they are likely to report the event to the local agent of marine insurance and it is only a matter of hours before all the underwriters who have so courageously taken upon their own heads a two-sevenths share of one three hundred and seventy-second part of the value of the hull and machinery are reduced to a state of nervous prostration through the sheer worry of wondering whether they may not now have to make do with two Rolls-Bentleys instead of three. We were of course far from the halls of Lloyds, but the *Commodore* was insured through a Groningen firm of brokers ('continental risks' thereby becoming 'home risks' with a cut of sixty per cent in the premium, although in fact the risk was still shared among the same ultimate London underwriters), and though this meant that salvage operations could quickly be laid on if they should really be needed we had no wish to cause any unnecessary alarm to a firm which had been charming enough to handle the *Commodore*'s affairs so sensibly. If we were still on the dyke at daylight the news would probably reach them — unless we took our can of blue paint out of the locker and painted out the Commodore's name from on her bows and stern. This, I believe, is something that any yachtsman should be ready to do in case of emergency, for it cannot conceivably do any harm and it may save him considerable trouble.

We did not however paint out the name. Within five seconds of the *Commodore*'s rising out of the waters of the Ijsselmeer all her lights were extinguished and we were over the side, not to save our souls but to examine the situation more closely. At the sharp end she was so far out of the water that we could see daylight, or rather moonlight, under her keel, and as she was therefore somewhat tipped up on her heels her stern was much lower in the water than usual. The water was in fact nearly a foot above the usual line. Walking round her we discovered that there was still a foot and a half of water below her rudders and the bottom was of mud tightly overgrown with something very like short grass but quite free of obstructions, so there was no danger to the propeller. At the front her shallow iron keel was lying neatly over the sloping slab of basalt and the whole bed of the lake was littered with unpleasant boulders covered with objectionably sharp little barnacles, but kneeling among the rocks and running our fingers carefully over the whole of the planking inch by inch we soon discovered that there was no question of her being holed. There was not so much as a scratch on her paint.

With this reassurance we were free to decide how to slide her back into a rather less humiliating position, and our next action was obviously to clear away all the rocks for several feet on either side of her, so that she could not possibly come to any damage on them if we should succeed in dislodging her. The boulders were heavy and many of them would have defied lifting if they had been on land, but under water the most surprisingly large stones can be rolled and trundled without much difficulty, because of the great reduction in their net weight when submerged. So, like children enjoying themselves at the sea-side, we knelt and lay down in the deliciously warm water to drag away the stones from beneath her and shift them well to the side. The work was energetic, but we did not find it at all an unpleasant occupation, and the long midnight bathe was very refreshing.

Once we had cleared a launching channel we found that she would swing quite easily on the single stone which supported her, but on account of its broad outline she was not able to slip off unaided. We pushed her out somewhat at the stern to bring her cooling intake clear of the sand, and then started up the engine and put her full speed astern. Nothing happened. Again and again we tried, with two of us heaving with our shoulders under the stem, but the stone obstinately refused to let her go. It was almost certainly the coating of rather crushed barnacles which gave it such an invincible grip on her keel.

When it was clear that we were achieving nothing, we stopped the engine and decided to lighten her at the bows. Right in the nose she had a tank which carried a quarter of a ton of water, and whilst this was running to waste through the tap in the galley sink we emptied the hold of six sacks of Dutch anthracite, a bicycle, coils of ropes, a mallet, a coil of hose-pipe, tyre fenders, two heavy anchors, and a variety of those weighty odds and ends which are always found in such places. We unshackled the bow anchor too, and drew out the chain to lead it aft, and then we piled all the miscellaneous hardware and fuel on the stern and on the roof of the after cabin with the object not only of lightening the bows but of tilting her backwards even further, so that perhaps she might slide when we again used the engine. Yet she still stuck fast, and try as we would we could not get an inch of movement out of her, even though she was so free elsewhere that we could swing her round through a quarter of a circle when we waded out, pushing on her stern.

It was soon very clear that the unaided power of the *Commodore*'s engine was not going to bring her off the dyke, and there was nothing to be gained by roaring it any more. It would be easier when daylight came, we decided, because we could then set about excavating the rock from beneath, but meanwhile we might as well return aboard. We changed into dry clothes and gathered in the stern cabin to consider the comical aspect of the matter over a glass of hot rum punch, and soon we were all so pleasantly warm that we dozed off on the bunks.

The very first hint of light came at about three o'clock. Out of the windows the rocky footing of the dyke now began to appear even more formidable, and it was obvious that we had done well to allow the *Commodore* to take the shock under her keel rather than on her ribs and planking. But though we were delighted to know that we would soon be able to examine the rock more closely on which she was so firmly supported we could not help noting that the surface of the water was ruffled by a measurable increase in the breeze. Every minute the wavelets grew larger, and soon there were waves more than a foot high slapping and splashing against her side. From minute to minute the wind was freshening, and it was blowing up from the south. This would have the advantage of raising the water level on the southern side of the island, but it would need a gale to raise it enough to float her off, and any advantage was more than outweighed by the fact that wind and wave alike were tending to drive her sideways on to the rocks. Even if we could dislodge her at the bows we could not hope to manoeuvre her clear of the shore under her own power, with such a strong onshore drift.

We tied all our ropes together to provide two very long lines which we attached to the spare anchors from the hold, and these were carried right out abeam of her with the dinghy and carefully dropped right side up on the bottom — which was only five feet below. The shallowness was something of a disadvantage too, for if the wind were to rise any further the waves would begin to take on the sharpness and steepness characteristic of Ijsselmeer choppiness, and would then push very powerfully on the side of the boat if she continued to lie across them. Still, this shortening of the waves made the adventure of rowing out the anchors a pleasantly exhilarating one too, and once they were placed it was not difficult to haul her stern round with Fred and myself wading and pushing whilst the strain was being taken up on both lines. Soon we had her lying more comfortably and at least held out so very firmly that she could not be driven on to the rocks unless the wind should freshen to something approaching a gale, which was inconceivable. Below such strength the anchors would certainly not drag out of the sticky bottom.

By now the colour of dawn was beginning to flush behind the island, and after a further fruitless attempt to dislodge the boat with the engine aided by straining on both anchors and some powerful shouldering at the bows it was decided that Fred and I should walk along the dyke and reconnoitre. We had no very clear idea of what we might find, but there was a possibility that we might find a fisherman preparing to go out, and that we could persuade him for a packet of tea to come round the point and give us the small extra pull on the stern which was all we thought to be necessary to get the *Commodore* afloat again. Better still, we might find a lever.

It was not more than a mile along the bank to the harbour. Four shapely fishing-boats lay at the jetty, deserted and with the nets hauled high up their masts beneath long fluttering pennants. Around the edge of the harbour the little painted wooden houses shone bright and clean in their coats of blue and black and green, but there was not so much as a cough from inside any one of them. The packetboat lay sleeping alongside the landing-stage, but there was no one aboard. We found a cottage bearing the harbour master's brass plate, and when we listened in the stillness we heard a deep breathing with just a touch of snore, but we had not the heart to wake anybody up in such a peaceful place and so we wandered into one of the lanes leading back from the waterfront to the low-lying land behind. In one of the houses a dog gave a yawning bark as we passed, and at once relapsed into slumber again.

Behind the harbour we eventually came to where a house was

being demolished, but though we searched among the debris there was no beam of any useful size. Across the top of the dyke however there was a fence with a gate to keep the cows in their own field. Dutch farmers often mount their gates not vertically, but with the hinge post at such a pronounced slope that the gate will swing shut and stay closed without a latch even in the highest wind. The gate on the dyke was of this type, and it fell shut against a solid rounded post, long weathered and seasoned and as strong as steel. It did not take us very long to extract it from the ground, and to prevent the cattle from straying we put in its place a sturdy enough roofing timber from the demolitions nearby. Then, armed with the gate-post, we softly left the drowsy village and made our way back along the dyke with the cows staring at us in sleepy surprise.

When we saw the *Commodore* from the land we had a shock. We had had no idea that she was really inclined at such an angle, and she looked for all the world like one of Monsieur Havard's wrecks. We could hardly believe that she had ridden so far out of the water at the bows, and I think that just for a moment we really thought that she was making water and that it was running through to the stern and taking her down at that end. But when he reached her we checked the level of the stern against a thumb-nail mark which I had earlier put on the paint as a guide and we found that she had not altered her tilt at all, and now that it was almost daylight it was possible to check round her sides nearer the bows and confirm that not a plank had received so much as a barnacle scratch. Satisfied that all was well, it merely remained, as before, for us to dislodge her from her ridiculous posture.

We went to work energetically. We were quite convinced that the *Commodore* had rested long enough on the island by this time, and there was the added incentive of getting her afloat again before the people in the farm across the field came out to milk the cows and discover a ship in a position which was, to say the least, in-triguing. Besides, we wanted our breakfast. It was therefore de-cided to shift one of the anchors further round and secure it amid-ships so that if she should at last come off she would swing out safely from the shore on a wide arc with the anchor as pivot at the centre of the circle. Fred was to haul on the other kedge-line and make sure that it did not foul the propeller, and my wife would take the boat full speed astern once more on the engine. Any other movable weight was to remain right aft, but I would stay in the water. A fulcrum was carefully built up with basalt rocks close against the keel, and on this the fence post was placed with its end under the iron. The dinghy was left floating by the shore, attached to the bows by a few fathoms of slack line, and it was agreed that if the *Commodore* came off the rocks too fast for me even to get into the dinghy I would walk round the dyke and meet her in the harbour, since the onshore waves would make it difficult to swim out in pursuit of her.

When all was ready I put my whole weight on the outer end of the pole and shouted for the engine to be run up full. Almost at once the post rolled slightly to one side, a sure sign that something was moving. With the fulcrum readjusted to the new position I put my feet on the pole and my shoulders under the flare of the bow and heaved with all my strength. I felt the ship lift bodily. There was a momentary tremble, and then the bows withdrew with such determination that I went over backwards into the Ijsselmeer where only a moment or two earlier the *Commodore* had lain. Spluttering more with pleasure than anything else I scrambled to my feet and just had time to lunge forward and grab with one hand the stern of the receding dinghy. We were away, and by the time I had hauled myself across the thwarts of the dinghy and up aboard over the bows, the *Commodore* was swinging out smoothly on her arc fifty yards off shore, and Fred was already hauling up one of the anchors over the transom. Ten minutes later we were moored outside the harbour master's house and the heap of fuel and bicycle and fenders was being stowed again in the hold. When at about six o'clock the first of the Markenaars began to throw open their shutters they no doubt thought that we had just arrived at their little island. Not one of them knew that we had spent the night half way up the dyke, and if the farmer may perhaps have scratched his head over the mysterious way in which his gate-post had changed from round to square during the hours of the night I very much doubt if he ever divined the cause.

I have said that I admire Marken, but the island had two very

different faces, one of which was infinitely more attractive than the other. The place was visited by a procession of trip-boats from Vollendam, Monnikendam and even Amsterdam, and it knew very well that it was a show place of considerable fame. And so did the inhabitants. Never have I encountered any other place in which the people could change their character to such an extraordinary degree, twice daily.

The Markenaars, up until nine fifty-nine in the morning, were the most natural and hospitable people. They would sit on a bollard and talk, they would show us their embroidery, they would proffer advice and help us with our shopping almost as though we belonged to themselves. The harbour master with his wooden leg, and his red pirate's sash above his white breeches, would take our harbour dues and then stay to carry on a long conversation which, as it seemed to be in some strange language of his own, was not fully comprehended by us. In fact we did not understand a single word of it, but the effect was pleasant enough and by signs and an occasional drawing on paper we managed to get along splendidly. Everybody had time to be genial and friendly — up until nine fifty-nine, at which moment the *Marken Express* bore down between the entrance jetties to disgorge the first hundred or more of those whose lives were being smoothly planned by Thos. Cook or the American Express.

In a moment the place was transformed. Women who had been about their washing now emerged to stand in their doorways, putting the last curl into place before striking a noble and picturesque pose. The children who had until that instant been romping beside our bows took on their stage roles of sweet little clean little Dutch little dolly-dears. The smiles faded from the faces of the men, to be replaced by long-studied expressions of mysterious but not unapproachable majesty — certainly not unapproachable to those who had money to spend. From an easy walk their gait changed to a hand-in-pockets roll, and those who had known insufficient English to converse with us in that tongue suddenly broke into a remarkable fluency confined to certain stock phrases.

'This way to see the fisherman's house. Yes, we can take dollars. You see that little girl, yes? She is not a girl, he is a little boy, ha, ha! You like to take a snap, yes?'

Whether or not Marken should be seen at all once it is on land, I rather doubt. The blessedness of its island existence was that between the departure of the last steamer in the early evening and the advent of the first one on the following morning the people could relax and be themselves — at least I like to think that it was their real natures which we met whenever we spent the evening or the early morning in their harbour. And the island really was a place of very great interest.

Just where the Markenaars came from seems not to be quite certain, but they do not in the least resemble the people living a mere couple of miles away across the Gouw Zee. There is something fair and broad-faced about them which is quite in keeping with the assertion of some of them that the island's inhabitants are derived in closed community from the sailors of a Norwegian ship wrecked on the island centuries ago, and their dress might be taken to confirm this. The costumes of Marken, however much they may now be donned for show, really are very lovely indeed and they have in their colours and in their embroidered designs a suggestion of some Scandinavian link. So too have many of the articles of painted wood inside the cottage homes, but this may of course all be nothing more than a case of what biologists term 'parallel evolution'. Certain historical records make it clear that there was once a monastery on the island, but after that the precise source of the settlers is less clearly recorded. Wherever they may have come from, their island life has led to the production of many exquisite things within their homes, and though no doubt all these objects will be carefully preserved even though the village has been swallowed in the mainland, the community itself is sure to lose much of its strange individduality now that its separation from the neighbouring land is undone.

The main livelihood was once of course centred on fishing. Today the fleet of plain but beautiful fishing boats still exists but in rather attenuated form. When the Zuyder Zee became transmuted into the Ijsselmeer the water gradually became fresh, but the change was exceedingly slow and so the fortunes of the fishermen declined by almost imperceptible degrees. Had the fishing been ruined even over the course of a year or two the men might have given up, but as each season was only very slightly different from the one before it they tended, like the men of the other Zuyder Zee ports, to roam further and further afield with their boats and even to devote their attentions to fish which once they would have scorned. Roach and perch are now taken in trawls which once brought in sole and plaice, and the boats sail in to Vollendam to unload cran upon cran of miserable pinkish miscellaneous fry which are slopped into lorries and taken to the fish meal factory. For Marken however the fishery is a dying trade, running to extinction as surely as the waters of the Ijsselmeer are still further pumped away.

Life was of course much safer after the closing of the dyke. Marken itself comprises a few hillocks separated by pastures, and all its low-lying land was inundated almost annually when the waters were tidal. For this reason the houses were concentrated on the humps until lack of space prevented further expansion, and then they were built elsewhere on stilts. The living floor was reached by a ladder and the ground floor was used for little more

than a store, which in winter had to be emptied of everything that might be damaged when the waters swept through beneath the parlour floor above.

This dependence upon the level of the ground is very strikingly shown by the hamlets themselves. Not a building on the island is of very great age — the villages have too often been destroyed by fire or sacked by invaders from Friesland or Guelderland for anything to have survived over the centuries — but those built before the sealing off of the North Sea are crowded on the hillocks so tightly that only in front of the church is there anything in the nature of a small unoccupied space, whilst the side alleys leading off from this miniature square are so narrow that in some of them it is hardly possible for two people to pass, and a full Marken skirt held out by all its array of petticoats may fill the breadth from side to side. But the stilt-raised houses of the lower land are not so compact. If one was forced off the edge of the hill there was no longer any need to crowd in upon one's neighbours, and there was plenty of room for expansion — and just as one can distinguish which of the houses were sited sufficiently high to escape flooding in the storms of Zuyder Zee days, so one can also recognize any houses on the low-lying land which date from after 1932, because however similar in general structure to their predecessors they were now able to sit safely on the ground, instead of having to perch in the air.

From Marken it was only a short run across the water of the Gouw Zee to the inland coast of North Holland. Monsieur Havard found the Gouw Zee one of the most fearful crossings in the whole of the terrifying Zuyder Zee and he related that the journey took two hours in a sixty-ton boat. Perhaps it did, even if the distance was only just over two miles. But he also noted that the Gouw Zee received its name from the 'very rich alluvion, forming a most valuable manure, found at the bottom of these shallows; hence the name of the Mer d'Or, the inhabitants deriving a golden harvest of hay from its employment on these meadows'. This might be so, or perhaps the name could be connected with the golden sand, or the golden shine of the water before sunset, even with the wealth of fish once caught there. Indeed any of these explanations would be just as convincing if the word *gouw* really meant golden, which it unfortunately does not.

Undoubtedly Vollendam, across the Gouw Zee, is attractive from a distance, if only because the housetops alone peep mysteriously over the shore dyke and reveal nothing of what the place is really like. The harbour is pretty enough, but the village is artificial to a degree, and though we put in there on several occasions to shop we were glad to escape as quickly as possible from the shifty men in their baggy pants who wanted us to photograph them and pay for the privilege.

Vollendam is really an adjunct of Edam, the cheese town, and though a mile or so inland Edam can be reached by boat. We had only to round the point beyond Vollendam and proceed a mile or more up the coast to the entrance of Edam harbour — this much was abundantly clear from the chart. Yet we went twice up and down the relevant stretch of dyke before finding the entrance at all, for it was sheltered from the north and east by a mole similar to the shore dyke, and bent round to run parallel to it for twenty or thirty yards, with the result that no gap in the stonework was visible. It would have been a bad entrance with any wind, for the sharp steep waves of the shallows swung round the end of the mole in such a way that they tended to slew a boat in the entrance — an annoying feature of construction because the two sides of the channel were no more than heaps of heavy basalt rocks. We had therefore to approach more or less at right angles, turn at full speed into the space behind the mole, and pull up before running down the sharp bend twenty yards further inside. It was easy enough in a comparatively small boat, but to take a laden barge into the channel-way when there was a strong crosswind would have been a reasonable test of skill.

Round the bend the cut ran up to a lock with huge gates recalling the days when the tide had once risen and fallen against the walls, and beyond the lock the prettiest waterway imaginable led up into the centre of the town. Along each side was a row of nondescript and unplanned building, cottages mingling with stately merchants' warehouses, municipal buildings, diamond-shuttered cheese stores, and simple brick houses of one floor or two with a gable above. Many of them dated back to the seventeenth century and a few even to before the days of Alva, and the general effect was quite unpretentious but very delightful.

Edam has many curious sights, and among them is a fine example of a floating cellar in one of the oldest of the houses beside the canal. It seems that the level of the water table varied with the season, and in order to build a cellar which was permanently water-cooled yet safe from winter flooding the house was built on piles over a walled pit excavated deep beneath it. In this hole floated a room lined out entirely with glazed tiles, and if the water should rise then too the room would lift upwards, floating like a square boat. The cellar was reached by a ladder which rose and fell through a trap in the floor of the house above, and altogether it represented a very ingenious piece of domestic equipment. No matter if it should develop a leak; it then had only to be baled out over the side.

Our progress through Edam was restricted to the speed at which the municipal *brugwachter* could open a bridge to let the *Commodore* through, close it again, open the barriers, and cycle round the block to rejoin the canal at each succeeding road crossing, but before long we were leaving the town behind us with the sound of its carillon drifting up astern to follow us on the breeze. Our course lay by a comparatively narrow and little used canal, green with duckweed, to the small town of Purmerend, where it joined the North Holland Canal just above Purmerend locks. Turning the *Commodore* to head northward we followed the winding course of this ship canal of a former era until after some ten or twelve miles it ran into the edge of Alkmaar. At our request the harbour-master arranged for all the bridges of the old town *gracht* to be opened for the *Commodore*, and squeezing her way through past gabled houses, some of which had been leaning outward over the water for more than four hundred years, she felt her way round to the quay oppo-site the Waag — a tall building complete with a carillon, a clock

with mechanical knights in armour and a model trumpeter to act as town herald. Dominating the Market Place the Waag is famous enough from prints and pictures, and its size alone is a sufficient monument to the importance of a local industry which can require such magnificent premises as a weighing-house for its product — the cheese that is not quite soapy and not quite creamy, neither soft nor hard, and which though not very exciting to the palate, is wholesome enough to find its way into grocers' windows from Limehouse to Piccadilly.

XI

Alkmaar and the cheeses — The secret panel — The carpenter's mission — Hoorn — The Eendracht's *venture — Enkhuizen — The patchwork boat — Staveren's doom — Waves on the Ijsselmeer — Lemmer — Dykes and polders*

Alkmaar's cheese-market is famous enough to have become one of the chief tourist attractions of North Holland, but the mere fact that visitors come from far and near to see some particular local speciality does not of itself mean that the thing is mere show or that it is necessarily to be condemned and avoided. It may be true that Alkmaar has an alert eye turned towards the tourist trade, but the market is genuine enough. Indeed the wholesaling of cheese takes place all the year round, but in winter there are no flags, no buses, and no visitors. The producers and the wholesalers gather in Alkmaar every Friday morning, and behind the diamond panes of the little cafes around the market-place cheese will be bought and sold by the ton without a visitor being any the wiser. If the market is carried on during the winter months with as much seriousness as when the tourists are there to watch, then clearly the summer-time performance with all its colour and tradition cannot be regarded as nothing more than a fancy dress parade. In fact the market, whether open or concealed, is the agency by which the current price of Edam cheese is fixed.

Like so much else in Holland, Alkmaar's strange cheese-selling is best experienced from a boat. Not that one has the most intimate view of the actual bargaining, but from a boat one is more likely to see all the little preparations which are over and done with before the overseas buses haul in from Amsterdam shortly before ten o'clock in the morning.

The harbour-master left his beautiful little watch-tower on the bend of the North Holland Canal to accompany the *Commodore* in person from bridge to bridge to make sure that her berth on the

Voordam was one from which we would have the best possible view of the early proceedings. Behind us the canal was bridged by the wooden bascule of the Bathbrug, so-named on account of the contractual friendship existing between the people of Alkmaar and the citizens of Bath — just as Bath itself has an Alkmaar Garden, and a marquetry picture of the Bathbrug hanging in the passage of the Royal Pump Room. Ahead of us was another similar bridge, the Scharensbrug, with the same primrose rails and pillars and massive counterweight of a type inseparable from any exhibition of the paintings of van Gogh. Beside us were the offices of the local newspaper and across the water the broad open space of the Waagplein, with the weigh-house itself somewhat off centre to leave plenty of room for the cheese.

We had purposely arrived on a Thursday evening, and at five o'clock on the following morning we were awakened by a banging and clattering from across the canal as a row of long boards was fitted into position along the side of the market place which ran down to the quay. We soon guessed what they were for — they were being put there as long-stops to prevent the cheeses from rolling down the slope into the water.

Shortly after six the first of the trucks arrived, fitted with racks of just the right dimensions to hold either the big cart-wheel cheeses or the more common rounder ones of two kilograms apiece. It backed up to the square, the tailboard was dropped, and a man and a boy jumped in to bend down and hurl out the yellow-orange rounds between their legs. One after the other the fat cheeses landed with a smack on the cobbles and bounced away like footballs to where a couple of men in yellow clogs knelt on the sets to stack the balls in rows. Some bounced past them and went merrily hopping down the square to be fielded by the boards set along the edge of the quay, from where a small boy bowled them back again. At about the same time a barge crept through from the North Holland canal to moor across the water from where we lay, and the moment the hold covers had been removed the skipper and his lad began to toss a few more tons of the round cheeses up in the air and over the stop-boards on to the cobbles beyond.

To simplify counting, the grey expanse of the market place was

N

inlaid with lines of a lighter stone marking out spaces just ten cheeses broad, which ran from side to side of the square. As each fresh lorry arrived the stackers got to work on a new bed, and by nine o'clock most of the cheeses were in position, neatly laid out in double-deck piles, and tarpaulins had been drawn over them to keep off the rain or dust or sunshine. More than thirteen thousand in number, the balls and rounds awaited the moment when the selling might begin.

At ten o'clock the weigh-house carillon announced the hour with a gay little tune. The knights in armour charged out of their door-ways, bore down upon each other, missed, and disappeared again through the little portals which opened at their approach and snapped shut behind them to keep them safe for their next hourly combat. The wooden figure of the trumpeter above them jerkily raised his arm and a fanfare floated away over the roof tops of the town. The farmers and cheese-factory agents drew back the covers and within the next few minutes the twenty-seven tons of cheeses had all been sold.

The actual selling was not done by auction. A wholesaler, a local man perhaps though probably with contacts as far distant as Knightsbridge or Piccadilly, would survey a pile of cheese and pick one out. Then he would pull from his pocket an implement like an apple-corer and bore a hole down to the centre of the cheese so that he could inspect the circular section which he cut out, and break off the inner end to taste it. Looking professionally not entirely satisfied he would then replace the rest of the boring in its hole and pick up another cheese to strike it hard with his fist. '*Kloppt goed*', the owner would reassure him, picking up another and hammering it with his fist. '*Kloppt goed.*'

The buyer would give another cheese or two a hearty *kloppen*, listening each time to the thud with all the attention of a tuner at work on a concert Bechstein. Then perhaps he might take another core, and yet another until having at last made his considered assessment of the quality he would suggest a price. The farmer would in his turn look dubious and suggest a somewhat higher figure, but soon a bargain would be struck and sealed in the tradi-tional fashion by something between a shake and a clap of hands.

With the cheeses sold it merely remained for the lot to be weighed and its price marked up on a board, and the weighing was of course the highlight of the proceedings. Alkmaar has an ancient Guild of Cheese-porters, who alone may take the lots to the giant balance of the municipal weighmaster which stands in the open base of the tower. The Guild is divided into four companies, and the six porters of each company are distinguished by the bright straw hats of red, yellow, green or blue, which together with a suit of spotless white overalls makes up their uniform. There is a regular hierarchy within each company of porters too, various strange insignia such as a ribbon and a silver badge or miniature cheese-barrow denoting the ranks of *provoost* or *voorman*, and there is a definite system of which man will work with which when a load is to be carried.

Portering is hard work, because even though the distance is short the conveyance is somewhat awkward and the weight heavy. A curved sled, painted in the colour of the company, is laid on the ground and the first layer of cheeses is piled on it in a rectangle several cheeses broad and six or seven cheeses long. Two or three other layers are added above, decreasing one cheese in each direction, until the load adds up to some eighty cheeses and weighs rather more than three hundredweight. Two porters take up their positions fore and aft between the protruding handles, stoop down, loop over the handles the ends of leather braces which pass over their shoulders, and at a command from the elder of the two they

shuffle away to the weigh-house at a jogging trot, with the younger porter always leading. Once weighed, the loads are cleared by lorries, or by boat, and by midday Alkmaar is back to normal for another week whilst the cheese finds its way to shops all over Europe.

On the evening after the market we were sitting in the *Commodore*'s saloon when the hatch door opened and an elderly Dutchman stood looking down at us, swaying unsteadily on the catwalk. Fearing that he would fall either backwards into the canal or head first into the boat we hastened to help him down the ladder, and as soon as he was inside the boat he greeted us with a somewhat exaggerated wave of his hat but with a smile which was not entirely due to the spirits which were so dangerously affecting his balance. He was unable to speak a word of any language other than his own, and as his speech was considerably slurred and thickened the conversation was somewhat one-sided, but eventually we grasped that we were to visit his house at eight o'clock that night, where he would have something to show us. We were quite unable to understand what this something was, but he was so insistent that in the end we agreed to go, not just because it was abundantly clear that he had no intention of leaving the boat until we had accepted his invitation, but perhaps also because we had no desire to give offence to any citizen of a town which had received the *Commodore* so kindly. He sketched us a map which showed that his house bordered on one of the narrow branch canals, and then we helped him ashore, where he took his farewell with more bowing and waving of his hat.

True to our promise, on the stroke of eight we stood below the leaning gable of his house and rang the bell. The door was opened by a manservant, and we were taken upstairs to the parlour, where the old bachelor himself received us with coffee and cake and wine. Though not strictly sober he was now steady enough to be able to lead us round the premises, and show us a few real gems of ancient furniture and some very lovely fireplaces of Delft tiles. But the object of which he was particularly proud, and which he had really invited us to see, was in the parlour. When we returned to it he began to grope over the oaken scroll-work panelling with his fingers until he found just the right spot. He pressed firmly on part of the carving, and one of the panels swung open to reveal a shallow cavity about eighteen inches high, which had been made to hold a secret possession. Carefully he took the object from the recess and opened it out on the table, a worn but beautiful specimen of a brass-hinged Bible of the sixteenth century.

There was little need for him to try to explain to us the circumstances of its concealment, although by signs and acting he managed to do so. The secret panel dated from the days of the book itself, the age in which the servants of the Inquisition were hanging and burning or burying alive those who dared to read the scriptures for themselves. The people who then had been living in that house had probably been only one among the households of Alkmaar which had been forced to read their Bible in deadly secret; and now that we ourselves were seated in that same parlour, still lit only by candle-light, we could imagine how each evening the master of the house had closed the massive bolts on the street door below and the family and servants had drawn the shutters close over the windows and gathered round the table to hear him read to them in a hushed voice from the forbidden book. The copy of the Bible was now perhaps no more than a private curiosity, but once it had been the treasured secret possession from which that long-forgotten family had drawn the strength to sustain them through the years of fear and persecution.

Of their possible fate, whether they read the Bible or not, the inhabitants of Alkmaar were left in no doubt at all when in 1573 the Duke of Alva, fresh from the slaughter of Haarlem, invested their little town and assured his monarch that if he took Alkmaar he was 'resolved not to leave a single creature alive. The knife shall be put to every throat'. With this object he surrounded Alkmaar with sixteen thousand experienced troops who would not have much difficulty, he thought, in overcoming the mere eight hundred men of the garrison and the thirteen hundred untrained burghers and their wives and children, and slaughtering the lot of them. The citizens however were soon trained, if only by force of circumstances, and one of the magistrates recorded at the time that he and his 'slumbering and sleepy fellow burghers were transformed into experienced soldiers by the Spaniard, who summoned them at every moment from their beds to defend the walls'.

Eventually the great assault came, but after a few hours of fierce fighting the Spaniards had lost a thousand men below the walls to the tarred hoops, quicklime, and rain of bullets and cannon balls to which the citizens subjected them, and Don Frederic had to order the attack to be called off. Some days before, however, a carpenter had managed to escape from the town, carrying with him a hollow stick in which was a letter requesting Prince William to arrange for the breaching of the dykes to the northward so that the surrounding land might be inundated. It was clear that such an action would devastate a great tract of North Holland and bring ruin to the farmers and villagers of the area, but William promised compensation and quickly secured their agreement to the scheme. Carrying hidden in his stick a copy of William's orders, and an assurance to the citizens of Alkmaar that very shortly the waters of the Zuyder Zee would roll furiously over the land and wipe the Spaniards off the face of the earth, the carpenter began his journey back to the city. This time, however, he failed to pass through the Spanish lines without being challenged, and although he managed to escape he dropped his precious stick. The papers were found.

Confronted with this interesting intelligence Don Frederic was alarmed. Already his soldiers were by no means anxious to renew an assault on a town which had mauled them so badly. They had seen their comrades writhing as the pitch-soaked and blazing coopers' hoops burned at their faces and necks and some had even preferred to be killed by the swords of their own officers rather than become involved in any further dealings at close range with the people of Alkmaar. If they should come to know that the sea was about to sweep over their encampment there might be open mutiny or panic. He therefore decided that the time had come to withdraw his troops while there was still time, and after seven weeks of siege the citizens of the little town were thus saved by the sudden and unexpected departure of the investing army. The breaching of the final dykes had not yet taken place and there was still time to prevent it, and so the land too was saved from devastation. In Alkmaar today the winged goddess of victory still stands looking

out over the fields towards Oudorp, where Don Frederic's encampment was arrayed, and October 8th of every year is still a local
occasion for flowers in the windows and flags on the housetops and
across the streets, and all the fun of waffle-stalls and roundabouts
and swingboats in hilarious commemoration of the day when the
Spaniards broke camp and departed.

Alkmaar still bears a few other reminders of its siege, and when
we threaded our way out between the barges moored along the
quaysides of the town canal we could see a Spanish cannon ball still
embedded in the wall of the upper storey of one of the older houses.
But modern Alkmaar is a prosperous modern town, thriving on
cheese, on the fields of gladiolus which we had seen in the distance
from the top of the weigh-house belfry-tower, and on its role as
market for the large area of North Holland. Flowers, dolls, fruit,
cloth, fish, and cheese are sold at the stalls in its streets, and those
who have blunt emotions can watch a stall-holder skinning eels
alive, running a sharp knife quickly round behind the head and then
deftly pulling back the black slippery skin as neatly as a glove to
toss the poor writhing creature into the pan of his balance. We had
sometimes caught our own eels below the *Commodore*'s hull at
night, but we had never had quite the same practical approach to
their preparation. We had preferred to sever the dorsal blood vessel
just behind the head and let the creatures bleed quickly into un-
consciousness and death before stripping them down and gutting
them. We would never have made good professional fishers of
paling, and though we always enjoyed a good eel I doubt if we
could ever have brought ourselves to eat them as some of the
country people did in the streets of Alkmaar. Buying at the stall the
pink and bleeding body of a freshly skinned and writhing creature
raw and wriggling and still staring with its beady eyes, they would
eat it from the tail upwards, with as little concern as if it had
been a banana.

Up the coast from the Edam entrance our next port was Hoorn,
a sleepy and forgotten little town which once held a very important
position in the world of shipping and which has left its name half
way round the world. In 1614, Isaac le Maire quarrelled with his
fellow directors of the Dutch East India Company over matters of

policy, and he decided to set up a rival concern, the Campagne Australe. The East India Company had received a monopoly from the States General, giving them sole right of navigation — as far as Dutch merchant ships were concerned—either round the Cape of Good Hope or to the Spice Islands *through the Strait of Magellan*, and they enforced the monopoly with their own armed patrol-ships. Le Maire believed that there must be access to the Pacific further south than Magellan's channel, and removing from Amsterdam to Hoorn he shared his belief with the Schouten brothers, two competent and experienced sea captains of the town. The mayor and aldermen and other local merchants were brought into the dis-cussions, and they enthusiastically provided enough money to fit out an expedition to find the new route to the Indies whilst at the same time all concerned preserved the most rigid secrecy about its destination.

Two good ships, the *Eendracht* and the *Hoorn*, were soon fitting out and arming in the harbour. Only the commanders and the merchants knew the true object of the voyage, and sailors were obliged to sign on as willing to go wherever the captains might re-quire. But the high pay and the strange attraction of the secrecy with which the voyage was surrounded soon attracted plenty of excellent seamen not only from Hoorn and other Dutch harbours but also from England, and when the expedition set sail from Hoorn with Le Maire's son as business manager it was properly equipped for a lengthy voyage and sufficiently heavily armed to deal with any-thing but an attack in force.

On the coast of South America the *Hoorn* was unfortunately burned when beached for careening, but there was plenty of room for her crew aboard the *Eendracht* and so with only one ship the Schoutens continued their voyage southward. The names of Staten Island (named after the States General of the United Pro-vinces) and the Strait of Le Maire still show the course they fol-lowed, and when at last on 29th January 1615 the *Eendracht* doubled the southernmost point of the outlying islands below Tierra del Fuego nothing was more natural than for Willem Schouten to name the great headland 'Kap Hoorn'.

However delighted the young Le Maire may have been that his

father's theory was vindicated, and that a way of breaking the monopoly of the East India Company had been found, that elation was not shared by the monopoly company itself and when the *Eendracht* reached the Dutch East Indies the ship and men were seized, the cargo confiscated, and the Schoutens themselves. shipped back to Holland by the western route in the steerage of the company's flagship *Amsterdam*. Disgraced, and robbed of the rich cargo which he had loaded on the *Eendracht* for the local company at Hoorn, Willem Schouten wrote up the journal of his voyage and it was published in Dutch and English, French, Italian and Latin. So great was the interest which it aroused that the Dutch East India Company was promptly ordered by a Dutch court to refund the value of the *Eendracht* and cargo. Hoorn's enterprising Campagne Australe had been forced out of business, but Schouten's claim to have rounded the tip of South America was vindicated, and though a few years later the Spaniards renamed the famous headland 'San Ildefonso' it was Schouten's name of Cape Horn which in the long run was to survive.

As the *Commodore* cut into the bay of Hoorn and ran slowly between the piles of the harbour entrance to draw in beneath the beautiful brick harbour tower of the Hoofdtoren she was certainly in a place of nautical memories. The Hoofdtoren itself had stood for more than eighty years when the Schoutens sailed out of that harbour, and we could imagine the shareholders of the Campagne Australe gathered on the same stone quayside in all their wealth and finery to bid the two adventurous ships farewell. Perhaps some of the wives and families of the Hoorn men among the crews had leaned out to wave from the same square diamond-shuttered windows round the base of the roof from one of which an official of the port now looked down on the *Commodore* to acknowledge her arrival with a friendly wave of his hand. And even before the days of the *Eendracht* the burghers had no doubt gathered in its upper storey to look out over the sea and watch with anxious hopes the fortunes of a great battle on the waters in which their own John Haring and many other men from their city were desperately engaged.

John Haring was a man of astonishing courage. He had only recently leapt to fame during an attempt to raise the siege of

Haarlem when, standing quite alone upon the Diemer Dyke, a narrow bank between the Ij and the waters of another lake now vanished, he had held in check more than a thousand of the Spanish forces seeking to advance along it to attack the remnants of a volunteer force from Edam. Because of the narrowness of the place where he had taken up his position the attackers could only approach in single file, but armed only with a sword and shield he fought and killed them one by one, and defiantly held his ground until the last of his comrades had escaped. Only then did he fling away his arms, dive into the chill February water, and swim to safety unscathed amid the rain of shot from the Spanish arms.

It was in October of the same year that Admiral Bossu sailed from Amsterdam with thirty ships, cruising off the same coast which we ourselves followed in the *Commodore*. From Hoorn and other ports of the Zuyder Zee a lesser fleet of rather smaller Dutch vessels shadowed his armada, waiting for the opportunity to sail in to close quarters and tackle the Spanish boats. Their chance came when Bossu's fleet was lying off the coast just to northward of Hoorn and the Dutch boats happened to be well to the windward side of them, and bearing down on the breeze they scattered the Spaniards, captured five of them, and set off in pursuit of the rest. Four small craft however had grappled with the flagship *Inquisition*, and the tangled mass of the five boats drifted before the wind towards the shore. Aboard the *Inquisition* the Spaniards, with sword and shield and bullet-proof mail, stood on deck waiting to repel any attempt to board her, whilst the Hollanders attacked with their familiar and primitive but very unpleasant armoury of blazing hoops, boiling oil and molten lead. Several times the men of the small boats forced an entry into the big ship, only to be driven out into the sea, and for more than twelve hours the fight continued — during which time the *Inquisition* drifted inshore until she stranded on a shoal off the point of the Bay of Hoorn. It was then that John Haring climbed up from one of the boats alongside, leapt aboard, and hauled down her flag. In so doing he was shot, and he died on the deck of the *Inquisition*.

Bossu's position however was hopeless. The rest of his fleet was routed and the flagship was fast aground on a shoal, hotly attacked by the ships attached to her side. The fight could have been endless, for the boatmen of the villages on the coast nearby were continually rowing out from the shore at Wijdenes to bring food and ammunition and reinforcements to the Dutch boats and to take off their wounded. Six hours after John Haring had tried to haul down the *Inquisition*'s colours they were struck on the orders of Bossu himself, and with only a quarter of his crew left to him he was taken ashore to be imprisoned at Hoorn, 'in which city he was received, on his arrival, with great demonstrations of popular hatred.' Considering that he himself was a Netherlander, this was hardly surprising.

The beauty of Hoorn is famous, and justly so. The city may have shrunk to a mere fraction of its former size and glory, but it has a great wealth of very lovely buildings remaining unscathed from the days of its maritime prosperity.

There is inevitably a sadness about any port which was once the scene of exploits such as those of Haring and the Schoutens and from which the ocean traffic has departed, at first through the silting of its approaches and then by the transformation of its waters into a great inland lake, and to a certain extent every former Zuyder Zee harbour town has this air of fading glory. It is felt most acutely however in the case of those which, like Hoorn, were truly great in the day when exploration flourished and the heavy sailing ships of the East Indies or West Indies trade sailed out of their harbours to fade away northward for a voyage of several years duration into the unknown. Hoorn was such a port, and so was Enkhuizen, a couple of hours run up the coast.

Enkhuizen lies at the western side of the twelve-mile narrows separating North Holland from Friesland, but it has one of the prettiest harbour entrances anywhere in the country. A lock, no longer used, leads through a black double wooden bascule bridge to the trading basin beyond, and here too the entrance is guarded by a heavy bastion, less ornamented than that of Hoorn but massive and sturdy, and still giving an impression of strength and confidence. This tower, the Drommedaris, must also have been a fine vantage point from which to view the fight with the *Inquisition*, but its interior is mostly made up of bare circular rooms, some of which served as cells for captives or for recalcitrant soldiers. It has however a very fine set of bells, so once again the *Commodore* was able to sleep amid the chiming of the bells of a master founder of the Low Countries. In fact the Drommedaris bells were cast by Michiels in 1929, but the church peal across the harbour is an authentic Hemony of 1647.

Our Dutch friend Piet paid us a visit at Enkhuizen, and he took us up to see the bells. There was something else however which caught our attention in the dim light of the upper floor where the pealing mechanism of the Drommedaris was housed, for there in a corner a strange little canoe lay, dusty and covered with cobwebs. Shaped like a kayak it was made entirely of odds and ends, a piece or two of motor tyre, some inner tubing, patches of canvas and roofing felt, all laboriously sewn together over a rough but well-shaped wooden frame. It seemed a ridiculous wreck of a boat and one in which nobody in their senses would put so much as a foot if it were afloat — though it hardly looked as though it would float — and we wondered that it should be kept at all, let alone in such a surprising place as the upper floor of a belfry. Laughingly we pointed out the absurd object to Piet.

'Ah,' he said, 'you would be surprised if you knew how many times that boat crossed the Ijsselmeer on a moonless night.' And then he explained the reason for its patchwork appearance.

The boat was built during the Occupation and it was indeed made of salvaged odds and ends, for to prevent unauthorized voyages the Germans had seized existing boats, and materials for a new one were practically non-existent. Secretly, with infinite care and patience the canoe was built, and however unfinished its appearance might have been it was nevertheless sturdy and buoyant enough to carry the weight of a passenger in the cockpit besides a navigator sitting astride the boat behind him to work the double-ended paddle. The passengers carried in this strange vessel were allied airmen shot down over North Holland during flights to and from Hamburg, Berlin, or the ports of the north-west German coast. They had been hidden and cared for, and then taken eventually to Enkhuizen, from where it was possible to carry them over the water to the relatively less heavily patrolled and occupied area

of the southern shores of the Ijsselmeer, or perhaps to the neighbourhood of Amsterdam where hiding was somewhat easier than
in the small hamlets and villages of the countryside.

At new moon, or perhaps on a night of fog, the boat had been
carried stealthily down to the water and the passenger and his pilot
had swiftly set out on the journey of thirty miles down the lake
which would carry the airman to safety — provided that the correct
landfall could be made before the first light of the next day came to
reveal the little boat still out on the open waters of the Ijsselmeer.
Each voyage had been a race against time and a very strenuous performance for some local lad of the resistance movement whose turn
it had been to make the journey, choosing his course by the stars
and by his own knowledge, aided by no more than a pocket compass. It was an enterprising undertaking but it had succeeded, and
men had been taken again and again to safety in this frail craft.

Enkhuizen was once a very flourishing port. There were several
ships from the city in van Tromp's fleet, and to be a seaman aboard
one of them was not always a pleasant experience. In his diary for
1639 the admiral wrote this entry: 'June 2nd. In the morning the
wind N., Portland N. by E. from us 4 miles off. We brailed up our
sails and held a Court martial; keel-hauled 3 sailors, each 3 times,
and whipped them with wet bums before the mast, mulcted of their
wages and discharged the fleet; they had run away from Captain
Sluijs.' Evidently the men survived the disciplinary action and two
of them were Swedes, Sven and Andries Andrieszoon from Gus-
tavus Adolphus' newly founded port of Gothenburg, serving as
seamen in the *Groote Christoffel*, of Enkhuizen.

A little earlier in its history Enkhuizen had earned her proud
claim to be the first city in all the northern provinces formally to
declare its rejection of Spanish rule and its adherence to William
the Silent — a remarkable act of confidence which was to bring its
proper reward in more ways than one. Amsterdam still remained
under Spanish rule and many of its merchants and business people
promptly removed themselves to Enkhuizen, where at least they
were not in daily danger of sequestration of their property, or of
death — provided of course that Enkhuizen could maintain its
freedom. The failure of the Spaniards to capture Alkmaar in the

following year, and the subsequent defeat of Bossu in the waters off Hoorn and Enkhuizen established the position of the city more firmly, and its prosperity soared still further. Within fifty years the population had increased to more than thirty thousand — about three times its present size — and it was among the richest and most flourishing cities of all the United Provinces. Another result of this new importance was that Enkhuizen was invested with the right to levy tolls on all ships navigating the Zuyder Zee, in return for which it performed the Elder Brethren tasks of lighting and buoyage through the area. This proved a very profitable business for the city and still further increased its prosperity.

Within a century however Enkhuizen was declining, and the years were approaching in which the houses of its abandoned outer streets were pulled down. In the middle of the nineteenth century it had shrunk to a mere five thousand inhabitants, and the shipyards, of which there were so many in the sixteenth century, had practically vanished. In the most recent years however the industry has revived. On the afternoon of the same warm summer's day, the dawning of which we had seen from our position on the rocks of the Marken dyke, we drew into the harbour of Enkhuizen just in time to scramble round to the basin and join the people of the town where they stood in proud anticipation on the quayside, which had thoughtfully been provided with bundles of heavy tyres in case the weight of the ship which was to be launched sideways from the yard across the water should prove too much for the drags and hawsers which were arranged to check her broadside surge.

The boat was a motorized barge of a thousand tons or more, and she lay black and shining on baulks laid across the slipway, with a collection of poles and wedges shoring her up from below. A couple of workmen were dislodging the wedges one at a time with heavy sledge-hammers, and each time a timber fell the people held their breath, expecting the ship to begin its short sharp slide into the harbour. The men knew better than we did however, for they walked with complete unconcern between the long hull and the water.

At last the moment came when all the props and wedges had been cleared away and the ship was only held by cables fore and aft, attached to the shoreward side. The men stood clear, a lady stepped forward from the cover of the slipway shed to give the signal with her hand, and at a blast of the foreman's whistle the cables were suddenly dropped. But, as is so often the case, all that the ship did was to demonstrate the truth of the mechanical principle that the force needed to overcome friction and initiate motion is greater than that required to sustain the same motion once it has been initiated — which is the mechanical engineer's way of saying that a ship sitting on a sloping slip is likely to stick, and it may need a push to get it moving. Quite a hefty push too, where a boat of a thousand tons is concerned.

Crowbars were brought to work without success, whilst the crowd watched in mixed hope and anxiety — except for the children, who were very glad of any prolongation of their special release from school classes. At last eight men picked up a fallen prop as thick as a telegraph post, and ranging themselves on either side they walked, trotted, and finally broke into a run to deliver a tremendous blow to one of the central trolleys just as the Sea Beggars must have attacked the town gate of Briel. Again nothing happened, and they charged a second time and then a third. And whilst they were retiring to consider their strategy the ship, as so often happens on such occasions, demonstrated the truth of the mechanical principle that at a certain angle the angular component of the vertical force represented by the weight of an object will be sufficient to overcome the opposing force of friction acting along the plane of contact of two smooth surfaces — which is the mechanical engineer's way of saying that a ship sitting on a sloping slip is likely sooner or later to slide. And slide quite rapidly where the rails are covered with grease.

The ship descended majestically down the incline to the accompaniment at first of a great gasp from the crowd and then of wild cheering as she lunged over, fell from the edge of the bank with a splash that raised the the water high over her side, and then righted herself to float proudly across the harbour, dragging down the slipway the bunches of yard-workers who had clutched at the dragropes to help check her thousand tons of bulk. A tug came speedily alongside to take up the strain, and the people of Enkhuizen broke out into tremendous applause, for this was indeed a great day. Their town was by no means the 'dead city of the Zuyder Zee' which once perhaps it had been. Even in the heyday of the East India Company no ship as large as this had ever before taken the water in the harbour of Enkhuizen.

In a country so rich in beautiful buildings it is not easy to select any one as outstanding, but I would doubt if Holland has any lovelier than the Pepperhouse, built on the Oosterhaven by a rich merchant and shipowner early in the seventeenth century and later the warehouse of the Enkhuizen chamber of the Dutch East India monopoly. It is now the home of the intriguing Zuyder Zee Museum, and its own mellowed appearance is beautifully enhanced by its surroundings. Viewed from across the water it is framed on the one side by magnificent weeping willows and on the other by one of the largest and most handsome wooden bascules in the country, whilst on the water below its windows floats a little fleet of representatives of every kind of ship, great and small, which traditionally sailed on the vanishing waters of the Zuyder Zee. There is a *boyer* with its broad fat hull and shallow lee-boards, a *boterschip* or butter-carrier, a little *tjotter*, a *hektjalk*, a *schokker* and a *blazer*, a whole array of craft whose names alone would be sufficient to intrigue, and even a remarkable boat called a *wyldsjitter*, a kind of duck-shooter's punt from the Frisian meres, armed with a seven-foot blunderbuss sited in a groove beside the stem and so powerful that its recoil would jerk the whole craft backwards through the water. Gay in their browns and greens and yellows, and with their tillers carved and curved for sheer beauty and delight, the line of strange boats from the past lie moored outside the Pepperhouse with their reflections curiously twisted and kinked by the play of the breeze on the quiet water.

Not far away is the St. Pancras Church, and after some difficulty in finding the man who kept the key — for the Dutch have a most annoying habit of keeping their churches locked except on demand — we climbed to the top of the tower, not only to look at the bells and to have the view over the gables and the streets below but also in order to look out towards the opposite coast and see in the distance the Frisian port of Staveren which was to be our next des-

tination. Satisfied that it was really there we put out from Enkhuizen
in the evening and on the last lingering remnants of daylight made
our entry between the Staveren moles into a quiet and decidedly
uninteresting harbour.

Before we left Enkhuizen we were talking to the master of a small
barge moored ahead of us, and we happened to mention that we
were bound for Staveren.

'*Staveren is een stad onder Godes straf,*' he declared roundly.

'Under the punishment of God? How was that?' we enquired.

Ei, but it was true. The people of Staveren had been *godslast-
eraars, godloochenaars,* blasphemers, atheists, impious, and they
had got what was coming to them, the skipper assured us. They
had been a wicked lot, and the worst of them all had been that
woman. What woman? Why, the one whose wicked wastage of the
mercies of God had ruined the port.

The skipper took up our chart and pointed to a great shoal extending for some distance off the port of Staveren and entirely enclosing it except where a dredged channel marked by leading lights led through the bank to the outer harbour.

'*Kijk hier,*' he said as he tapped the spot with his finger. '*Vrouwenzand; ziet U?*'

Yes, we saw the Vrouwenzand right enough, and we knew that it had a bad reputation because a ship driven on to it by a southwester could very easily be smashed to pieces by the waves breaking on the shallows. And of course if we had thought about it we would have known that the name meant 'Woman's Sand' or 'Women Sand', but we certainly did not know that there was a story behind the title.

The skipper unfolded the tale as related in Enkhuizen, and told us that Staveren had once been a great place, a rich walled city with heathen palaces and later with many churches. It occupied an unrivalled position on Lake Flevo, and about the tenth century its sailors managed to reach the North Sea through the meres and creeks and soon they were trading round the Skaw and through the Sound into the Baltic. Trading treaties were concluded with Sweden and Scotland and Denmark, and when the Zuyder Zee was formed Staveren became one of the greatest of the cities of the Hanseatic League. So powerful was she, that she even turned against the ports of Lübeck and Hamburg and attacked them.

But prosperity led to vanity, and the merchants forsook the humble ways of honest trading and began instead to rival each other in show and ostentation. One of them, a woman of great wealth, was determined that her house should put those of all the other merchants in eclipse and so she ordered one of her ships to sail to Danzig and return with the most priceless cargo of riches that money could buy. Spices of the Orient, jewels from Russia, peacocks, perfumes, dishes of gold, it did not matter what she should bring provided it was exotic and costly.

Many weeks later the same ship was sighted out at sea, making down the coast from the north. Impatient to inspect the rare cargo which would soon be unloading in the port of Staveren, the woman was rowed out to meet the vessel and a short distance off-shore she boarded it. The captain then explained that he had been unable to find at Danzig any articles sufficiently rare and unusual for her, and rather than return unladen he had loaded a valuable cargo of wheat.

Incensed by this practical and seamanlike attitude to things the owner ordered her men to jettison the entire load, and where it was thrown overboard there arose a dreadful sandbank which grew year by year until the port was entirely closed and the town ruined. Which served them right, the bargemaster pointed out. It was a just fate, and the wise retribution of Providence upon a people who could be so vain that they could thus destroy the mercies of God when there were many people in the land who were impoverished and lacked their daily bread.

It is easy to discount this tale, and yet it is certainly very possible that given the right circumstances a mass such as a cargo of wheat might have initiated sandbank formation. Light or moderate winds will build up a bank, and the dominant wind of the area blows towards Staveren across the Zuyder Zee. Once begun, a sandbank may steadily increase in area, and with the resulting alteration in the tidal currents almost anything can then happen. Bruges was entirely ruined by the silting of its approaches, and the inlet of the sea which once led to that city has now vanished without leaving a trace, and though the connection between the fate of Staveren and the haughty action of its rich woman merchant cannot be proved the bargemaster of Enkhuizen was only one of those who were convinced that the tale of Divine retribution was a sufficient and natural enough explanation of the downfall of a city of *godloochenaars* — whatever a liberal theologian might think of the view of God implicit in the story.

The crossing of the twelve-mile gap between Enkhuizen and Staveren is not a particularly arduous one, but the course is only a degree or two to the east of north and after half an hour one loses the benefit of the lee of the protruding land on which Enkhuizen is situated, and the wind is free to blow from the west over eight miles of shallows to raise a most uncomfortable slop on the beam. The Ijsselmeer is in fact of just the wrong depth. If it were much shallower, then the waves could not build up at all — though for that matter ships could not sail its waters either — whereas if it were considerably deeper they would constitute a pleasant swell rather than the array of short sharp crests and troughs so characteristic of the area.

Usually — that is, with water of adequate depth — a considerable strength of wind and a long distance from land is required before waves of much size can be developed, and even in a gale the largest waves will only have a height (from crest to trough, measured in feet) of about one and a half times the square root of what a sailor calls the 'fetch' — the miles, that is, over which the waves are being built up by the wind crossing the water. From this it follows that even a gale cannot raise waves of more than nine feet in height at Dover if it blows from the south-east, whereas a south-westerly gale can drive thirty-foot waves before it as it sweeps in over four hundred miles of the open Atlantic.

The exception to the 'usually' is when the waves run over water of restricted depth. If the bottom is no deeper than the wavelength — that is, the distance between two consecutive crests — then the drag which it will exert on the waves is very marked, and as the waves themselves move more slowly their height is necessarily increased because all good waves know that if they are to abide by the laws of physics their momentum must remain constant, and thus if they are to move more slowly than they would like to, then their mass must be correspondingly increased by growing in stature. So the waves become sharper and travel closer to each other than they would over deeper water, and once they become sharpened it is not very difficult for the wind to catch their ridges and push the top edges still further forward. The result of all this is that quite a moderate wind can raise waves which, though not in any way dangerous, can roll a boat surprisingly well. The *Commodore* has a bilge as rounded as the rollers of a rocking-horse, and if waves of the right frequency take her straight on the beam her mast will sway from side to side with all the regularity of the finger of a metronome, reaching an angle which the needle mounted on the saloon bulkhead declares correctly to be between twenty and thirty degrees to either side of the vertical.

The Ijsselmeer might have been purposely constructed by

nature, aided by the Dutch reclamation engineers, in order to give the *Commodore* the biggest possible rolling for the least expenditure of energy by the wind. If there were waves at all they seemed always to be on the beam and of precisely the right length and frequency for each one to catch her as she lay back on the rebound of the tilting caused by the one before. We did not mind, except that it made it difficult to stand up and enjoy the distant scenery, and virtually impossible to cook.

By some strange oversight of the weather the breeze which habitually blows uninterrupted by any hills or other obstacles across the flat Dutch countryside was absent when we first made the crossing, and our journey to Staveren was over water so flat that the reflection of the setting sun was as round and smooth as if we were seeing it in a mirror. Fishing boats were lying idle by their nets or chugging slowly to haul their trawls in a wide sweeping circle, and the evening was warm and breathless. But our second crossing was different. Though the breeze which had begun to embarrass us on the Marken dyke had eased during the day, in the early evening it had freshened considerably and even if the air was comparatively still in the shelter of Enkhuizen harbour we could see the smoke from the tall funnel of a steamer at the railway jetty fleeting swiftly over the mole and out across the water. We put out just after darkness had fallen and we were not in the least surprised to find the *Commodore* wanting to wallow like a walrus from the moment she drew out of the lee of the Oosterdijk headland and had the full delicious benefit of a beam sea built up to the maximum which was possible in the depth available. In fact the waves, though not very large, were continually overstepping the limit of stability and were breaking — a familiar habit of waves when the conditions are such that they have too much energy to hold within their regulation shape and form. The slapping of their curling fronts against her fat flank helped to remove some of the oil which she had picked up in the traffic of the Amsterdam canals, but after a while she seemed to think that she had had enough and she kept continually turning her head in a more easterly direction as though she did not want us to hold her any longer on course toward the defunct city of blasphemers and atheists.

The Staveren lighthouse was now only eight miles distant and we could have kept her wallowing towards it. In daylight we might have checked the rolling too by watching for the bigger waves as they bore down from the side and quickly turning her head to sidle them, but in the dark they had a way of taking her rather by surprise and so we very properly allowed the *Commodore* to have her own way and make for Lemmer instead. It was a longer voyage by several miles, but for most of the way she would have the waves helping her, not only by their repeated pushes on her stern but also by providing a net forward movement to the water through which she would be moving. And push they certainly did, with all the helpful power they could muster, so that it was not very long before we saw some way ahead of us the dark flat line of the containing dyke of the North-East Polder. We kept the dyke well to starboard until we saw the flasher on its northernmost corner, and then we closed right in to within fifty yards of the wall, to make sure that we were well inside the limits of the dredged channel outside which the bottom rose in banks and shoals which were almost awash. Soon after midnight we had nosed our way round the wave breaks to the barge-pier beside Lemmer Lock.

In the morning light we were more able to appreciate the straight smooth line of tall dyke which represented the latest conquest of the Dutch engineers in their endless enterprise of robbing the sea of its hidden land. Behind it lay the wide expanse of a brand new area of Dutch soil which was now in full cultivation, the third of the seven polders to be laid down in an area where once the Zuyder Zee had risen and fallen on the tide.

The story of Dutch land drainage is an impressive one, and its success can be measured by the fact that without the dykes along the river banks and lakes and sea-coasts more than two-fifths of the entire country would be under water. Efforts to defend the land by dykes from the encroaching sea date back to the beginning of the thirteenth century, but the first great advance in drainage came with the invention of the windmill pump three hundred years later. These mills, many of which are still in use in North Holland and around the Lake of de Kaag, were used to drive an Archimedes screw and lift water from field ditches up to drainage lodes and

canals raised at a considerable height above the surface of the land. In the first quarter of the sixteenth century alone more than a hundred thousand acres were reclaimed by wind-power, one third of this land being won from lakes, and the rest from the sea. The advent of steam-power next made it possible to dispose of the Haarlemmermeer and a few other scattered lakes, but the most ambitious scheme of all was later drawn up by Dr Lely. In 1918 the Dutch Government gave its formal assent to his plan, which involved the closing off of the Zuyder Zee and the reclamation of more than half a million acres of its bottom by poldering and pumping. There were other advantages too in Lely's idea. The great dyke at the northern end would carry a road and perhaps later a railway to join Friesland and North Holland. The length of coastline along which sea walls had to be maintained against flood and storm was reduced from 186 miles to 19, and the conversion of the Zuyder Zee into a freshwater lake would provide a reservoir from which water could be drawn to supply the towns and cities to the west and south of the area.

The building of the Afsluitdijk was an immense undertaking, and as the gaps grew narrower so the difficulties of the racing flow of the tide increased, but millions of tons of sand and stone and boulder clay were dumped along the line, and wicker mattresses covered with boulders were sunk on the sides to prevent erosion by waves. Finally a heavy stone covering was added, and in 1932 the last gap was closed in a dyke which measured a hundred yards broad at the water-line, and was raised to twenty-five feet above sea-level. Quite apart from the locks for shipping, the dyke was provided with twenty-five automatic sluices which drained out some of the Zuyder Zee water at low tide but held out the sea during the return flow.

Even before the dyke was completed the first small polder was laid down at Aandijk, north of Enkhuizen, and cleared by pumping. The area was only about a hundred acres, but its purpose was experimental and it was designed to provide all the necessary information upon crop selection and cultivation of land which until recently had lain under salt water. Soon afterwards the Wieringermeer or North-West polder was banked off and two pumping stations drained its fifty thousand acres whilst the building of the main dyke was still in progress. The newly revealed bottom was a vast plain of salty mud, but giant trench ploughs were constructed to cross it with deep furrows into which the rain water would run, leaching out the salt from the soil through which it trickled. Within a couple of years this first of the main Zuyder Zee polders was ready to carry crops of grain, and the leaching ditches were filled in again so tha the area could be parcelled out into rectangular lots half a mile long and 800 feet broad, each of them having one of its narrow sides bordering a metalled road and the other flanking a canal of sufficient size for navigation by farm craft and small barges. New villages were built, transport canals were dug, and within a few years the area was growing some of the richest crops in the country. In 1945 the Germans breached the dyke of this polder to flood it, but by good fortune — or perhaps from lack of explosives — they did not break down the Afsluitdijk and thus convert the whole Ijsselmeer area once more into the salty Zuyder Zee from which it had been so laboriously salvaged.

The North-East polder, stretching south from Lemmer and swallowing up the former islands of Urk and Schokland, was next on the list. Enclosure was completed in 1939, and the pumping dry of its eighth of a million acres was put in hand by the three pumping stations at De Voorst, Urk and Lemmer. Canals were cut even before the bottom was exposed, and three hundred miles of new roads were laid down when the land emerged. Less trenching was

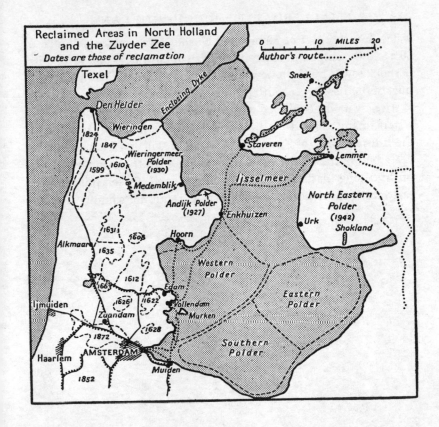

Reclaimed Areas in North Holland
and the Zuyder Zee

Dates are those of reclamation

0   10   MILES   20

Author's route......

needed in this case, because the soil had lain for several years under fresh water and so most of the salt had already disappeared. Crops could be grown almost at once.

When the work is finally completed the Lely plan will have added one tenth to the area of the Netherlands, a country in which the density of population is forty per cent greater than in Britain and fifteen times that of the United States. From just south of Enkhuizen the Ijsselmeer will have vanished entirely, though certain narrow areas around its present shores will be left under water, partly to facilitate transport but in the main because the coast is in many places fringed with sand which is of little use when reclaimed. Marken, though no longer an island, will thus have access to the water on its western side, and the Orange Locks of Amsterdam will still lead out through the eel-nets into a shrunken patch of fresh water, but the port of Hoorn will be shut away on a small inland lake and the ships will reach it not from open waters out beyond its harbour tower but by a new canal leading over land to an artificial inlet of the Ijsselmeer south of Enkhuizen.

Already a post equipped with a beacon light stands far out in the waters, many miles from the nearest shore, to mark the position of the future capital of Zuyder Zee Land. It will not be many more years before the *Commodore* may have to give the standard signal of three long blasts for a bridge to be opened, fifteen miles to the eastward of the dyke on which she spent a summer's night.

XII

Friesland, land of black and white — The scientific view —
Farewell to Holland — The Baltic lies ahead — The Com-
modore goes to bed

At Lemmer, the *Commodore* was in Friesland where, as Pliny
wrote, 'the ocean hurls itself in an endless flow over the boundless plains, so that in this struggle of nature one is uncertain whether
the earth of these Lowlands is of the land or of the sea.' The countryside was one of meres and lakes and waterways radiating in
every direction, and as she set her nose northward out of the town
to pass through the lakes of Groote Brekken, Koevorden and Lang-
weer she was once again travelling one of the main inland routes
and meeting some of the heavy barges which move more than
25,000,000 tons of goods through the country every year — a total
almost as great as that of all the traffic of the railways and roads
combined.

She carried us steadily onward between rich marshy pastures
and past huge low-eaved and reed-thatched farms standing stolidly
in the wide fields where thin black-and-white storks prodded in the
ditches for frogs, and fat black-and-white cows paused for a
moment on the canal-side track to blink at her before continuing
on their casual way to the black-and-white barns where they would

be milked. By boat the voyage towards the provinces of Drenthe and Groningen was a sweet and story-book journey, but then a traveller by boat may perhaps miss the things of real importance. Two social scientists from the United States had been making a very profound study of the life of a village in this same area, and of course they discovered things which we as humble boatmen could never find — for instance that the village 'constitutes a functioning microcosm that has grown out of its deep natural and cultural roots. . . . Repetitive patterning is extended to almost every phase of social life . . . even to the time of clipping the farmyard hedge.' The inhabitants 'exhibited marked social retardation', they found. Not that the research workers always had a dull time, for when they gave a lecture to the inhabitants of the functioning microcosm on the subject of life in the United States 'there were audible sounds of interest and pleasure'.

On this journey the *Commodore* passed quickly through Friesland, and the Sneekermeer and Bergumermeer were already astern before she drew in to a side arm of the canal at a small village to lie there for the night and to replenish her bread and butter and milk. Perhaps we were surprised to find the Frisian language so very similar to our own, for bread and butter were no longer *brood* and *boter*, but *bred* and *butter*, and for the first time we were able to speak and understand a foreign tongue without previously knowing a word of it.

What was the weather like in the Channel when we came over, the bridge-keeper asked as we stood beside him while he swung the big span for a heavy barge to ease her way through in the dark. '*Wier de wind goed?*'

Yes, *de wind wier goed*, we said. Had they had a good summer in Friesland?

On the whole, yes. Sometimes there had been storms and '*nou in dan ien schoer heyl in rain*'. If the man who was talking with us had been a shepherd from the Cheviots and not a Frisian bridge-keeper his words would not have sounded very different. 'Nou'n than a schoer o' heyl 'n rain.' It was certainly easier for us to talk Frisian than to follow the Welsh hymns in the upper room of the English Church on the Groenburgwal in Amsterdam.

Next morning we were following the Caspar Robles Diep across the drier land towards Groningen, and the following day the *Commodore* was squeezing towards the bank of the Eemskanaal to let the Dutch coasters pass her on their way inwards to their home port of Groningen. At Delfzijl she passed through the lock into salt water again and with wind and wave and tide behind her she was soon flying up past the sands of the Dollart to leave Emden on her port side and swing round in midstream to draw alongside the Emswachtschiff and report her arrival in Germany. A week later she had threaded her way through the waterways of the northwest corner of the German Federal Republic to emerge in the Baltic and oblige us to change language yet again. *Pain et beurre, brood en boter, bred in butter, brot und butter*, now it was *brød och smør* which we had to buy before breakfast in the shops.

Denmark was certainly a long way from the reaches of the Thames up which the *Commodore* had carried us on our first exploratory voyages, but she seemed strangely determined to roam continually further afield. We felt sure that she would be satisfied now that she had reached the Baltic, and we expected her to wish to return at least as far as Warmond for the winter. But we were mistaken. Continually we had to write to her insurers asking that her permitted cruising grounds should be extended by just one more area of water, and long before the end of the summer holidays she had made it quite clear to us that she had no intention of turning southward just yet. At the beginning of September she drew into a little fishing harbour within sight of the castle of Elsinore, and consulting our phrase book we asked a question of the village shipwright on her behalf.

'*Vil De vaere så venlig at rede en køje til mig?* — Will you make up a bed for me please?' We really meant that we wanted her slipped for the winter, but it was the best we could do.

And so she stayed beside the Sound until the following spring, hauled up high and dry in a comfortable shed. She evidently knew — which we ourselves at that time certainly did not — that in Norway and Sweden there were canals lovelier than any which she had yet been through and that John Ericsson, the inventor of her propellor, had had a brother Nils who had cut a most ingenious waterway leading from one of these countries to the other. The Dalslands canal had been open for ninety years but no boat from England had ever yet reached it, and with just the slightest touch of conceit the *Commodore* was secretly determined to be the first to explore it. And in the following year she did so — but that part of her northern voyage must be reserved for telling on another occasion.

We ourselves were to return to England by packet boat from Esbjerg, and it was a sad parting when the village taximan came to pick us up from beside the slipway and we left the *Commodore* patiently waiting for Mr Hinrichsen to make up her bed. Ahead of us lay the months at home in our own country, but we knew that throughout the winter evenings our thoughts would tend to return to the places to which she had taken us. To Lisse and the gerbera farm at Noordwijk, to the Rembrandts and the Ruysdaels and the pictures of Frans Hals, to Dordrecht with its bustling tugs, Warmond with its solemn sheep placidly taking the ferry from the village to the fields, Enkhuizen and its patchwork kayak, the Vliet with its memories of the English refugees; to Alkmaar, where the unknown Dutch family had come together at night to read from the big family Bible during the dark days in which the Dutch nation was being forged; to a people who now were constantly driving back the sea as tirelessly as once they had repulsed the Spanish terror; to a nation which had unpretentiously given the world so much of indestructible beauty and abiding value.

APPENDIX

WATER transport is so highly developed throughout the Netherlands that any yacht will have an easy passage through the main traffic routes, which are innumerable and of very large dimensions. Fresh water is available in almost every town and village, and on account of the flatness of the land there are very few locks. Fees are negligible.

The main canals are open on Sundays as well as weekdays in most areas, and though on some routes the bridges are not manned between midnight and six in the morning, on others they are opened at any hour.

The following books are useful:

Inland Waterways of Holland, by W. E. Wilson, published by Imray, Laurie, Norie and Wilson. A catalogue of the 123 chief waterways of the Netherlands with dimensions, number of bridges, etc., but no general information.

Thorpe's Yachtsman's Guide to the Dutch Waterways, revised by John Howlett, published by Stanford. This work contains excellent maps of tidal streams and of the great majority of the canals and rivers. The information is much more extensive than in the former book, and moorings, yacht clubs, water-points and the like are given.

Almanak voor Watertoerisme, Deel II, published by the Bureau Voor Watertoerisme, Keizersgracht 590, Amsterdam C, is an admirable alphabetical guide of more than 600 pages in which the minutest details are given of every harbour and waterside village in the country, often with scale plans and always with all the vital information such as availability of locks on Sundays and the telephone numbers of shipyards.

The Bureau also publishes excellent water maps of all areas of the country where waterways are abundant, giving the height of every bridge and the depth of even the smallest waterway. Scale about $1\frac{1}{4}$ ins. = 1 mile. Besides this the Bureau will supply a chart of the Zuyder Zee (which should be corrected *up to the day of the voyage*), a small map showing through routes in the Amsterdam canals, and a most useful sheet giving the times at which each of the railway bridges throughout the country is opened. This is particularly valuable, as hours can be wasted by arriving at the wrong time at a low bridge on a busy line — though such bridges are not common.

An invaluable and accurate map is the *Schipperskaart van Nederland*, published by Born N.V. of Assen. Scale 1 cm. = 4 km. This is the standard map used by bargemasters, and is excellent for planning lengthy routes.